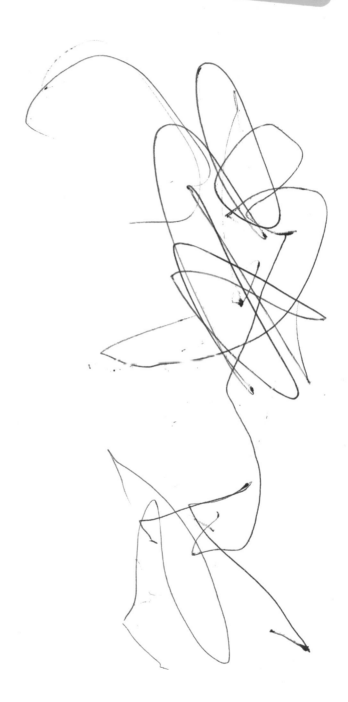

HOW TO SURVIVE YOUR KIDS

FROM PREBIRTH TO PRETEEN

HOW TO SURVIVE YOUR KIDS
FROM PREBIRTH TO PRETEEN

JOSEPH R. NOVELLO, M.D.

McGRAW-HILL BOOK COMPANY

New York   St. Louis   San Francisco   Bogotá   Hamburg
Madrid   Mexico   Milan   Montreal   Panama
Paris   São Paulo   Tokyo   Toronto

To Sam, Mayra, Billy, Francisco, Yaritza,
John Edward, Crystal, and Diego

1 2 3 4 5 6 7 8 9 DOC DOC 8 9 2 1 0 9 8 7

ISBN 0-07-047590-3

LIBRARY OF CONGRESS CATALOGING-IN-PUBLICATION DATA

Novello, Joseph R.
  How to survive your kids.

  Includes index.
  1. Child rearing—United States.   2. Parent and child—
United States.   3. Child development.   I. Title.
HQ769.N68 1987   649'.1   87-16803
ISBN 0-07-047590-3

Contents

Acknowledgments

You know who you are. Children, mothers, fathers, and grand-parents who have visited my office, written to my magazine column, phoned my call-in radio programs, participated in my television segments, attended my lectures and seminars. You are true coauthors of this book because it's based directly on the questions you've asked me. You've kept me on my toes. You've enriched my life and you've made me a better physician along the way. I've respected your anonymity in these pages, but you're not anonymous to me.

I'd like to acknowledge several clinical associates in my private practice in Washington, D.C.: Dan Goebl, Joyce Goebl, Judy Graser, Jim Holmes, Randy Roberts, and Teresa Villani. When you're sur-rounded by such top-notch people every day, your own professional growth is continuously stimulated.

The students, residents, and staff of Georgetown University's School of Medicine are also found between the covers of this book. The good teacher learns while teaching. These colleagues and colleagues-to-be have taught me well.

Then there's *Woman's World* magazine. My column, "You and Your Child," debuted in 1981, at about the same time that Dennis Neeld took the reins as Editor-in-Chief. Much of the material in this book has appeared in the column. Thanks are due to my editors over the years: Maris Cakers, Norm Zeitchik, Joan Klein, Karen Kreps, and Gus Gustaitis.

Many people at WMAL radio in Washington have contributed to the success of my call-in program. Special acknowledgment is due to Eileen Griffin, Program Director; Jim Gallant, Operations Manager; Len Diebert, News Director; and Fred Weinhaus, Gen-eral Manager.

And, even though 1 o'clock in the morning seems an unlikely time for a psychiatrist to be taking calls from over 200 cities across the United States, NBC radio's *Talknet* has provided me that opportunity—while reminding me "Joe, remember, it's only 10 o'clock on the West Coast." Thanks, Maurice Tunick and Dave Bartlett.

Noon. That's more like it. My television segments "Family Matters" and "Healthscope" have aired for over four years on WJLA-TV's *Noon News* in Washington. Thanks to my producers Laurie Bernard, Stu Rivchun, Louisa Hart, and Prenella Neely. They are good idea people, and some topics treated in this book were first explored on Channel 7.

My syndicated radio program, *Healthtime*, is primarily a medical feature, but I do manage to sneak in a few scripts on child raising every now and then. Child psychiatrists are like that. Thanks to Tony Rudel, Larry Krents, and Warren Bodow, the good people at *The New York Times* and WQNR radio in New York who helped get the program launched, and to Pam Pulner, who helped keep it afloat. Thanks also to our sponsor, Pfizer Pharmaceuticals, where Chuck Frye, John Song, and Peter Carlin have provided steady, reliable support. And special thanks to *Healthtime*'s producer, Loren Robinson, who has raised *that* "child" from a network of 7 to over 250 stations.

For the material adapted from my articles in *The Washington Post*, I would like to thank Marsha Mason and Phyllis Krucoff, editors who know what parents want to know.

Thanks to my literary agent, Marilee Heifetz, for bringing me to McGraw-Hill and to Tom Quinn, my editor.

When you get right down to it, most of the material in this book originated in some fashion from my clinical practice of child and family psychiatry.

And did someone say "secretary"? Make that secretaries—three good ones. Cheryl Chadwick, Dana Rector, and Sabina Timlin all contributed to the effort.

But they had backup, support, and guidance. Lo Ann Ward, my Administrative Assistant and right arm, has now been through two books with me. This one, though, was special. Lo Ann and her husband Jim experienced the birth of their first child, Danielle, somewhere between the first and second draft of this book. For LA the experience must have been something like delivering twins. I'm pleased to report that she carried both children beautifully.

For my wife, Toni, this is book number four. She contributed to my previous books through her roles as critic, companion, and cheerleader. She contributed to this one, however, in a new role: consultant. A live-in pediatrician for an author of a book about raising children. Now *that's* just what the doctor ordered.

Introduction

"Doc," said a frustrated father, "my kids have me well trained. It's not supposed to work like this is it?"

"Just give me a little help, okay?" asked a harried mother, "like what to do until the grown-up arrives."

These parents are typical of most I encounter: well-intentioned but—overwhelmed.

Now I don't belong to the school that believes children get up in the morning plotting how they're going to wreck Mom and Dad's day. I'm not a hard-liner. But I'm not a softy either.

I believe that someone has to be in charge of a family. I believe that "someone" should be a parent—not a tyrannical child. And that's why this book was written. It's for parents who want to stay in control of their children, who wish to pass along their own values, who will dare to teach discipline, who want to work hard at the difficult task of talking and listening to kids, who wish to learn all they can about child development so youngsters can grow happy and healthy and realize their full potential in life.

This is a book for parents who long to love and be loved in the process.

Impossible? No way. It can happen to you.

My formula is based on three "gets": *Get* informed, *get* involved, *get* in charge.

How to do it? Don't just read this book. Study it. Live it. Make adjustments, as necessary, for your own personal values, but please keep an open mind for learning new ways of dealing with the surprises, big and small, that your children will throw at you.

Parenthood is an art and a science. You'll find both in these pages. I've included the latest relevant research information along with practical tips on everything from what to name the baby to the best toilet-training tactics, to what to do if you catch your 9-year-old son "playing doctor" with the little neighbor girl.

You may be tempted to use the index and go directly to a problem that's currently got you baffled. That's fine. I want this book to be immediately helpful. After all, it's based on real questions from real parents. Learn from their experiences. But I also urge you to read the book from cover to cover. It's designed as a developmental sweep through the various predictable stages of childhood.

I want you to understand your child's changing needs from one phase to the next. Who knows, you might even get out ahead of your youngster—that's real survival.

And the quizzes. Don't forget the quizzes. I've included them to help you sharpen your skills. They're also for fun, so don't be intimidated. Good parents are made, not born. We have to work at it, each in our own imperfect way.

But while none of us is perfect, we have an obligation to our children to give them our very best effort.

That's what *I've* tried to do in these pages. If you return the favor, we all benefit: you, me, and, most of all—our children.

Joseph R. Novello, M.D.
Washington, D.C.

CHAPTER 1

Before the Baby Arrives

Welcome to the first stage of parenthood—the anticipatory stage. You're awaiting the arrival of an event that will forever change your life. In fact, things are changing already: your relationship to your spouse, your relationships with family and friends, and your own self-image. You have a lot of questions and a lot of secret fears, especially if this is to be your first child.

Relax. It's not easy, but it doesn't have to be so tough. I've collected a number of questions from expectant parents just like you. I hope my answers will provide some guidance over the rough spots and that they'll stimulate you and your spouse to further discussion.

That's what this stage of parenthood is all about: discussion and planning. Use your pregnancy not only as a physical event but as an opportunity to examine yourselves as mates and parents-to-be. For what purpose are you bringing a child into the world? What kind of person do you want him or her to be? What will be the values of your new family? What place will your marriage take in relation to your family? If there are other children, what will be the impact on them? Examine. Plan. Think.

Good parents are made, not born. You have to work at it. I've found, in my clinical practice of child psychiatry, that reactions during the pregnancy itself are very accurate predictors of what kind of parents you'll be. If you work at it now, you'll one day be the proud parent of a happy young adult. He or she will love you for it. You'll rejoice in your success and, yes, maybe even breathe a sigh of relief that you've finally worked yourself out of a job! So use

1

this time effectively. There's no looking back, and for that you should be prepared—and be pleased.

As Kahlil Gibran has written so eloquently:

For life goes not backward nor tarries with yesterday.
You are the bows from which your children's living arrows
     are sent forth.
The archer sees the mark upon the path of the infinite and
     He bends you with His might that His arrows may go swift
     and far.
Let your bending in the archer's hand be for gladness.
For even as He loves the arrow that flies, so He loves also
     the bow that is stable.

What Children Want from Parents

Q: What do children really want from their parents? It's a question I keep asking my wife since we're planning to start a family soon.

A: For the answers I've gone right to the experts themselves: a group of children aged 6 through 16. Their answers are amazingly consistent regardless of sex or age:

   1. *Nurturance:* Children want parents to take care of their basic needs, such as food, clothing, and shelter.

   2. *Protection:* Children expect mothers and fathers to protect them from dangers—but they chafe at overprotection. Their basic attitude: "Keep me safe, but let me make a few of my own mistakes."

   3. *Honesty:* Children want parents to be truthful, even about difficult matters such as marital problems.

   4. *Consistency:* This is a big item and is stressed by virtually all the children. They especially complain about the parent who is strict one day and lenient the next. Such inconsistency confuses them.

   5. *Discipline:* Surprised? Yes, children want discipline. They want firm discipline that is not rigid or punitive. The youngsters

prefer praise over criticism. A common complaint: "My parents always tell me when I make mistakes, but they ignore a lot of the good things."

6. *Love:* Children want to be accepted for who they are, with their own strengths and weaknesses. They want to know that parents will forgive them when they make mistakes.

7. *Fair treatment:* Nothing upsets youngsters more than if they believe a brother or sister is favored over them.

8. *Communication:* Many of the children on my unofficial "panel of experts" complained that parents do not take time to answer their questions or to explain the reasons behind their decisions.

9. *Friends:* The teenagers stress that they wish parents would be more tolerant of their friends.

10. *More of mom and dad:* The single item stressed most by all the children, each in his or her own way, is that they really want more time with their mothers and fathers.

Your Marriage Comes First

Q: My husband, Tom, and I are expecting our first child in six months. Some of my girlfriends have warned me that having a baby will have an enormous impact on the marriage—for good or for bad. Maybe my question is impossible to answer, but what I wonder is this: What should come first, my husband or my baby?

A: Your question is tough but not impossible to answer. It is my opinion that your marriage should come first.

Now, before you charge me, a child psychiatrist, with being antichildren, let me explain. I'm very much prochildren. It's just that a sound and happy marital relationship is one of the best guarantees of having happy children. And let's face it, just as your relationship with Tom existed before the baby will enter the scene, you hope that your marriage will still be strong when your child is grown up and has moved out of the house.

Parenthood is only one stage in the adult life cycle. It is not the first stage, and it should not be the last stage. Husbands and wives who become too preoccupied with their children, too "child-centered," risk losing each other—and, paradoxically, their children too in the process. Your baby will need you. Tom will need you. While sensible "balance" is the name of the game, make sure that your marriage gets plenty of attention. Cherish it just as you do the baby, and you can enjoy the best of both worlds.

How Children Affect Marriage

Q: My husband and I have been married for one year. We're very happy—but we're concerned about what's happened to so many of our married friends after they have children. Do marriages tend to fall apart after children arrive on the scene, or is it just our imaginations?

A: A recent study by a University of Minnesota researcher suggests that your imaginations are on target: A couple is twice as likely to contemplate divorce after the arrival of the first child.

But hold on. Remember that most American couples are fairly pleased with their situations. In the same study, Olson and McCubbin found that 77 percent of the individuals surveyed were satisfied with their family life.

Are you ready for a child yet? Your marriage must be the solid foundation upon which your family will be built. Talk it over with your husband. Maybe your hesitation is a sign that you're not quite sure of your relationship yet. No problem. If you use this as an opportunity for honest self-examination and work to improve your marriage, you can turn your hesitancy into a strength. As a child psychiatrist I'd like to see more parents take time to consider the state of their marriage before they decide to have children.

Establishing Family Values

Q: We are expecting our first child in four months. We'd like to be as prepared as possible. Can you recommend some good books on parenting?

A: While there are many fine books on parenting, I would suggest that you start with the best book of them all: you and your husband.

By this I mean that now is the time for each of you to examine, or "read," yourselves. You are about to start a family: I'll refer to you as the "Jones" family. What will it mean for your child to be a Jones? What will be the values of the Jones family? Before you read any books, these vital questions about family values should be answered. Why? Values define us as individuals and as families. They give ultimate meaning to our lives. They also aid tremendously in the practical day-to-day raising of children. For example, parents who know what really counts in their family (the core value system) know where to draw the line with their children—and they know when they can give the kids some slack.

Family values distinguish between what is "negotiable" with youngsters and what is not "negotiable." Children raised in this kind of consistent environment grow up with a clear sense of right and wrong, of duty, and of self-identity.

While you can be sure that your children will occasionally put your family value system to a test, it is better for them to have something clear and resolute against which to define themselves—rather than being left to drift in a sea of ambiguity. Some day your son or daughter should be able to stand up and say: "I'm a Jones, and we Joneses believe that...!"

Will Baby Be Healthy?

Q: I am five months pregnant with my first baby. Everything is going well, but I'm afraid. I can't get it out of my mind that there's something wrong with the baby. My obstetrician says not to worry. So does my husband. But I'm worried.

A: Some amount of worry about the birth of a firstborn is natural. But I sense that you are preoccupied with the matter. There are many possible psychological explanations for your predicament. Some women find it hard to imagine themselves as mothers, so they unconsciously project "damage" onto an unborn infant. Some women suffer guilt during pregnancy. These psychodynamic explanations go on and on.

I cannot diagnose your problem without considerably more information. I would suggest, as a starting point, a talking session with your obstetrician; he, or she, is trained to help women with the emotional, as well as the physical, problems of pregnancy. If necessary, your obstetrician could refer you for counseling. Don't be discouraged. The problem you describe is not so unusual. Most mothers work it out just fine.

A Baby's Sex

Q: I am eight weeks pregnant. My husband and I aren't sure if we want to know the sex of our baby before birth, but as a starter, can you tell me what determines, from a genetic standpoint, a baby's sex?

A: The basic unit of inheritance is the *gene*. There are thousands of different genes that determine the entire spectrum of inheritance: sex, hair color, eyes, facial features, height, etc. These genes are bunched together into larger structures known as *chromosomes*.

Your baby has inherited half of his (or her) genes from you and half from your husband. But—this may surprise you—sex has been determined by your husband's sex chromosome, not yours.

Let me explain. Women have twenty-three pairs of chromosomes called XX. Men have twenty-two pairs of XX chromosomes and one mismatched pair XY. As you can see, a baby will always inherit an X chromosome from his mother, but he may inherit either an X or a Y from dad. If the sperm that fertilized your ovum was carrying an X chromosome, the baby will be XX: a female; if the sperm was a Y carrier, you'll have an XY child: a male.

Breast vs. Bottle

Q: We are expecting our first child in five months. What is your opinion about breast feeding versus bottle feeding?

A: I'll outline some of the current thinking on this still controversial subject, but I'd like to begin by emphasizing a very important point: From a purely psychological standpoint, the most crucial factor is the warmth, security, and love in the mother-child relationship—not the method of feeding.

In fact, the only method of feeding that should definitely be avoided is simply propping up a bottle for the infant on a pillow. The act of feeding an infant, you see, goes far beyond meeting the purely nutritional needs of a baby: It is the path of love and human bonding. Although breast feeding does tie mother and baby closer together in a physical sense, the psychological closeness can be injured by a mother who is nursing because of pressure from others or out of a sense of obligation. Conversely, a bottle-feeding mother can accomplish wonderful closeness with her baby through her act of cuddling the infant in her arms, cooing to her, rocking her gently.

Now let's look at some of the advantages of breast feeding:

1. *Superior nutrition:* Breast feeding has nutritional advantages. Breast milk is superior in its specific protein content to cow's milk and formula. Recent studies, however, suggest the need for supplemental feedings after four to six months to avoid "weight faltering" of the infant.

2. *Fewer infections:* An infant's body does not produce antibodies to infection. Breast milk, however, does pass maternal antibodies directly to the baby. Studies suggest that breast-fed infants have fewer infections and develop fewer allergies.

3. *Less obesity:* Breast-fed infants may have a lower tendency to obesity in later life. Studies now being conducted are shedding interesting new light on this phenomenon. In related research, scientists at Harvard have found that adults who were breast-fed as infants have lower cholesterol levels, even if their fat intake is high. The medical significance of these findings, however, is still inconclusive.

4. *Cheaper:* Finally, some mothers point out that breast feeding is cheaper. They also stress that breast feeding is less work than hassling with bottles and formulas and packing them along on trips.

On the other hand:

Fathers, who wish to play an active part in taking care of a new-born, derive great pleasure from feeding a baby. Dads sometimes feel left out when moms are breast-feeding. Mothers themselves sometimes feel too tied down by the demands of breast feeding. Older siblings sometimes develop a case of jealousy, but the issue is usually related to all the attention that the new baby is getting, rather than the fact that he is breast-feeding; at other times the breast feeding itself can be an unspoken source of conflict for the older kids. Finally, it is paradoxical that some mothers who successfully nurse their babies come under pressure from friends or families to give it up. "Is he still on the breast?" they'll ask incredulously. Why? Maybe they're jealous too.

The answer? Breast feeding does appear to have several advantages, but there are some disadvantages as well. Look over my facts; then make up your mind—but don't neglect your own feelings and the feelings of your husband. Whatever you choose, the most important factor is to make the feeding experience the vehicle not only for nutrition but for positive emotional bonding between yourself and your little one. Best wishes!

Breast Feeding and Intelligence

Q: We're expecting our first child in two months. I wasn't really planning to breast-feed until I read somewhere that breast feeding can help a child develop a higher IQ. Any truth to this?

A: I know of no direct cause-and-effect relationship between breast feeding and IQ scores. You may, however, be referring to one study that discovered, retrospectively, that many gifted children were breast-fed as infants. In this report, the researcher learned that 70 percent of the gifted youngsters he studied were breast-fed.

No, there's certainly no mental magic in mother's milk. The answer is probably psychological. Mothers who breast-feed often develop a stronger attachment to their infants. This attachment can later blossom into a continuing, close, warm relationship which, of course, provides the right environment for a child to flourish intellectually, emotionally, physically, and spiritually.

Rocking Chairs: Myth or Fact?

Q: I'm due to have our first baby in six months. My mother insists that I buy a rocking chair. She says that she rocked me when I was a baby and that her mother rocked her. I don't need a rocking chair. What's it all about anyway? Is it just one of those old myths, or is there really something to it?

A: There *is* something to it. Motion research conducted in several medical centers in the United States and Canada has concluded that babies are tremendously soothed by the rhythm provided by rocking chairs. In fact, rocking chairs (maybe the ultimate in low tech) are standard equipment in many of the best hospital nurseries in this country. Looks like a case of grandma knowing best after all.

Here's to a Long Life

Q: I've heard a lot of talk lately about how the life span is increasing. My first baby will be born in two months. Just what are her chances of living a long life?

A: A child born this year has an average life expectancy of 74 years. Make that 78 if you're sure your baby is going to be a girl.

The life expectancy of Americans has been increasing at an astonishing rate. A baby born in 1900, for example, could only expect to live to age 47. But a baby born back in the year 3000 B.C. could expect to live only to the ripe old age of 18! In other words, the average life expectancy has increased as much in the last eighty-plus years as it did in the preceding 5000 years. And guess what? It's still going up.

Here's to your baby. May she lead a long, happy, and healthy life!

Successful Child, Successful Adult

Q: We'd like our child, who's due in three months, to grow into an adult who is productive and successful in his or her work. Do you have a formula for success?

A: Success means different things to different people. The adult who is "productive and successful" in *work* generally was a child who was successful in school and in hobbies. A recent Harvard Medical School study, for example, suggests that goal-directed children who derive satisfaction from a job well done tend to grow into adults who have rewarding jobs. These children, from an early age, demonstrate a high degree of perseverance: They stick to a task until it is done right. They receive a lot of praise from parents for such efforts. These children also develop hobbies and special skills such as music and athletics. They develop a self-image of mastery, of competence, of being *good* at something.

What can you do to breed this kind of success? A few tips:

- Set a good parental example of responsibility and honest, hard work, but balance your work interest with good humor, love, and personal relationships.

- Require your children to do their best.

- Expect children to complete tasks.

- Praise the accomplishments of youngsters.

- Teach firm, but graceful, discipline. Remember that the goal of all parental discipline is the ultimate *self*-discipline of the children themselves.

- Encourage your youngsters to develop their own special interests. Success at work, of course, isn't everything, but as your question implies, it sure beats failure.

Permissive vs. Authoritarian Parenting

Q: We're not quite ready yet, but we're getting there. Lately we've been talking about how we'd raise our children, and there seems to be a very basic disagreement here. My husband is what you'd probably call "permissive." I'm the authoritarian one. Here's our question: Is it better to be permissive or authoritarian in raising children?

A: First, few parents consciously select a certain "style" of parenting: They just grow into it on the basis of their own temperament and life experience. This is too bad because there is a lot of information available about effective parenting. One way is not necessarily just as good as the next for all children.

Second, the question seems to presume that there are just two parenting schools from which to choose and that, once the selection is made, parents will apply the philosophy on a consistent basis. In fact, there are intermediate alternatives between the permissive and authoritarian extremes. And it is the unusual parent who can consistently apply a single set of parenting principles. Many parents actually tend to shift back and forth, unknowingly, from pole to pole: a confusing state of affairs for children.

The *authoritarian parent* demands respect and obedience from children. She is the leader. The children are the led. "Do it because I say so" might be the credo. Children who grow up in this repressive atmosphere tend to be passive. If the tone of the family is angry and nasty, kids tend to be resentful or revengeful. Authoritarian parents, however, who mix firm limits with humor and love can avoid many of the pitfalls.

The *permissive parent* adopts a laissez faire attitude. Rather than adopting an authoritarian dictatorship, he turns over much of the family leadership to the children themselves. These youngsters are encouraged to make their own decisions, sometimes to the extent of "reinventing the wheel." Many children, however, become unintended victims of this parenting style: They get run over by the wheel before they ever have a chance to discover it. These youngsters tend to wear their problems on the outside. Their unrestrained misbehavior leads them into trouble with the world around them. On the other hand, creative children with a high degree of self-motivation tend to blossom in this type of environment.

What happens if one parent is authoritarian and the other is permissive? It can result in a heap of trouble. It can lead to the well-known *good parent–bad parent syndrome:* Permissive parents say yes a lot and are, therefore, seen as "good guys" in the eyes of children; authoritarian parents tend to set limits and say no and are seen as the "bad guys."

The answer? A middle course. Parents, not children, should be in charge of families. But children must be given a chance to grow in responsibility and the ability to express themselves. I prefer a parenting style that might be called *participatory parenting:* Mothers and fathers establish the core family values and make the crucial decisions, yet children are encouraged to participate by expressing their opinions and to gradually assume responsibility for making their own decisions; first in minor things, later in important matters. The goal of all parents, after all, is to raise a loving, self-disciplined child who possesses the necessary skills, values, and attitudes to become a successful, autonomous adult.

Planning a Family

Q: I am 24 years old and have been married for two years. My husband and I are beginning to think about starting a family. We'd like to have three children. Here is our question: Is it better to have children very close together in age, or is it preferable to space them apart by a few years?

A: Strictly from the standpoint of psychological development, it is preferable to space children two or three years apart. Children who are only twelve to eighteen months apart in age tend to be very competitive since their needs, wants, and interests are always so similar. When children are spaced at two- or three-year intervals, their individuality is enhanced. Their differences are defined naturally and chronologically. There is less sibling rivalry expended in their attempts to define themselves in comparison to each other.

So much for the theory. In practice any parent can tell you that you sign up for a certain amount of sibling rivalry any time you have more than one child.

Another factor to consider is your own personal development and the development of your marriage. What are your own life goals? Over the span of how many years, for example, do you want a child in diapers? Do you have career plans? Be sure to crank these factors into the equation too.

Parental Example

Q: We're expecting our first child in two months. We've talked a lot about raising children, but we can't seem to agree on *self-discipline*. What is the most effective self-disciplinary technique?

A: The single, most effective technique to teach children self-discipline has nothing to do with spanking, withholding the weekly allowance, or restricting the kids from watching *Fantasy Island* reruns. The single, most effective way to teach your children the joys of self-discipline is your own parental example!

For example, the parent who insists upon keeping rules and maintaining respect in the family while secretly cheating an employer or the Internal Revenue Service and throwing temper tantrums himself when things do not go his way is sending a mixed message to his child.

Children are more aware of what we adults *do* than of what we *say*.

What are your family values on self discipline? Whatever they are, you will communicate them daily to your children through your own behavior. This is not to say, of course, that parents must be perfect. We are people. None of us is perfect. Children are marvelously forgiving of our faults—if we demonstrate our love to them and if we demonstrate, through our own behavior, the value of self-discipline.

Love Is Not Enough

Q: We're going to have our first child in three months. Both Darryl and I want to be good parents. Isn't *love* really the key?

A: Yes and no. Love is certainly the first step. I presume you're bringing a child into the world out of love. But love will not be enough. You'll have to *understand* your child's needs as he or she passes through the various stages of development. This will take some active effort, and study, on your part. You'll also have to understand your own reactions as your youngster grows; after all, parents go through stages too.

You'll have to develop some new skills along the way too; especially communication skills and discipline techniques. Finally, you ought to examine what you mean by *love*. Love is more than a feeling. Love is action. In the words of Harry Stack Sullivan, love is when the happiness or security of the other person matters as much to you as your own happiness and security. As a parent you'll have daily opportunities to put love into action in many ways great and small, utilizing all your new understanding and skills. If you do, your child will love you for it.

Parents as Teachers

Q: We're expecting our first child in four months. We both agree that it will be important to spend a lot of time with the baby. My question is this: How important is it to actually *teach* things to a baby versus just being there as a nurturer and supporter?

A: It can make a world of difference. In one study undertaken by the New Parents as Teachers Project in Missouri, it was found that when mothers and fathers, with the guidance of child development specialists, spent a lot of time teaching and encouraging their children in the first three years of life, these youngsters scored significantly higher on achievement tests than other children. For example, the youngsters in the study scored in the 85th percentile in school-related skills, compared to the 61st percentile for children who were not in the study group.

Popular Names

Q: My husband is John. I'm Mary. We're expecting our first child soon. We'll be darned if we're going to saddle him or her with a name as common as our own. Please help. What have been the most common names for American children over the years? We'd like to avoid them.

A: Although the naming of children does reflect changing cultural attitudes, demographic shifts, and even contemporary fads, the consistency is surprising. In 1900 the most popular names were Mary,

Catherine, Margaret, John, William, and Charles; in 1928, Mary, Marie, Anne, John, William, and Joseph; in 1948, Linda, Mary, Barbara, Robert, John, and James; in 1964, Lisa, Deborah, Mary, Michael, John, and Robert; in 1972, Jenniffer, Michelle, Lisa, Michael, David, and Christopher; and in 1982, Jenniffer, Anne, Jessica, Michael, Jason, and Matthew.

In general, I find that names of boys tend to change more slowly over a period of time than the names of girls; therefore, the names of boys tend to be much more traditional and biblical than the names of girls. For example, the name *Mary* was tops in 1900 and 1928, second in 1948, and third in 1964 but failed to make the top ten in 1982. *John*, however, was most popular in 1900 and is still among the more popular names for boys today.

Baby M*A*S*H

Q: We're expecting our first child in one and a half months. We've been told it will be a boy. My husband wants to give the baby an unusual name: M*A*S*H. No kidding. I can't believe it. My husband says that such names are helpful in getting ahead in life, that people remember you. I say forget it. What do you say?

A: Research substantiates what reasonable parents already know: The name you choose for your child can have an enormous impact on his self-esteem, development, and success in life. Your husband, however, is reading the results backward. When you give a child an unusual name, you are likely to do more harm than good.

For example, when M*A*S*H goes to school, he may be ridiculed or shamed by his classmates. This could cause him to shun their company, to become shy, and to suffer in self-esteem. Researchers in one study asked a group of 10- to 12-year-olds to rate the popularity of children at their school. The youngsters with odd or unusual names were almost always at rock bottom of the list.

The naming of a baby reveals more about the parent or parents than about the child. What are your husband's aspirations for his son? He wants his son to "get ahead" and "be remembered." Ahead to where? Remembered for what? As a TV series *M*A*S*H* topped the charts; as a name for your son it's got to rank very low in the ratings.

Naming the Baby "Junior"

Q: I am eight weeks pregnant with our first child. If it is a boy, I'd like to name him after my husband. I've heard that boys can grow up to resent being named after their fathers because it implies that they are always "second." What is your advice?

A: There is nothing inherently harmful about naming a son after his father or about *not* naming him after his father as long as both you and your husband respect his birthright to grow into his own individual self-identity.

Boys who eventually resent being named after their fathers do so because they resent pressures that force them to be just like dad in terms of temperament, interests, and career choice.

Boys who are named after their fathers but whose individuality is respected can grow up with a healthy identification with dad.

The naming of a baby, at any rate, should be a collaborative effort between you and your husband. Similarly, now is the time for both of you to have some serious discussions about a value system for your developing family. If your name is Smith, what will it mean to be a "Smith"? What will be the values of the Smith family? For what purpose are you bringing a child into the world? Too few parents stop to consider these questions; most of us are too busy living life to stop and philosophize about it. But just like the selection of a baby's name, these questions have enormous practical importance. Your answers will determine your parenting roles, your disciplinary practices, and the development of your child.

By the way, I sense from your letter that you have a strong preference for a boy. You did not ask at all about names for a daughter. Careful. Please examine this matter and talk it over with your husband. You may be courting trouble if you are not prepared to welcome a little girl into the world.

Should the Children Call Us by Our First Names?

Q: My husband and I are expecting our first child in two and a half months. We are toying with the idea of raising her (or him) to call us by our first names. It seems more warm and friendly. What do you think?

A: Warmth and friendliness grow out of the nature of the parent-child relationship, not out of names or titles. If you are warm and loving to your child, you will receive warmth and love in return, whether you are addressed as Mommy, Mother, or Mary Jane.

Some parents prefer to be called by their first names because they are actually unsure of their parental role. Going on a first-name basis with their children, therefore, has a leveling effect and blurs the parent-child boundary. This effect can be dangerous. No matter how a youngster refers to a parent, it should be clear to all parties that a distinct difference in role exists.

Although a few child psychiatrists actively advocate first-name parenting, I do not advise it for most families because of the blurring of the parent-child boundary and because it can confuse youngsters. One 7-year-old boy asked his mother why his friends all had "Mommies" and he had a "Lucille."

How-to-Parent Classes

Q: We're expecting our first child in five months. My husband thinks we should sign up for one of those how-to-parent classes. What is your opinion?

A: In general I'm very positive about them. But as you can imagine, such programs come in many sizes and shapes. Therefore, I suggest that you ask a few questions. First of all, what is the general philosophy of the course you're considering? Is it conservative, liberal, or something in between? Is the course broad-based, or does it really turn on one basic technique such as communication? Also, who is responsible for the course? Who designed it? Who teaches it? What are the credentials of the leaders? Finally, I recommend that you talk to some parents who have completed the course. Has it worked for them? That's the acid test.

Friend Lost to Pregnancy

Q: I'm eight months pregnant, and I'm ecstatic. My husband, Rudy, is ecstatic too. There's one thing, though, that hurts. My girlfriend, Paula, has pulled away from me. And I know why. Several years ago Paula had a hysterectomy. I'm sure that my own pregnancy is a sharp reminder that she will never bear children. I feel so bad. Paula is my closest friend on earth. We went all the way up from grade school together. I hate to see this happening. Any advice?

A: This phenomenon is not unusual in the last trimester of pregnancy. Jealousy, envy, rivalry, competition, and resentment are commonplace. Just ask any woman who's ever been pregnant. But Paula's pain is special. It's probably based on her own deep sense of loss rather than her resentment of your happiness. In this case, it will have to be *you* who must reach out to *her*. Do it now.

Competitive Mother Syndrome

Q: I don't have any children yet, and maybe it's harder for me to understand, but I can't stand mothers who are always competing with other mothers through the exploits of their children. Why do they do it?

A: The most common cause of the *competitive mother syndrome* is overidentification with the child. These mothers feel empty and incomplete so they strive to achieve satisfaction vicariously through the accomplishments of their children.

Another cause is the overvaluing of competition and winning. Some mothers are natural competitors themselves: in work, in sports, in social events. They expect their children to follow in their nimble footsteps.

I've described two extremes. There are other causes. The danger to children, however, is similar in any case. Children who feel that they are merely extensions of their parents are trapped. They feel loved only for what they do, not for who they are. Some of these children are indeed driven to achievement. Each success, however, is empty. It must be topped to ensure the parent's love.

Other youngsters, perhaps less gifted, dig in their heels and refuse to run the fast track. Their "success" is failure—and it is their revenge as well.

By the way, fathers can be just as competitive as mothers.

Pride in a child is a must. Occasional boasting? Why not. But a persistent attempt to fill your own personal needs through the development of your child is not healthy. It robs the child—and the parent too.

Pretty Baby

Q: Our baby is due in three months. We just want her to be healthy and intelligent. If she's "pretty," that's okay, but we couldn't care less. But recently I've heard that babies who are considered to be pretty or cute actually get more attention from parents than other babies. It's hard to believe. Is it true?

A: It may be hard to believe, but research findings suggest that it may well be true. A University of Texas psychologist, for example, has found that mothers who have pretty babies (as judged by independent observers) actually cuddle them more frequently.

Our society places a high premium on physical attractiveness. It should not be too surprising, then, that preferential treatment begins in the cradle—and that it continues through childhood, adolescence, and even into adult life.

Is this a good thing? No. It is not good for a child to grow up building his own self-esteem and identity upon such a flimsy foundation. Another downside risk is that parents often give an attractive child more slack than her brothers and sisters. The "cute kid" sometimes gets away with too much. This, of course, is not good training for later life.

And what about the unattractive siblings of these nubile beauties? They may suffer. They may be scapegoated.

Pretty babies are fortunate, but their good looks can boomerang on them and on other members of the family if parents are not careful.

Adoption and Intelligence

Q: My husband and I are both college graduates, and we place a high value on academic achievement. Because I'm not able to conceive a baby of my own, we're planning to adopt. My question comes down to inheritance versus environment. Will the child's basic intelligence be determined more by the genes he inherits from his biological parents or by the kind of stimulation, encouragement, and environment that we'll provide?

A: This is not an easy question. The determination of intelligence is a complicated matter. Although many genes from the mother and father go into the equation, a youngster's eventual environment is also a most important factor.

Our knowledge in this area comes mostly from studies of twins—and from adoptions. Identical twins who have been separated at a young age tend to have very similar IQs when tested years later. Another argument for heredity is that the IQs of adopted children tend to be more similar to their natural parents' than to their adoptive parents'.

On the other hand, inherited traits of intelligence must be given the proper atmosphere to be developed. After all, a perfect seed may not grow into a tall tree if it's denied good soil, while a less-than-perfect seed may grow unexpectedly tall if it's supported by fertile soil, water, and proper sunlight.

I wouldn't be overly concerned about this matter. Even if you had children of your own, their intelligence could vary considerably from each other. There are no guarantees. Love your child for who she is—not for what she might become.

Adoption Benefits?

Q: We are working with an adoption agency and look forward to adopting our first child. At a meeting the other night, I learned that some companies now give "pregnancy benefits" for adoptive parents. True?

A: True. And it's a great idea.

At this time several U.S. companies provide "adoption leave" and other benefits. A major reason is that adoption agencies, recognizing the fact of women in the workplace, have loosened up on the old requirement that adoptive mothers must be full-time home-makers. Now that employed women are turning more frequently to adoptions, their employers are beginning to respond. If your em-ployer doesn't offer such benefits, talk to your personnel manager about it anyway. You could break some new ground for yourself, your child—and other women too.

Adopt a Latin Baby?

Q: My husband and I have been waiting three years for an adop-tion with a local agency. Last week we learned that we can quickly adopt a baby from South America. We're elated but cautious. We're both blond, blue-eyed Yankees. Would we be doing the child a disservice by raising him or her in a foreign environment?

A: There is very little hard data upon which to answer your ques-tion in spite of the fact that thousands of babies from Latin Amer-ica have been placed for adoption in this country over the past twenty years.

One study, completed by a psychologist at California State Uni-versity, finds that so-called transethnic adoption is not as prefera-ble as same-ethnic adoption. Estela Andujo, Ph.D., reports that transethnic adoptees tend to be more confused about their identi-ties. She also speculates that because these adoptees have physical characteristics different from most American children, they may ul-timately experience role confusion and discrimination.

On the other hand, both groups of adoptees scored about the same on tests of basic self-esteem.

What to do? Your sensitivity shows. Use it wisely. If possible, talk to other parents who have adopted transethnically. If you de-cide to go ahead, try to raise your child with a healthy and positive appreciation for his or her own heritage.

Bilingual Jitters

Q: I am six months pregnant with our first child. My husband, Carlos, is a native of Venezuela. I'm American. Carlos wants to raise the baby to speak both English and Spanish. I think it's basically a good idea, but there's one hitch. I don't speak Spanish. I'm worried that I might somehow get "left out." Yet, on the other hand, I hate to deny our child the chance to be bilingual. What is your advice?

A: This is not an uncommon situation. In fact, with the heavy influx of Spanish-speaking people into the United States, we're going to be seeing a lot more bilingual concerns.

Your worry about being left out might be a bit exaggerated, but I have observed subtle differences in how children relate to the parent who shares a special language with them. It injects a certain exclusivity into the relationship. The nonfluent parent may not be left out, but she (or he) is excluded from something special. The problem, by the way, can be exacerbated in the presence of foreign-speaking in-laws. The spouse who can't communicate in the foreign tongue feels even more awkward and conspicuous.

The best solution for your problem would be for you to learn Spanish. It would be fun—and relatively easy if you learn it right along with your child.

Bilingual Children

Q: Our first baby is due in four months. My native language is Spanish. My husband speaks only English. We both want our children to grow up to be bilingual. What is the best way to do it? Should we raise our child to be bilingual from birth or add the second language at a later time?

A: This subject has interested me for several years, and I have spoken to many bilingual parents and bilingual child psychiatrists about it. While there is some difference of opinion, the following guidelines represent the general consensus:

1. If you really want your child to be bilingual, begin at birth.

2. Be careful not to establish a very private "mother-child" language that excludes your husband. In the best of all worlds, it would be best if your husband would also learn Spanish. In that way, the

entire family shares all modes of communication; your husband will not feel left out of an important part of the relationship.

3. Be prepared that your child, at some point, may well disavow his non-English language. This usually happens when a child enters school, when he fears being "different" from the other kids. If this happens, do not worry. Gently continue speaking Spanish at home, but do not push it unduly in other settings. Most such youngsters eventually pride themselves on being bilingual, and they will thank you for insisting on it. ¡Buena suerte! Good luck!

Depression during Pregnancy

Q: My daughter is six months pregnant. She's seeing a psychiatrist because of depression. My question is this: Is there any risk that her baby will be harmed by the depression?

A: The greatest immediate risk to the baby would be from possible side effects if your daughter is taking medication. She should consult with her physician in this matter.

The near-term risk to the baby would be if your daughter's depression extended to the postdelivery period. In that case her illness may prevent her from providing adequate mothering. Women who are ambivalent about motherhood are susceptible to depression. Babies born to depressed mothers are very definitely at risk. For example, these infants often fail to thrive or develop normally. Help from a mother substitute (father, grandparents, etc.) can be effective in avoiding such failure to thrive. Continued treatment for the mother is crucial.

The long-term risks, of course, would be that your daughter's form of depression might be genetically passed to the baby. Some types of depression are hereditary; others are not. Her physician can offer some predictions based on the nature of her illness and on a comprehensive family history.

The single most positive element in this case, however, is that your daughter is receiving treatment. Too often, depression during pregnancy goes unrecognized. That's when mother and child are in greatest danger.

Schizophrenic Baby?

Q: My husband is schizophrenic. He's been hospitalized twice in his life—for about two months each time. He's doing pretty well now on medication and occasional visits to his psychiatrist. We recently learned that I'm pregnant. I'm overjoyed, but suddenly it's hit me: What if the baby is schizophrenic? I've heard that the illness is inherited. True?

A: Yes, there is a definite genetic factor where schizophrenia is concerned. But don't panic.

You have to realize that most schizophrenic fathers have normal children and many normal fathers have schizophrenic sons and daughters.

On the basis of major research studies, your child probably has an 8 to 16 percent chance of developing the illness. The incidence in the general population is slightly less than 1 percent.

What really causes schizophrenia? We're not entirely sure yet. There are strong genetic factors, but there are environmental factors too.

Current treatment, combining proper medication and supportive psychotherapy, offers considerable hope.

Don't be scared by the word *schizophrenia*. Like your husband, most people with schizophrenia aren't that much different from anyone else. And they're a lot better off than many other people whose own inherited illnesses are far more damaging—even fatal.

Children of Alcoholics

Q: My son, Kenneth, is 25 years old and, unfortunately, is an alcoholic. We've tried to get him to go for treatment for the last two years, but he refuses. It pains us, but we've come to the conclusion that it's his problem: He's not ruining anyone except himself. Well, all of that has changed. He recently got married, and his wife is expecting a baby. Can you tell us anything about children of alcoholics? Maybe it will open my son's eyes.

A: Children of alcoholics are four to five times as likely to become alcoholics than are other children. I hope this fact opens Kenneth's eyes.

Here's another eyeful: A frequent symptom of parental alcoholism, according to a study prepared for the governor of New York,
is child abuse. And hyperactivity is especially more frequent in cases
where the father is alcoholic.

Children of alcoholics often bear other scars: shame, difficulty
with expressing feelings, and problems with trusting other people.

I suggest that you and your daughter-in-law start attending meetings of Al-Anon, the self-help group for relatives and friends of al
coholics. Learn as much as you can about the disease called alcoholism.
Then consult with an experienced alcoholism counselor about doing an "intervention" with Kenneth, that is, confronting him with
his illness. It could be the best thing you've ever done for him—
and for his child.

Drinking during Pregnancy

Q: I am four months pregnant. Last week I went out with a girlfriend to celebrate her promotion, and I, well, went overboard. I
mean I got totally smashed. I couldn't even stand. My friend had
to call my husband to pick me up. The next morning I felt so guilty.
No, doubly guilty because I had forgotten all about the baby. I've
been very careful up to this time. Now I'm frightened. Have I
harmed the baby? What should I do?

A: You are probably aware that a fetus subjected to *chronic* alcohol ingestion has a strong chance of developing birth abnormalities. There is no evidence at this time, however, that binge drinking
(one or two intoxications during pregnancy) causes problems. But
there is no test that can be done on your baby at this time to confirm my reassurance.

Let's face it. Alcohol has never been implicated as being good
for the developing fetus. My best advice: No more drinking at all
during your pregnancy. But if you've minimized the amount of your
drinking in your question to me, please reassess yourself.

The key is not so much how much or how often you drink, but
why you drink. If you habitually drink to change your mood you
may be knocking on the door of alcoholism. The next step would
be that your life would become increasingly unmanageable as a result of your drinking.

I don't mean to alarm you. Maybe you don't have a drinking problem. I hope not, but if you do—face it and do something about it.

Fetal Alcohol Syndrome

Q: I'm sure my sister is an alcoholic, but I've been too chicken to talk to her about it. She's been married for two years, and now she and her husband are beginning to talk about having children. Suddenly, I think I see a chance to talk to her about her drinking. Doesn't alcoholism cause physical problems in the newborn? If you could give me some facts, I'll discuss them with her. Maybe she can be persuaded to quit for the baby.

A: First, the facts you've requested. The fetal alcohol syndrome includes several symptoms and signs: low birth weight; malformed eyes, nose, mouth, and ears; heart and kidney defects; brain malformation; and others. In a recent study of twenty babies of heavy-drinking mothers, 45 percent had at least three of these abnormalities, 20 percent had more than seven! Yes, newborns can suffer tremendously from mom's alcoholism.

Now, about your sister. Don't feel too guilty about being "chicken." Such a hush-hush approach by families is common in the early stages of alcoholism. It's called *enabling*; that is, anyone who suspects the problem but, for whatever reason, fails to confront it is actually enabling the loved one to continue the illness. I salute you now. You've decided to stop enabling. But will your sister listen? She'll probably deny or minimize the problem. So get some help. Talk to her husband privately. If he'd join you, you'll be in better shape to get results. If her husband turns out to be an enabler himself (not an unusual scenario), you've got a bigger problem on your hands. Try Al-Anon and an alcohol counselor. Good luck.

Smoking and Pregnancy

Q: My sister, Monica, is three months pregnant, and she smokes almost two packs of cigarettes a day. She says she knows that smoking is bad for the baby, but she thinks the risks are exaggerated. What can I tell her?

A: Tell her to stop smoking. Cold turkey.

Your sister is ruining her own health. Since she's an adult, I guess we can take the position that it's her free choice. But the baby doesn't have a choice. Your sister is forcing her baby to be a smoker too. After all, every time your sister lights up, she's smoking for two.

Nicotine, carbon monoxide, and the other toxic substances in cigarette smoke pass from Monica's lungs to her bloodstream through the placenta and right into the baby's bloodstream. What happens then? The fetal heart rate increases, blood oxygen content decreases, and the fetus is robbed of vital nutrients that it needs for proper growth.

Monica is running a higher risk of uterine bleeding and miscarriage. If the pregnancy continues, the odds are strong that the baby will be born prematurely and underweight. If that happens, research studies conclude that the baby runs a higher risk for physical and mental impairment, respiratory illness, skin problems, and slow growth rate.

Please show this answer to Monica. If she won't quit for herself, maybe she'll quit for the baby.

Stop Smoking

Q: I'm five months pregnant. I've smoked about a pack of cigarettes a day for the past eight years. I'm scared for the baby's sake. Is it too late to stop? Has the damage already been done?

A: No, it's not too late to stop. Many studies have shown that mothers who stop smoking *completely* in the last three months of pregnancy can even the odds—as far as perinatal death is concerned.

You wouldn't dream of deliberately lighting up a cigarette and blowing the smoke into a baby's face, would you? But what you're doing to your own baby is far worse. Quit now—for good.

Preparing a Child for the Birth of a Sibling

Q: I am four months pregnant. We have a 3-year-old daughter, Becca. When should we tell her that she's going to have a baby brother or sister? Are there any tips you can give to prepare her for the event and to minimize sibling rivalry?

A: Don't look now, but your daughter probably knows about the coming event already! Well, she may not know *exactly* what is going to happen, but she probably senses that there is something exciting brewing in the family. Children are marvelously adept at picking up our emotional cues, even at Becca's tender age. As a matter of fact, Becca may well feel "left out" of the excitement at this point.

When to tell her? Now. Waiting any further will probably lead Becca to suspect that something is being hidden from her. She'll become suspicious, and you'll have a tougher time convincing her that the news is good news when you do finally break it to her.

If Becca is part of the process from the beginning, she can grow with you and your husband into an awareness of what a new baby will mean to your family. Be sure to answer her questions directly and factually, but do not overwhelm her with unnecessary details that she cannot comprehend, such as the mechanics of labor and delivery.

One of Becca's first fears will be that Mommy will go off to the hospital and abandon her. Anticipate this fear, and help her to deal with it. Explain how she will be taken care of while you're in the hospital. One of the best ways to accomplish this is to playact the drama with dolls: The daddy doll drives the mommy doll to the hospital, the grandmother doll comes to stay with the "Becca" doll, and so on. It would be wise to repeat this game several times so that your daughter can gain some real mastery of the facts and of her feelings.

It also helps youngsters to visit their mothers in the hospital, particularly if the hospital stay is at all prolonged for any reason. I hope your maternity ward has a liberal visiting policy for children.

How to minimize sibling rivalry? While a certain amount is to be expected and almost goes with the territory in such situations, there are a few tips:

1. Assure Becca, even in the doll game, of your love. She is still very special to Mommy and Daddy. Your love for her will not diminish.

2. Allow Becca to play with the baby and to help you in caring for it. Appeal to her as the big sister.

3. Beware of the trap of promising to treat both children equally. Such a promise is not only unnecessary, but it's impractical. Each child has different needs. You will love both of them and attempt to meet their unique needs to the best of your ability. That's the most that any child could wish. Overemphasis of "equal treatment" only magnifies all the everyday inequities that children naturally experience.

4. Since the baby will require special attention, try to arrange some "Becca time" each day for just the two of you. Your husband should do the same. This, of course, does not have to be equal time, just special time. Becca will love it.

Birth of Sibling

Q: I'm pregnant. The baby is due in three months. My husband and I have gotten used to the idea of another child. Our 14-year-old daughter, Monica, is not very happy about it. Her sister, Tabby, who is 7, is delighted. Frankly, I'm surprised. I thought it would be the other way around. Any comments?

A: Tabby, on the surface, is the child being displaced. She'll go from being the youngest to being the middle child. Monica, on the other hand, will still be the oldest. I suppose these facts led you to believe that Tabby, not Monica, might resent the intrusion of a baby brother or sister.

Sometimes, though, these things go beyond simple arithmetic. There are developmental factors to consider too. Monica, for example, is an early adolescent. Your pregnancy might be conflictual and even embarrassing for her. Teenagers can conceive of almost anything except their parents as sexual beings. Then, too, Monica might be worrying that she'll get stuck with a lot of baby-sitting duty.

Tabby appears to be adapting well. Maybe she relishes the possibility of becoming a big sister. Maybe she's just putting up a good front.

Whatever the case, don't accept either girl's reaction at face value. Sound them out—privately and separately. Sibling rivalry is part of everyday life. It can become a problem if it's not talked about—openly and honestly. Following the private chats, why not have a full-family discussion about how *all* your lives are about to change? All four of you have feelings about that—right?

Father in Delivery Room

Q: I'm six months pregnant with my first child. I'd like Bob, my husband, to be in the delivery room, but he's not too sure about it. What's your opinion?

A: My opinion, in general, is that it's a very good idea. Researchers at Johns Hopkins University recently surveyed a large number of fathers who had attended the births of their children. Two out of three were very pleased. Many of them were ecstatic about the experience. Most of them felt it made them better fathers by bringing them closer physically and emotionally to their children than they ever imagined they would get. As far as Bob is concerned, I wouldn't push it. The delivery room is not for everyone. Instead, talk it over with him. If he has technical questions, direct him to your obstetrician. Give him the facts; then respect his feelings.

Fathers Are Not Expendable

Q: We're expecting our first child soon, and we've been reading a lot of books. Most of these books about infants focus almost exclusively on the mother-child relationship. What part do fathers play in the life of infants—or are fathers really expendable?

A: Fathers are hardly expendable. Yet you are quite correct to point out that the importance of *fathering* has been largely ignored by the experts for many years. The basic theory has been that an infant's relationship pattern is a *dyadic* (two-person) one until the age of 3 or 4. The dyadic *bonding* occurs between the infant and the mothering person, usually the biologic mother. Unless the father is actually providing the primary mothering function (such as in a role-reversal situation or death of the mother), his importance is secondary; his impact on the family is felt primarily through the degree of support he provides his wife in her primary mothering role.

Current research, however, suggests that fathers can have a significant direct influence on children during infancy. Studies in the United States and England have shown, for example, that fathers are fully capable of nurturing and caring for infants. The myth that men inherently lack the competence to empathize with and respond to infants has been debunked. Furthermore, research at the National Institute of Child Health and Human Development has demonstrated that the more active fathers are with their 5- to 6-month-old infants, the higher the little ones score on the Bayley Index, a test of intellectual and motor development. Another study has shown that infants whose fathers are actively involved in dressing and bathing them withstood stress and frustration better than infants whose fathers are not actively involved in their daily care.

No, fathers are not expendable. They can and should play an important and unique role with their babies, right from day one.

The Art of Fatherhood

Q: I'm an expectant father. In your opinion, what is the single most important trait for successful fatherhood?

A: Good fathers share many traits in common: They maintain a strong marriage, they share parenting responsibilities with their wives, they're available to the children, they establish firm family values, they communicate well with their youngsters, they care enough to provide firm but fair discipline, and they gradually work themselves out of a job and back into a comfortable one-to-one relationship with their spouses.

But you ask for one *most important* trait. If I had to select a single trait above all others for successful fatherhood, it would be *empathy*. Why? Empathy is love put into action. Empathy is the ability to see with a child's eyes, to hear with a child's ears, and to feel with a child's heart. The father who has empathy is a surefire success. His fatherhood is, indeed, an art.

Pregnant Fathers?

Q: I'm pregnant with our first child. The pregnancy is going pretty well for me—but not for my husband, Andy. If I didn't know better, I'd say he was pregnant too! He's tense, suffers frequently from upset stomachs, and has difficulty sleeping. Comments please.

A: Your husband may be suffering a variant of the *couvade syndrome,* a condition where expectant fathers express some of the symptoms of their pregnant wives. The psychodynamics can be complicated, but in general such men tend to overidentify with their wives and may even envy their ability to give birth to a child. But don't worry. It's not so ominous as it might sound.

In fact, your husband's identification with you may be a healthy sign of his closeness and his sensitivity as a father.

You should also consider, of course, that your husband's symptoms may be part of his prefatherhood jitters. Parenthood is serious business. Andy may be a bit overwhelmed.

I suggest a private chat with your obstetrician. If a psychiatric consultation is indicated, he or she will know and can help arrange it.

Recycled Fathers

Q: I will soon marry a man who is fifteen years older than me. It will be my first marriage, his second. He has three children from his previous marriage who live with their mother. He says that he wants us to have children. My question is this: Do men make better fathers the second time around?

A: Yes. Most "recycled" fathers report a higher level of satisfaction from raising children in a second marriage. Their basic attitude is much more positive. For example, three times as many of these men attend childbirth classes with their wives than do first-time fathers. This early involvement leads to a feeling of intimacy and closer participation in the parenting process. These men feel more "bonded" to their infants. Therefore, they tend to communicate better and to share responsibilities with their wives—which, of course, is mighty good medicine for the marriage.

This information is generalized from interviews by researchers with several hundred men. Your own man is an individual with his own unique attitudes and aptitudes. My best advice? Discuss your question openly with him. He's the real expert on how he'll fare the second time around.

The Changing American Father

Q: Our first baby is due soon—and I smell a rat. I'm talking about my husband. Let me explain. When we discussed having a family, he promised that he'd be involved with the baby. You know, diapers, feeding—the whole 9 yards. But now? Now that little Anthony is scheduled to arrive any minute, Big Anthony, my husband, is having second thoughts. He says it's the woman's role to do these things. Macho stuff. I remind him of his promise, but it does no good. What should I do?

A: You might remind Big Anthony that he's out of step with today's fathers. American fathers, in fact, are getting much more involved in the care of their infants.

A recent Gallup poll, for example, reported that 80 percent of new fathers change diapers, 79 percent attend the delivery of their child, 67 percent feed the baby, and 43 percent bathe the little ones.

As a child psychiatrist I can tell you that fathers who get involved early in the raising of their children tend to stay involved. And that's good for everybody: little Anthony—and Big Anthony too.

He Can't Accept My Pregnancy

Q: My husband and I have been married for three years. Last week my doctor told me what I suspected: I'm pregnant. I thought my husband would be elated; after all we've been trying for this the past several months. Instead, he's gotten very quiet, kind of pulled back into himself. He says he's happy but that it hasn't hit him yet, that he can't accept the pregnancy yet. I'm trying to understand him. It does mean a tremendous change in our life. But I'm worried.

A: Psychological "acceptance" of pregnancy is really one of the first stages of parenthood. Most people coast through it without even recognizing it, but your husband is having some trouble with it.

It's as though he has accepted it in his mind initially (he did want the pregnancy, remember), but he hasn't worked through an emotional acceptance yet. It may take some time. You can help by urging that he talk to you about it. Don't rush to judgment. In my own clinical experience I've found that this type of emotional uncertainty does not necessarily foreshadow rejection of the baby and the parental role at all. Your husband, like other men and women, may require a period of thoughtful reflection, emotional working through...and ultimately be a better parent because of it.

My Husband Wants a Baby but I Don't

Q: I'm 29, and I've been married for two years. My husband wants us to have a baby—but I don't. I'm just not ready for it. There are too many things I want to do. I say we've still got time. My husband says no: The time is now. I love him, and I'm tempted to go along with it just to make him happy, but isn't this the wrong reason to have a baby?

A: From the standpoint of a child psychiatrist I know that children who are genuinely wanted by both their parents come into the world with an important advantage. You say you're not ready to bring a baby into your life, and I'm inclined to take your statement at face value. But, on the other hand, I sense some ambivalence in your question. Part of you, at least, is "tempted to go along with it." Be careful. Ambivalence can be a dangerous motivation for pregnancy.

You may be heading for a crisis in your marriage, especially if your husband equates your reluctance to have a baby with the possibility of your not loving him. You and I know that the two are not necessarily related, and I bet your husband does too, but these matters can become very emotional. That's why the decision to bring children into the world can be so complicated. The good news here, though, is that the two of you are talking about it and seeking consultation.

Dad's Great Expectations

Q: We're expecting our second child in about three months. It's going to be a boy. Our daughter, Karen, is 2. I know my husband is very happy that we're having a son, but I didn't know just how happy he is until I overheard him talking to his buddies. They were in the kitchen drinking beer, and Rad, my husband, was bragging about what a great guy his son is going to be. He has it all planned: honor roll, football scholarship, law school—you name it. The funny thing is that he's never mentioned these plans to me!

A: Maybe just a little boozy braggadocio here. Don't get too alarmed. On the other hand, studies have shown that parents who fail to communicate their private expectations for their children to each other tend to have more misunderstandings and disagreements about child raising in later years.

Also, although you don't raise the issue, I wonder if you're concerned about Rad's possible preference for your son over Karen. If so, the time to talk it over with Rad is now.

This is preparation time. Use it wisely.

Quiz

Test your parenting skills on the following questions, taken directly from this chapter. Nobody's perfect, but you should score at least 80 percent if you really want this book to help you become a better parent.

1. True or false? Babies, contrary to popular belief, are not soothed by rocking chairs.

2. True or false? Breast-fed infants have fewer infections.

3. True or false? The "ideal" spacing of children is twelve to eighteen months.

4. True or false? The proper role of fathers in the raising of infants is to support the mother. Fathers have little actual impact on the development of babies.

5. On the basis of a survey of children (aged 6 to 16) what do youngsters really want today? Select the three correct answers:

   ☐ A. More time with parents
   ☐ B. More freedom
   ☐ C. More discipline
   ☐ D. Higher weekly allowance
   ☐ E. Honesty

6. True or false? Men who marry for a second time and who had children in their first marriage generally do better as fathers in their second marriage.

7. True or false? Allowing your child to call you by your first name (rather than Mommy or Daddy) is good. It helps create closeness.

8. True or false? Children should always take priority over your marriage.

9. True or false? Smoking during pregnancy can result in premature birth.

10. True or false? A female infant born today will (based on statistical averages) outlive a male infant by ten years.

11. True or false? Most couples are more susceptible to divorce after the birth of their first child.

12. The single most important technique in teaching self-discipline to children is:

   ☐ A. Consistency
   ☐ B. Parental example
   ☐ C. Rewards
   ☐ D. Punishment

13. True or false? Children with unusual first names are more apt to be popular with their classmates.

14. True or false? Pretty babies get more attention from their mothers.

15. Identical twins who are separated at birth:

    ☐ A. Tend to develop the same intelligence levels
    ☐ B. Are more influenced by their environment where intelligence is concerned

16. If you wish a child to grow up bilingually, it is best to:

    ☐ A. Teach both languages from birth
    ☐ B. Add the second language at the age of 3
    ☐ C. Add the second language at the age of 6

17. Children of alcoholics:

    ☐ A. Have a greater incidence of alcoholism than other children
    ☐ B. Have a lesser incidence of alcoholism than other children
    ☐ C. Have the same incidence of alcoholism as other children

18. True or false? Infants whose fathers are actively involved in their care score higher on tests of motor development and intelligence.

19. True or false? Infants who are breast-fed generally require supplemental feedings after four to six months.

20. The best approach to raising children is:

    ☐ A. Authoritarian
    ☐ B. Permissive
    ☐ C. A middle ground between the two

Answers

1. False	6. True	11. True	16. A
2. True	7. False	12. B	17. A
3. False	8. False	13. False	18. True
4. False	9. True	14. True	19. True
5. A, C, E	10. False	15. A	20. C

CHAPTER 2

Infants and Toddlers (Birth to 2)

A miraculous time: Your child will go through more change in these two years than in any two years of her entire life. You will also change and adapt to her needs. The newborn is a helpless creature. She'll depend totally upon you for her survival. She'll need heavy doses of protection, nurturance, stimulation, and, of course, love. The warmth, consistency, and encouragement you bring to her will help her develop a basic sense of trust, security, and optimism: If things go bad, Mother and Father can be counted on to make them better.

But enough of this passivity. Soon your baby will begin to crawl, then walk. There's a big, wide, wonderful world out there, and she wants to be a part of it. You'll have to let her explore, of course, while still providing a physical and psychological safety net.

Baby will also learn to talk—and then to talk back. The 2-year-old's favorite word, of course, is "no," and she uses it in an effort to control the world around her. Control is also a core issue in toilet training. She wants to be in control—and she doesn't want to be in control. These ambivalent swings between dependence and independence will try your skills and your patience at times, but the right blend of encouragement and proper limit setting will carry the day.

The Newborn

Q: When does a baby really begin to use her senses such as sight, hearing, and feeling?

A: The newborn baby is alive, in all senses of the word, at birth. She sees, hears, tastes, smells, and experiences tactile sensation and movement too.

This question, of course, is more than just theoretical. It has enormous practical implication for mothers and fathers. For example, some parents believe that the basic needs of the infant are limited to feeding and physical safety. Not true. Infants, from the first day of life, also need stimulation: visual, auditory, and tactile, or "touching."

Research by the renowned Reneé Spitz demonstrated, many years ago, that infants who do not receive such stimulation simply do not thrive well, either physically or psychologically.

This stimulation, by the way, represents your infant's first real experience with learning. She will require variety but do not *overload* her. With time she will develop preferences. For example, some infants seem to react more to visual than auditory stimuli; these children may later tend to learn better visually (reading) than auditorily (lectures).

So you can see that your infant's special senses are special in many ways. The basic formula for newborns: nurturance, protection, and—stimulation.

The Nose Knows

Q: Please settle an argument between me and my girlfriend. I say that my son was able to distinguish me by smell alone when he was only 1 month old. My friend says that humans do not have such a highly developed capacity for smell.

A: Your girlfriend is going to have to pay up on the bet. Infants can distinguish smells within the first week or two of life. Researchers at Oxford University have demonstrated an infant's preference for the natural body odor of his mother as early as 7 to 10 days of age.

Do Babies Dream?

Q: I've heard that babies dream. I suppose it's possible, but how could you ever prove it since babies can't tell you about their dreams?

A: Researchers in neurophysiology and sleep laboratories have long known, from research on adults, that dreaming takes place during a particular phase of sleep called *rapid eye movement* (REM). When a sleeping person is hooked up to an electroencephalogram (EEG, or brain wave tracing), the record suddenly changes when his eyes, under his closed eyelids, begin moving rapidly (REM); if the person is suddenly awakened, he will report a vivid dream. Awakening a person in other phases of sleep does not result in a dream report.

We know that infants do experience REM sleep. In fact, they have more REM sleep than adults. So technically you might say that they dream. But you're right, of course, when you point out that babies cannot verify a true dream. If an infant has anything like a dream, it's probably a scattered perception of sound and light, unorganized into any concept. With time, however, these images become organized by the developing brain into dreams as we adults know them.

Accelerated Bonding?

Q: I've heard that babies are capable of distinguishing between various caretakers at a very early age if they can perceive obvious differences. What I'm thinking about is this: I want to make sure that my 1-month-old infant becomes bonded to me rather than to my sister who will take care of him when I return to work. If I always wear a distinctive piece of clothing (such as a bright-red blouse), will it speed up the process?

A: It might, but the "gain" may only be temporary. And what if you go to your baby without the red blouse? He could get very confused. So relax. Don't be in a hurry. Spend as much time as you can with baby. The bonding process is natural. It takes time. Enjoy it.

Infant Stimulation

Q: We have just brought our premature daughter, Gayle, home from the nursery. She's 4 weeks old now and doing fine thanks to the wonderful care of those doctors and nurses. I was especially impressed by all the physical touching, stroking, and holding that the staff used in Gayle's care. One of the nurses explained that it was based on a theory of *infant stimulation*. Can you explain? Can I use it at home with Gayle myself?

A: Yes, by all means. Gayle, like all infants, has three basic requirements: nurturance, protection, and stimulation. While it's easy to understand the dangers of withdrawing food or physical protection from an infant, the dangers of understimulation are less apparent. But, believe me, stimulation is absolutely crucial—especially for preemies, like Gayle.

Infants who are not stimulated by touch, sound, sight, and smell do not thrive. They may fail to gain weight or to develop physically and psychologically.

Here are some tips for an at-home stimulation program:

1. *Tactile stimulation:* Babies love to be held, cuddled, and rocked slowly. You might add some gentle stroking with your fingers along the side of Gayle's face. Also, introduce soft textures such as cotton.

2. *Auditory stimulation:* What's a baby's favorite sound? Her mother's heartbeat. Should you talk baby talk to Gayle? Yes. There is evidence that the falsetto-pitched adult voice is pleasing to an infant's ears. Soft music and lower tones help to soothe an infant.

3. *Visual stimulation:* Even newborns react to colors and shapes. If you watch closely, you'll find that Gayle probably has some favorites already. But don't go overboard in the first several weeks: Too much of any stimulus can lead to overload and confusion.

4. *Olfactory stimulation:* That's right. Smells are important too. Infants prefer the odors of mother's breast milk and sweet-smelling substances.

There you have it. A prescription for close mother-child bonding: nurturance, protection, and stimulation.

Smiley

Q: Our baby, Lark, is 6 weeks old. I first noticed her smiling at me when she was only 2 to 3 weeks old. But my husband points out that she smiles at everything—not just me. What does this mean? Is she basically happy? Doesn't she recognize me yet?

A: Your baby is happy as a lark. Her smile is a good sign. But, no, she's not really smiling at you—yet.

Lark's smile is what we call a *social smile*. Observe her carefully. I bet she'll smile at pictures of the human face too. She's not developmentally ready to distinguish pictures from the real thing. And she's certainly not ready to distinguish your face from other familiar faces.

Lark will probably begin to smile selectively to familiar faces at about 3 to 4 months of age. She will associate your face with warmth, nurturance, cuddling, security. Researchers at the National Institute of Mental Health have identified the baby's smile as one of the most powerful indicators of a strong mother-infant attachment.

Keep smiling.

Abandoned Baby

Q: I was shocked. A few nights ago I went out to close the garage door, and I found a baby on our doorstep. I've heard about such things happening, but you can't imagine what it's like if it's never happened to you. My girls, aged 8 and 15, wanted to keep it—and for a moment I did too—but we finally called the police. We can't imagine why someone would have picked us; maybe it was just at random. Why do people do this anyhow? And what happens to these infants?

A: Mothers and fathers who abandon children generally fall into one of these categories:

1. *The destitute:* These parents usually have a great love for their baby but are financially destitute. They may carefully choose a family that they believe is better able, financially, to care for their baby.

2. *The depressed:* A woman suffering postpartum depression may feel so hopeless about herself and her ability to "mother" that she abandons her infant.

3. *The disturbed:* A mother or father suffering from severe mental illness such as schizophrenia may precipitously discard a baby because "voices" say to do it. This kind of abandonment is more haphazard, less planned, and is more apt to jeopardize the safety of the infant.

What happens to abandoned infants? The Washington, D.C., police department reports that about 75 percent of the parents are found. Typically, Protective Services takes the infant while the parent or parents are being counseled and evaluated.

I'm told that 50 percent of these infants are returned to their parents but that the other 50 percent are placed for adoption after a sixty-day waiting period.

Infant Psychiatry

Q: My girlfriend told me she saw a doctor on a TV show who was talking about psychiatry for infants. This seems a bit farfetched. What good can a psychiatrist do for an infant?

A: A lot —in some situations. Infant psychiatry is a special interest of a small group of child psychiatrists. They consult with parents and pediatricians in cases such as failure to thrive, abuse and neglect, repetitious vomiting, and other developmental disorders.

The psychiatric assessment is accomplished through the medical history, physical exam, interview with parents, and direct observation of the infant. Treatment is conducted through counseling of parents and, at times, direct work with the infant. No, the psychiatrist cannot use "talking psychotherapy" but relies instead on games, social stimulation, and behavioral learning through special techniques.

Three Types of Crying

Q: My baby is 1 month old. She cries a lot; just like most babies, I guess. The thing that interests me is that I'm learning to distinguish her various cries. There's a hunger cry, a pain cry, a fussy cry. I've heard that babies have these different kinds of cries, right?

A: Right. A Harvard researcher has identified three basic types of crying as early as the first week of life:

1. *Hunger:* The hunger cry generally lasts about a half second, is followed by a pause, and is then repeated after a high-pitched in-breath.

2. *Anger:* Mothers recognize the anger cry as distinctly different from the basic hunger cry. The cry of anger is shrill and may contain a mixed tone quality. It's just not as pure as a hunger cry.

3. *Pain:* The pain cry is clearly different. The basic outcry lasts much longer: several seconds. Babies tend to hold their breath for several seconds and then repeat the cry. There may be a burst of several short cries before the long wail is repeated.

Remember, there is variability from one infant to another. There is no substitute for your understanding your own daughter's unique brands of crying. After all, it's her first attempt to communicate verbally with you. Yes, crying is communication. I'm glad you're listening so carefully.

Baby Toys

Q: My baby is 1 month old. My husband gave her a rattle that was his when he was a baby. So far she's ignored it. When will she show interest?

A: Most babies are ready for their first toy by about 1 month of age. But, as you might have guessed by now, rattles are not their typical favorites.

Your baby spends most of her time in her crib. She's relatively passive. She spends a lot of time watching in wonderment at the world unfolding before her eyes. That's your clue. Make her first toy something she can look at. Something like a mobile. By the way, it's best to position it from 12 to 24 inches away from the baby's face; she won't show much interest in things located more than 2 feet away from her. The rattle? Still plenty of time for her to shake, rattle, and roll.

Is She Normal?

Q: I'm a first-time mother, and maybe I'm just a little anxious. My precious little one, Andrea, is 2 months old. I keep worrying about whether she's normal. Don't get me wrong—I don't think there's a problem—but, just to be safe, what should I watch for?

A: Don't feel self-conscious. It's entirely normal for all new mothers and fathers to be a little anxious about this kind of thing.

Generally we assess newborns on three basic criteria: physical, intellectual, and social development. Here are a few guideposts to the normal expected development of the average 2-month-old:

1. *Physical:* Andrea should be able to hold her head up for a few seconds at a time. She should be startled by sudden sounds and it should show in her facial expression.

2. *Intellectual:* Andrea should be starting to distinguish between you and your husband. She may also begin demonstrating a preference for left and right.

3. *Social:* Andrea should be interested in other people. She should follow them with her eyes. She should also be soothed by cuddling or by a soft voice.

These are just a few guideposts for you. If in doubt, consult with your pediatrician. He or she can do a complete infant assessment if it's indicated.

Weaning

Q: How soon should I wean my 2-month-old daughter from her bottle? How should I do it?

A: Slow down. There's plenty of time.

At this point your daughter's bottle-feeding is meeting not only her nutritional needs but her instinctual and emotional needs as well. Her sucking reflex is powerful and must be satisfied. It is her way of exploring the world and of attaching herself to you. This period of dependency is important in establishing an infant's sense of basic trust; that is, your baby depends entirely on you and comes to learn that Mom is available and trustworthy. Such an infant can grow into childhood with a healthy optimism about the world. On the other hand, there is some danger in weaning an infant too soon. Abrupt weaning can lead to tension and anxiety in an infant; it can create problems in later life, such as poor frustration tolerance and a brooding sense of pessimism.

Don't be in a hurry. Sometimes we place too great a premium on independence in our society. There's plenty of time for your little one to grow up into an autonomous, independent adult.

While weaning should be done gently and gradually, it would be a good idea to establish a "game plan" to gradually phase out the bottle—to wean your daughter.

Some additional tips:

1. Stick to your game plan. Don't leave weaning up to your baby. Many babies would *never* give up the bottle if it was left entirely up to them.

2. Don't use the bottle for anything but milk.

3. Don't allow your infant to wander off with her bottle. If you insist that feedings take place on your lap, your daughter will eventually, on her own, give up the joys of sucking for the greater joy of crawling and exploring; in this way you'll harness your little one's natural developmental drives and get them working for you, not against you.

4. Recognize that waiting too long to wean can also be detrimental. Some mothers fall into this trap because they enjoy the continued dependency of their infants. Careful. The 3- or 4-year-old who's still sucking from the bottle can become the 23- or 24-year-old who's still clinging to Mom's apron strings.

Multiple Baby-Sitters?

Q: My baby, Caroline, is 2 months old. I've had to return to work immediately because of personal and financial problems. My sisters take turns caring for Caroline at their homes during the day. I've been concerned that having so many different caretakers will confuse my baby, but they tell me that she "can't tell the difference." What is your advice?

A: Your sisters are largely correct—for now. But in another month or so they will not be correct. At about 3 months of age, an infant becomes *bonded,* or attached, to her mother or to the person who is providing the primary mothering functions. Moving from caretaker to caretaker could, indeed, cause problems at that time. What kind of problems? Caroline might find it very difficult to make attachments, to feel protected, to feel safe. Infants learn basic trust in their mothering relationship: If things are bad, there is that *one* special person who can be counted upon to make it better.

My advice? Settle on a single, consistent baby-sitter. But, more importantly, spend as much time with Caroline as possible so that she identifies you, not someone else, as her mother.

Babies and Color Vision

Q: Our baby is 2 months old. I've placed a lot of colorful objects in her crib so she'll be stimulated. My sister says that it's useless; she insists that babies don't really tell the difference between colors until they're about a year old. Comments?

A: Congratulations on providing the colorful visual stimulation. Along with holding (i.e., tactile stimulation) and talking (i.e., auditory stimulation), such stimulation is crucial to proper development.

Most infants are able to distinguish colors by about 4 months of age. A number of research studies have demonstrated, for example, that such infants tend to prefer brightly colored toys over black, white, or gray toys.

Rug Rat

Q: Our 2-month-old, Christina, is a regular rug rat. She loves to lie on the carpeted floor. I even think she's trying to crawl. My girlfriend says it's too early for crawling. Comments?

A: Your girlfriend is right—but let's give Christina credit for trying.

A 2-month-old infant who is developing her motor skills quickly may look as though she's crawling. While on her stomach, she may lift her head and flail her arms and legs. She doesn't really get anywhere with all this motion; it's an infant's equivalent of running in place. But it is a good warm-up for the real thing: crawling, which Christina should accomplish by 6 to 7 months of age.

Hand Development

Q: Lawrence, our 2-month-old, had a very strong grasp reflex almost from birth. Now he's using his hands to grab things, such as toys. I don't remember too well, but I don't think his brothers and sisters developed so fast. My questions are these: (1) Is Lawrence's development really extraordinary? and (2) What does it mean?

A: Lawrence is certainly ahead of schedule as far as hand development is concerned. Most 2-month-olds have very little hand coordination. About the best they can manage is to suck their fingers. However, a hand itself becomes something of a plaything when they're 4 months of age: Infants are fascinated by their fingers; they grab them, pull them—and yes, learn to grab for any object within reach. By the time they're 6 or 7 months old, the hands are even busier: Now an infant can actually pick things up—usually to drop them.

So, you see, Lawrence is at least 2 months advanced beyond the average for hand.

Lawrence's accelerated hand coordination may indicate that he's blessed with very good "fine" motor coordination and will be dextrous as an adult—just as early speech (or lack of it) is often a good indicator of intelligence.

Encourage Lawrence's skill. I'd suggest toys that will further stimulate his interest in handling things. My formula is to build upon successes.

The Eyes Have It

Q: My 2-month-old daughter has very expressive eyes. Can she, at such a young age, really be using them to communicate with me?

A: Yes, in her own way, she is communicating with you. In fact, from the moment of birth babies are immediately attracted to the human face. Research has demonstrated that even in the delivery room a baby will stare at faces and even follow them as people move from place to place.

This kind of early eye contact works both ways. Mothers, too, have an early fascination with their babies' eyes. Researchers have found that in the very first "conversations" between mother and child, 80 percent of what is said relates somehow to the babies' eyes.

This eye-to-eye communication between you and your daughter can be the marvelous beginning of a loving and trusting relationship. The eyes really do have it!

Disco Baby

Q: My daughter, Mary, is 3 months old. She's been irritable for the past few weeks, and I've tried everything to quiet her down. I've finally found the solution: disco dancing! That's right. She loves the disco beat. I play the music on the stereo and dance with her. She quiets down every time. It never fails. I've tried other music such as rhythm and blues, waltzes, and so forth, but no luck. Only disco does the trick: Why?

A: A baby's need for motion is real. Motion is a subtle organizer of psychological and neurological development. Babies who are rocked regularly, for example, show better coordination of muscles and even better development of vision and hearing than babies who are allowed to remain relatively motionless for long periods.

Studies at Ohio State University have demonstrated that spinning also leads to enhanced development.

Mothers know intuitively, of course, that rocking and spinning are pleasurable and even gleeful experiences to most infants. Why? The vestibular system, the tiny organ located in the inner ear which controls our response to motion and change of position, is highly developed in infants. It may be, therefore, a logical early source of sensory input and primitive pleasure.

Why Mary's disco craze? Most infants opt for a slower beat such as a normal walking motion or a slow rocking chair cadence. Mary is keeping time to a different drummer, that's all. Dance on!

Child Abuse

Q: There was a story in our local newspaper recently about a mother who drowned her 3-month-old baby in the tub. The next day there was a story about a mother who was thrown in jail because she was caught burning her 2-year-old son's arm with a cigarette. Now I've heard that she's been released. I'm afraid she'll murder him now. We're going to have another "killer mother" on our hands. How can the courts be so stupid?

A: The first principle of intervention in serious child abuse cases is to separate the offending parent from the children. Although the mother you describe may have been released, I doubt that she has custody of her son.

Abusing parents need help. I hope this mother gets it promptly.

There is not a clear relationship, however, between child abuse and *filicide*. In other words, mothers who abuse their children rarely commit murder—and, interestingly, mothers who commit filicide do not usually have a prior history of abuse. This is a surprising finding and points to an essential difference between the two groups of women.

Filicide is usually the impulsive act of a severely disturbed parent. In one study of mothers who killed, the majority were found to have major psychiatric disorders; many of them, for example, heard voices telling them that their babies were evil and had to be destroyed.

Of course, mothers who abuse their children, physically and emotionally, are "disturbed" too, but the nature of their problem is different. Many of them, for example, were themselves abused as children, and they are acting out an unconscious replay of their own trauma.

An Infant's Personality

Q: My 3-month-old daughter seems to have a totally different make-up than her four older brothers and sisters. When they were infants they all seemed to be much more active and demanding. Most mothers would not complain about my baby: She's mild and easy. But, still, I'm a little concerned. She seems so different from the other children.

A: Babies come into the world with different temperaments. In a sense, a baby's temperament is her personality. Your older children might actually have been considered to fall into the category called *difficult* babies: They nurse very actively, they scream when they're hungry, they do not keep a regular schedule, they actively reject changes in routine. Your newborn, on the other hand, appears to be what is sometimes called a *slow-to-warm-up* baby: They appear shy, are slow to feed and to respond to stimuli. Nevertheless, if she is gaining weight and is developing her motor milestones normally, there is no need for concern.

Your baby will probably need more tolerance and more time to do things than did your other children. For example, it will take longer to feed her. Do not pressure her. The greatest danger could be your own impatience and the expectation that she should be just like her siblings or that there must be something *wrong* if she is so slow.

Do not be worried. Instead, get to know her as an individual. Your best opportunity will be to observe her when she's feeding. For example, the way she reacts to her first few mouthfuls of solid food will tell you a lot about how she's likely to react to other kinds of changes in her daily routine. If you can anticipate her reactions, you can preserve a smooth, nonconflictual mother-child relationship. With this relationship to sustain her, you can be sure that she'll grow up to be happy and secure—even if she may grow up to be a bit less active and assertive than her brothers and sisters.

A Jumpy Baby

Q: My husband and I are new parents. We're getting very concerned because our 3-month-old daughter seems to be so "jumpy": Everything seems to make her frightened and tense. She cries at the slightest noise. Picking her up seems to make her worse. Please help.

A: Some babies are more high-strung or jumpy than others. Your daughter may well have come into this world with such a temperament. She lacks a well-developed "stimulus barrier" at this time. In other words, extraneous noises or other stimuli that some babies are able to ignore impact on your little one with shrill and equal intensity. She is probably being bombarded from all directions: a door closing, a new sight passing into her field of vision, the telephone ringing, a plane flying overhead, a blanket brushing on her face. She is simply oversensitive to auditory, visual, and tactile stimulation.

Until your baby's natural stimulus barrier matures sufficiently, she will remain overly vulnerable to sound, sight, and touch. The answer? First of all, do not lose confidence in your mothering. Do not let her sensitivity cause you to be frustrated, since a vicious cycle could result: Your frustration could frighten her even more which, in turn, could heighten your frustration, etc. Your approach to your little girl should be seen as something of a challenge. Try to become her temporary stimulus barrier by shielding her from as many extraneous sensory "surprises" as possible: Be gentle with her and keep handling to a minimum. Also, for the next two or three months try to limit other people from handling her. Try to "soundproof" her room as much as possible. Bring things into her field of vision slowly, deliberately. Shield her but do not attempt to completely isolate her from the world; *stimulus deprivation* can be as dangerous as too much stimulation. Over the next few months the natural maturation of her stimulus barrier should take place— and relieve Mom of the task of being a "substitute barrier."

Crybaby?

Q: I hate to say it, but my 4-month-old son, John, is a real crybaby. He cries ten times more than his older brother and sister did at his age. He doesn't have colic, and our pediatrician has given him a clean bill of health. Is he unhappy?

A: Not necessarily. According to actual research, infants spend about three hours a day crying; it's an uncontrollable reflex to all forms of distress: hunger, discomfort, and just plain old temperament. This crying is automatic; it goes with the territory. Some infants just cry more than others.

By the age of 6 months, however, John should be able to control his crying to some extent. He'll learn that Mom is available to help him and that he can expect you to respond to him. He'll learn basic trust and optimism: If things are bad, they'll get better because Mom is near. In essence, he'll have less reason to cry.

Let Him Cry?

Q: Whenever my 4-month-old son cries, I tend to go right in and pick him up. My husband says I'm making a mistake because I will cause our son to become too *dependent*. Should I let him cry?

A: This is an important question about infant development. I'm sure that both you and your husband want your son to grow up into a reasonably autonomous and independent person. You are both aware that children who are too pampered or overprotected tend to become very cautious and dependent individuals; they can suffer from lack of confidence, shyness, school phobia, homesickness, etc. You don't want your son to fall into this kind of dependency trap.

But trying to force independence on a 4-month-old is doomed to failure. Your baby still has legitimate dependency needs which must be met. Frustrating his dependency needs will only lead to more frustrations—not to independence.

Your son's cries, of course, mean many different things: hunger, pain, irritability, loneliness, need for attention, etc. Your response to these cries assures him that, if things are going badly for him, help is just around the corner—in the person of Mom and Dad. He is reassured. He learns optimism and trust.

Nevertheless, it is important to have a general game plan in mind for gradually, over several months, allowing him to experience some frustration in his life. Your husband seems to be aware that a certain amount of frustration or tension is actually a necessary ingredient for proper growth, learning, and development. The key is to introduce this frustration slowly and in doses that your little one can tolerate.

Reading to Infants

Q: I've heard that if you want to raise your child to be a good reader and a lover of books, you should read aloud to her at an early age. My daughter is 4 months old. Is it too early to start reading to her?

A: No. Infants learn to respond selectively to stimuli: touch, smell, taste, sight, and sound. While they need all of these stimuli, you would want to emphasize sight and sound. How? Start by reading to your infant while she's in the cradle. Progress to picture books and songbooks. This early experience with the written word coupled with your own enthusiasm and love of books will be a powerful combination.

Mirroring Mother's Moods

Q: I've noticed that my 4-month-old son picks up most of my own moods. It's as though I'm a mirror and he reflects back my unhappiness and sadness. Is this normal?

A: Yes. Infants when only a few days old respond to their emotional environment. They respond to facial expressions, the tenseness of Mother's arms as they are held, the pitch and tone of her voice, even to the rate of her heartbeat as they are nursed or cuddled.

I would not want you, however, to be overconcerned about these facts. You can be free to express the full range of your emotions. The greatest dangers exist only when a negative feeling tone (such as anger or tension) prevails continuously in the mother-child relationship—or when the relationship is so neutral that it is devoid of any feeling at all. So let those feelings flow.

How Much Sleep?

Q: Our 4-month-old, Heidi, is a fitful sleeper. She wakes up several times during the night. We thought she'd be sleeping through the entire night by now. What's wrong?

A: Probably nothing. By the age of 3 to 4 months, about 70 percent of infants will sleep from about midnight to dawn. But keep in mind that 10 percent don't sleep through the entire night in their first year. Heidi is certainly still well within the range of normal.

My advice: *Relax*. Some parents start taking it personally if a baby doesn't sleep through the night by 3 or 4 months of age. This only makes matters worse. Your worth as a parent is not on the line. While you should certainly respond to Heidi's cries of pain or hunger, don't overreact; you could unwittingly encourage her awakenings if you give her unnecessary nighttime attention.

Floppy Disk

Q: My husband, a computer salesman, calls our 4-month-old "the floppy disk." It's because Merry is so loose and floppy when you pick her up. She's like a little rag doll. Is this normal? Could she have a muscle problem?

A: All infants are "programmed" to be floppy for the first few months of life. Muscle tone and motor control come with maturation of the neuromuscular system.

Merry, at 4 months of age, should certainly be more in control of her body than she was at 2 or 3 months. For example, you should be able to pull her to a standing position. She should actively reach out for her toys. And she should be able to hold her head upright and steady after you've placed her in a sitting position.

I hope these basic guidelines help. Unfortunately, babies are more variable than computers. There is a range of normal for motor development. If you're still concerned, why not check with your pediatrician? He has the best hardware to make the diagnosis.

Walking Tall

Q: Our baby, Eddie, is just 4 months old. My husband and I (according to our parents) both walked at an early age. What should we watch for as we watch Eddie's attempts at walking?

A: Keep in mind that all the various milestones of development express a *range* of normalcy. There is a great deal of variability among individual children. Also, youngsters tend to develop unevenly; that is, they may be a bit slow in accomplishing a particular task and then catch up very rapidly.

With this in mind, you might use the following guidelines:

- 3 to 4 months: Sits up, when propped, for 10 to 15 minutes

- 5 months: Sits without support and stands holding on

- 6 months: Pulls self to stand

- 8 months: Walks while holding onto furniture

- 9 months: Stands briefly

- 10 months: Stands alone easily

- 11 to 12 months: Walks

- 14 months: Walks up steps

- 22 months: Balances briefly on one foot

These guidelines are, generally speaking, the *earliest* you would expect to see any of these accomplishments. So don't be alarmed if Eddie is as much as two or three months delayed in any of these categories. Give him time. Soon enough he'll be walking tall.

Fussy Baby, Fussy Daddy

Q: I don't know any other way to say it: Aimee (4 months of age) is a fussy baby. She cries all the time: when she's feeding, when she's being held, even when she's sleeping. It bothers me, but it's really driving my husband up the wall. He shouts things like, "Why can't you shut her up?" This is obviously starting to cause some real friction in our home. Can you help?

A: Sounds like you've got two fussy ones on your hands. Aimee's fussiness is to be expected, but Dad's is not. He's going to have to pull himself together. On the other hand, a fussy baby can certainly bring out the worst in fathers—and mothers too. So let's attack this problem step by step.

   1. *Physical causes:* There are many physical problems that can lead an infant to become irritable: Allergies and gastrointestinal symptoms lead the list. Ask your pediatrician to examine Aimee.

   2. *Physical contact:* Most infants respond to cuddling. Try doing it in several different ways (skin to skin, head next to your heart, crooked in your right arm, i.e., different positions) until you discover Aimee's preference.

   3. *Motion:* The gentle act of rocking works today just as it did in grandma's day. Try it. If it works, do yourself a favor and buy a rocking chair.

   4. *Your own reaction:* Infants can tell if a mother is tense. They respond with tenseness of their own. Try to relax. Some babies do go through a period of being *fussy*; there's probably no better word for it. You can get through it, but you'll need the active support of your husband. You don't want him to turn off to Aimee now. It could be a very poor sign for the future.

Temperament

Q: Kerri, our 4-month-old, is very *fidgety*. She startles easily. She's supersensitive to everything going on around her. She doesn't like to be held. By comparison, my older daughter (Kathleen, now 3 years old) was as peaceful a baby as you've ever seen in your life. Nothing fazed her. What causes this difference? What effect will it have on their future personality development?

A: The role of temperament is poorly understood, but, as you suggest, it is a crucial element in child development. Differences in temperament, in fact, can often be experienced in the womb. I'll bet, for example, that Kerri did a lot more kicking during your pregnancy than Kathleen did.

On the other hand, the "fit" between parental temperament and a baby's reactions is also an important factor. A very active mother who loves to "roughhouse" with her infant may be disappointed in a passive baby. An easygoing mom, on the other hand, may become tense with an active child. In each case, the baby's development will be affected in some important way.

The key: Try to respect the individuality of both Kerri and Kathleen. It seems that you're more comfortable with Kathleen's temperament. That's okay. But let Kerri be Kerri. With the right combination of protection and encouragement she may translate her infant "fidgetiness" into a high-energy, inquisitive personality in later years. Yes, temperament during infancy does influence later personality development.

Sleepy Baby

Q: Miriam, our 5-month-old, is a real sleepyhead. She sleeps about 16 to 18 hours a day. Even when she's awake, she seems sleepy. She'll even fall asleep in the middle of a feeding. My pediatrician has told me not to worry, but I am concerned. Should I try to keep Mimi awake?

A: No. Mimi is the best judge of how much sleep she needs. I don't advise you to forcibly keep her awake.

The amount of sleep that babies require differs widely from one child to the next. In the first few weeks of life, for example, most infants sleep about 16 hours, but some may sleep as little as 10 or 12 hours.

On the other hand, I do share some of your concern. As a child psychiatrist, for example, I'd want to know how much stimulation Mimi is receiving when she's awake. If her environment is placid and unstimulating, she may decide that sleep holds more attraction. So be careful.

Have fun with Mimi. Make sure that all her senses are stimulated while she's awake. Put mobiles over her crib. Cuddle her. Coo to her. Sing to her. Cradle her on your arm when you feed her. Allow her to become accustomed to soothing odors, including your own body. The five senses (sight, touch, hearing, taste, and smell) must all be actively stimulated. In this way Mimi will get a powerful message: She's missing a lot when she's sleeping.

Early Riser

Q: Our little Felicia is 5 months old. She's become a very early riser, like with the crack of dawn. If she'd just lie there quietly, like she used to, it would be okay. But not Felicia. She bangs, cries, and bangs some more—until she wakes up everybody. We've tried a few things like keeping her up later at night (doesn't work) and putting black shades on her window (doesn't work). Any ideas?

A: It's not unusual for the sleep cycle to shift a bit at about 5 months of age. I would guess that Felicia had been on a fairly regular 9-hour sleep cycle until recently. The problem is that she is on the verge of some developmental breakthroughs. She is about to use motor and social skills that have not been available to her until now. She's excited, and she wants you to know about it. I'm not surprised that your efforts like the black shades have failed. Felicia is keeping time to an internal alarm clock. You can't fool mother nature. You might try moving Felicia to a more distant part of the house from your own room, if that's possible. Also, try some daytime exercises with her. It would be good for both of you, and it might help to channel her energy.

I'm pleased that you haven't tried restraining Felicia in her bed. That's one thing *not* to do.

Infant Depression

Q: My 5-month-old daughter is not gaining weight and seems to cry all the time. The pediatrician says that there is nothing physically wrong but that she might be suffering from "depression." Is this possible? What can my husband and I do about it?

A: Yes, it is possible. Your pediatrician is probably making a very astute observation. Infants can, and do, suffer from depression. The early warning signs include failure to gain weight, failure to reach normal developmental milestones, poor eye contact, lack of a spontaneous smile, lack of interest in surroundings, poor sleep patterns, and frequent crying that does not respond to holding or cuddling.

At the age of 5 months your daughter should have approximately doubled her birth weight. She should turn her head to sounds and smile and vocalize her delight at your presence. She should actively reach out for objects and grasp them. Cuddling should soothe her rather than cause her to arch her back in an infantile attempt to flee your embrace. The absence of these normal milestones of development could signal infant depression—particularly in the absence of physical illness.

What causes such depression? Researchers at the National Institute of Mental Health and other centers are actively pursuing this question. One thing is known: Mothers who are themselves depressed can pass along some of these symptoms through the early mother-infant relationship. This is why a pregnant woman who is depressed or who is highly ambivalent about the coming birth of her baby is urged to seek consultation with her obstetrician or with a psychiatrist. Pediatricians and child psychiatrists are increasingly interested in this phenomenon and can offer helpful suggestions for both mother and child.

On the other hand, there are probably other causes (genetic, neurological, environmental, etc.) that have little to do with the mother-child relationship. Please do not assume that it's all your fault.

What can you do about it? Quite a bit. Treatment recommendations by a child psychiatrist would be focused on the baby's developmental stage and the nature of the environmental problems. The treatment would include suggestions for specific forms of stimulation, exercise, and communication. Parental guidance to help you understand your daughter's needs and your reactions to her would also be provided.

Early identification of such "at-risk" infants is the key. You and your pediatrician have made an early diagnosis. Your daughter should now benefit greatly from early intervention.

Sneaking Out on a 5-Month-Old

Q: My 5-month-old daughter won't let me out of her sight. She gets especially upset when my husband and I try to leave her with the baby-sitter. Should we put her to sleep before we go out for the evening? Should we sneak out the door? What works?

A: The *good news* is that your daughter is developing normally. Her intense attachment to you causes her to suffer *separation anxiety* when you are away from her. This is part of normal development. At about 4 to 6 months of age most infants will do anything they can in order to keep Mom at their side: They will cry and they will cling. Such tactics, of course, can make life difficult for a mother since you have frequent needs to be away from the baby for periods from a few minutes to a few hours. Obviously, an infant's separation anxiety can be especially tough on a mother who works outside the home.

There are a few things that you might try in order to help your daughter through this conflict of normal development. Try playing peekaboo with her. This simple game can teach her a very profound psychological lesson: What seemingly vanishes has a permanent existence and returns—with a smile! The child who has excessive fears of abandonment when her mother is out of sight assumes that Mom ceases to exist when she is no longer visible, that is, out of sight, out of existence. The game of peekaboo is really a game of mastering separation anxiety.

You might also try to assure your daughter that you'll be right back whenever you leave her for a few minutes. Again, this teaches her something about your own permanence in her life. As your daughter comes to realize that Mom can be counted on to return, she will gradually exhibit less separation anxiety. She should also develop a healthy sense of optimism: "Things may get bad occasionally, but they do eventually get better since the person I need so much is so reliable."

As far as the baby-sitter is concerned, I would not suggest sneaking out on your daughter because it violates this sense of basic trust. Choose the baby-sitter carefully and arrange for her to spend some time at your home with your daughter when you are present. In this way you'll not only be able to observe how the sitter relates with your child but also help build a nonconflictual relationship for the two of them. Tell your little girl beforehand that you and your husband are going out and introduce her to the sitter before you leave the house. Even if you do all these things, your daughter, of course, may still cry, but her tears are more likely to be tears of disappointment than tears of rage or abandonment. You'll be helping her to conquer separation anxiety, and you'll feel a lot better, too, about occasionally leaving her. After all, mothers also have needs.

Guilt over Crying

Q: Our 5-month-old, Jenny, cries a lot. I don't get too upset over it. I try to determine why she's crying; then I respond accordingly. My husband, Bob, however, can't stand to see me take my time. He expects me to react immediately. In fact, he'll often go right to Jenny and pick her up. I think he's trying to make me feel guilty or something, but I've been through this twice before with my own children—this is his first. How can I get him to take it easy?

A: Babies cry for many reasons: hunger, tension, tiredness, colic, pain, loneliness, dirty diapers—and a host of other reasons. It's amazing how experienced mothers can so often discern the reason by the quality of the cry itself. You're experienced at translating cries; your husband is not.

But you suggest a thicker plot. Why would Bob want to make you feel guilty? I'm concerned about your suspicion. Does Bob need to prove he's a better parent than you? Is there some covert competition with your former husband? Is Bob already on the road to overprotecting *his* child to the exclusion of *yours?* There are many possibilities. I hope a frank discussion with Bob will yield the answers.

Peekaboo

Q: Our 6-month-old daughter, Larissa, just can't seem to get enough of peekaboo. Why should she be so fascinated by this game?

A: Larissa has discovered one of the games that babies play. Although it is full of fun, it marks an important psychological milestone.

Peekaboo is a way that infants master the fear of separation from Mom and other loved ones. It usually begins with Mom hiding her face in her hands, then removing them—all to the squealing delight of the little one. Later, babies learn to cover their own faces and to invent other creative variations of their own.

What is the meaning of this innocent play? It means that Larissa has learned to tolerate your absence, that she has a fixed memory of you, and that she is optimistic about your *being there* after the playful absence of peekaboo. It is a first step toward a crucial psychological attribute called *object constancy*. Although play is sometimes known as the "work" of children, my only advice to you and Larissa is—to enjoy!

Daddy's Rockaby Is No. 1

Q: My 6-month-old daughter is doing very well, but I'm puzzled by one thing. When she gets especially cranky, my husband is much more successful than I am in calming her down. Can you explain it?

A: Research studies have shown that babies are soothed by lower-frequency speech tones. This fact helps explain why fathers, with their lower voices, are often able to calm down a crying infant more quickly than mothers.

Another tip: If your baby's crankiness makes you tense, you may communicate that tension to her by your grasp and even by a quickened heartbeat which she hears if she is held with her head over your heart.

There are probably a number of other possible explanations. But why not relax and enjoy the support that your husband is giving?

"Sending Power"

Q: On my last visit to our pediatrician she remarked that our 6-month-old, Clark, has low "sending power." The way she said it made me think that I'm supposed to know what it's all about, and I'm too embarrassed to ask her. What is *sending power*, and why doesn't Clarkie have it?

A: *Sending power* is a term used by some pediatricians and child development experts. It's a concept that describes an infant's ability to get parents and other adults interested in him. It can't be measured very easily, but it can be described—by pediatricians and parents too.

For example, some babies are quite active, "cuddly," or playful; they send good "vibes" to adults who respond by paying more attention to them. This produces a positive feedback loop that can enhance a child's self-esteem.

Sending power is often a matter of temperament. Maybe Clark is naturally passive. On the other hand, there may be a more serious underlying problem such as developmental delay, failure to thrive, or infant depression. Your pediatrician is the one with the answers. Talk to her. Forget the embarrassment. Fire up your own sending power.

Development Screening

Q: Our firstborn, Jewell, is 6 months old. Our pediatrician's office called the other day to set up an appointment for Jewell to have some routine developmental testing. What is it exactly? Should we have it done?

A: Routine and periodic developmental screening is excellent pediatric practice. In fact, most pediatricians do it as a matter of course; your doctor may have a more elaborate or formalized way of doing it.

Generally these are tests of motor development, language skills, social skills, basic learning, and psychological maturity. Sometimes they are divided into four basic categories: (1) gross motor (standing, walking, etc.), (2) fine motor (use of hands, etc.), (3) language (receptive and expressive), and (4) personal-social.

These tests are very important since early detection is so crucial to the proper treatment of any developmental disability. Tests such as the standard Denver Developmental Screening Test (DDST) are often given at 6 to 8 months and again at 18 to 20 months of age.

Should Jewell be tested? Yes, it's certainly in her best interest. But why not ask a few questions first? Which test will be used? Why? Will it be repeated later? How much will it cost? If your questions are answered to your satisfaction, you're all set and so is Jewell.

Keeping Up with Her Cousin

Q: We have a unique situation. My sister, who has a 6-month-old daughter, lives with us. My husband and I have a 10-month-old son, Billy. My sister is always pushing Mary, her daughter, to keep up with Billy. Nobody seems to mind the competition—except Mary. She just can't keep up. Will she be harmed by this?

A: The four-month gap between Billy and Mary at their current ages is enormous from a developmental point of view. For example, Billy can probably sit, creep, pull himself to his feet—and maybe even take a step or two. Mary? The best she can do right now is probably to sit up and lean forward on her hands.

The "competition" cuts two ways for Mary. While the efforts to keep up with Billy may help propel her a little faster in her development, it could lead to a lot of frustration. The maturation of her neuromuscular system is out of everyone's control. She needs time. I'd discourage the competition; the results are too loaded in Billy's favor at this stage of development for the two cousins.

I Don't Love My Baby

Q: I'm 25, married, and the mother of a 6-month-old girl. Something's wrong. I just can't feel any love for my baby. I don't hate her or anything, and I do take care of her. But I resent her, and to be honest, I often wish she'd never been born. I was very happy as a childless married woman—now my world has been turned upside down. But what can I do? I mean, I'm stuck. I can't turn her back in or something. Please advise.

A: You've got a tough problem, but it's not as rare as you think. In fact, I admire your candor. Many women would either hide from the fact or feel so guilty and ashamed that they'd never be able to face the issue. You're confronting your dilemma, and that's the first step to solving it.

There are many possibilities. Was the baby planned? Was she your husband's idea? Did you feel pressured by others (friends or family) to have a baby? Did you feel pressured by some idealized image you had of yourself as "wife and mother"? Pressured motherhood can obviously breed unhappiness.

But there are other possibilities too. For example, sometimes a woman and her baby simply don't "fit" each other. It's a complex physical and psychological matter. Neither mother nor baby is really at fault. But both of them have a problem.

So how do you solve your problem? You've taken a giant first step by admitting it to yourself and to me. Now let's get a team together. It will have to include at least the following players: your husband, your pediatrician, and a psychiatrist. Together you can win. Best wishes.

Child-Proofing

Q: Cathy, our 6-month-old, can roll over now on her own. I hear that's a sign that she'll be crawling before too long. Do you have any tips about child-proofing our home?

A: Here are a few of the basics:

1. Don't leave Cathy alone anymore unless the area is secure.

2. Remove all sharp-edged furniture and breakable objects.

3. Be sure that electric outlets are covered, and be careful of electric wires trailing across the floor.

4. Install approved safety gates at stairways.

5. Don't leave anything on a table or stove that Cathy could reach up and pull.

6. Keep toxic substances out of reach. Be especially alert to the cupboard beneath your sink.

This list is a starter. I'm sure you can improve on it based on your own special circumstances. Child-proofing calls for common sense: something most mothers have in abundance.

Catching Cold at the Doctor's Office

Q: Last week I took Sue Ellen (6 months old) to the pediatrician for a well-baby checkup. When I walked into the waiting room I knew I had made a mistake, but it was too late. There were four or five children there—all of them coughing and sneezing. I just knew Susie would catch a cold, and, sure enough, two days later she came down with one. Why don't doctors schedule well babies separately from sick ones?

A: Some pediatricians do. Many others have separate waiting areas. But do you know something? It may not matter quite as much as you think.

A pediatrician in Massachusetts assisted by researchers at Children's Hospital of Boston has studied this problem. He found that 32 percent of the "well" children who visited his office came down with a contagious illness (mostly sniffles) within one week of visiting his office. This looks like a very significant number—until you hear the rest of the story. At the same time the doctor found that

30 percent of his patients who had *not* visited the office also developed these symptoms during the same week.

The key, of course, is that infants and young children have about six to nine viral illnesses a year whether or not they visit the pediatrician's office. So you can take some reassurance about taking Sue Ellen to see her doctor.

On the other hand, the study did not investigate the transmission of things like measles or chicken pox which have longer incubation periods than covered in the Boston research. In fact, two reports last year suggest that measles may often be transmitted within doctors' offices. The bottom line: Some infectious disease is, no doubt, picked up at the pediatrician's office but the risk of contracting common viral illnesses (such as gastroenteritis, or a cold) is less than you might think.

Baby-Sitting Boyfriends

Q: I warned her. My niece (aged 19) is an unwed mother. When she had to go back to work and couldn't find day care for her 6-month-old baby, her boyfriend (not the baby's father) volunteered to baby-sit. "What does he know about babies?" I asked. "You're looking for trouble." But my niece wouldn't listen. She insisted that everything would be fine. Well it wasn't. Her boyfriend abused the baby—something we figured out after taking the baby to the local emergency room for the third time in three weeks. Please warn your readers about this danger.

A: Boyfriends as baby-sitters is a growing phenomenon largely because of the increase in teenage pregnancy and the relative unavailability of good day care.

While I'm sure that many of these fellows are adequate and safe custodians of infants, there does appear to be a growing danger. For example, researchers at the University of Washington studied child abuse cases from 1973 and 1983. In 1973, 37 percent of the known abusers were men. In 1983, the number had soared to 80 percent. The researchers attributed the increase mostly to the baby-sitting boyfriend phenomenon.

Warn our readers? You've already done it. Baby-sitters, whether they are male or female, must be carefully screened for experience with children and for their personal habits. Be sure to get references. Be sure to check on them closely—including some unannounced visits.

Is Baby Normal?

Q: Our baby, Joey, is 7 months old. He seems okay, but he's developing more slowly than his older sister did. I realize that there is a range of average development, and maybe I shouldn't be so concerned, but I can't help it. For example, he's not sitting up yet. Can you give me some guidelines?

A: Yes. At 7 months of age, most infants are able to do the following things:

1. Grasp objects

2. Transfer objects from hand to hand

3. Sit up for brief periods

4. Repeat vowel sounds

There are other so-called motor milestones, but this list is a good start.

How does Joey fare on my list? If sitting up is the only problem, don't worry. By the way, he may be able to sit up if you support him at the hips; many infants do not really sit unaided without support until 9 or 10 months of age.

If you have continuing concerns, why not check with your pediatrician?

Baby Talk

Q: My sister has a 7-month-old son. He's a darling, and I'm a very proud aunt. My sister and I, however, got into a serious disagreement recently about the way she talks to him. She uses all this "baby talk." It sounds horrible. Examples: *horsie, doggie, bow-wow, wa-wa.* I'm 28 and single, and I realize that I've been out of touch with babies and children for many years, but it sounds so foolish. Why do mothers talk like this anyhow?

A: A very good question. Baby talk flows naturally from most parents. You might be interested to know, by the way, that this infantilized form of communication is not limited to the United States. Linguists have studied this phenomenon in many cultures and have concluded that it is almost universal.

Why? Although the baby talk itself flows naturally, the reasons behind it are complex, and few mothers, for example, could tell you why they refer to a dog as a *bow-wow* or a *doggie*. There are probably several reasons: First, infants and toddlers are so responsive to sound that they can more easily identify a thing or animal by the sound it makes (*choo-choo* for train, etc.). Second, it is very interesting that parents tend to repeat those vowels and sounds which are most easily imitated and remembered by their little ones. Mothers and fathers also learn to vary the pitch of their voices; they learn that infants are most excited by a high pitch.

Parents also learn that the basic rules of communicating verbally with infants are (1) repetition and (2) keep it simple. These are obviously not the ground rules for the kind of adult conversation that dominates your world.

Yes, baby talk sounds foolish at times to adult ears, but to your nephew it makes a lot of sense. Your sister is just doing what comes naturally.

Stranger Anxiety

Q: My son, Francisco, is 8 months old. Up to this time he has been very accepting of anyone who comes along and showers him with attention. For example, he has always enjoyed being picked up and cuddled, even by strangers in the supermarket. Recently, however, he seems to be deathly afraid of people. Whenever anyone approaches him, he screams and clings to me. Why has he become so insecure?

A: Do not be alarmed. Francisco is not becoming insecure at all. As a matter of fact, he is exhibiting a phase of normal development.

Francisco's fear of nonparental adults is nothing more than *stranger anxiety*—a predictable phenomenon at about 6 to 8 months of age.

In fact, this anxiety is actually a good sign. Why? It tells us that Francisco has accomplished adequate bonding to you. He prefers you to anyone else. You have achieved specific value to him as a mother. He will not accept, willy-nilly, any substitutes.

Children who do not exhibit stranger anxiety, who accept "mothering" indiscriminately from adults who pass quickly in and out of their lives, may be in trouble. Such infants may grow into adults who cannot make strong attachments to other people, who form easy superficial relationships with "strangers," but who lack the depth and constancy that is required for meaningful, sustained relationships.

This phase should not last more than several more months. With time Francisco should become less clinging and dependent upon you. He'll even become more ambivalent toward you. And he'll learn to judge new people in his life on a person-by-person basis.

Walking Her Way to a High IQ?

Q: Our daughter has begun walking at 8 months of age. I've heard that early walking is a sign of high intelligence. True?

A: Unfortunately, no. The early development of gross motor skills is not related to intelligence in any way. It is not even related to the later development of athletic skills.

Enjoy your daughter for who she is. Raise her in a way that maximizes all her potential, but don't raise her to compete against norms or standards. Remember that intelligence, as measured by IQ tests, is only one ingredient of success in life.

Lost Memories?

Q: Please settle a friendly argument for my husband and me. We have an 8-month-old infant, Chad. My husband says that Chad will be able to remember events of his infancy if he develops a good memory. I don't think that anyone can remember things that far back. Who's right?

A: You are. But this is not an easy question to answer. Freud's classic explanation is that since so many infantile memories are unpleasant, we unconsciously repress these recollections for the rest of our lives.

Piaget had another explanation: The infant's mind works differently until about the age of 3 when he's capable of expressing ideas in speech. Memories before this age, therefore, are stored in the brain—but in the nonverbal code of infancy. This is why we do not have access to them.

But what if we did? We probably wouldn't understand them unless, of course, we could again learn how to think like a baby.

My Husband Feels Left Out

Q: I have a big problem. It's about my husband and my 8-month-old son, Gregg. For the past four months I have been out of work and home with Gregg. He has become very attached to me, and that's the problem. My husband feels left out of things, especially when Gregg reaches and cries for me when his Daddy tries to pick him up. What can I do?

A: Gregg's reaction is entirely normal and so is your husband's.

At 8 months of age, Gregg is expected to have a primary attachment to you. But he may be overdoing it a bit: making up for lost time in an effort to recapture what he missed in the last four months.

Gregg may see his father as something of an intruder into his special relationship with you. Gregg may also be reacting to Dad with a dose of something else that is normal at about this stage of development: *stranger anxiety*. The good news is that this is normal development and that the bonding between Gregg and you seems solid.

I suggest that you involve your husband in Gregg's daily care: bathing, feeding, changing diapers. In this way he will be more familiar to Gregg and less a stranger. Your husband should benefit by feeling more involved, and as the tension lessens, he'll get more positive reinforcement from Gregg.

Looming Large

Q: I've noticed that our 8-month-old daughter, Diana, is easily startled if I surprise her by coming through the door too rapidly or by entering her field of vision very quickly. If I walk up slowly, she seems to be much more relaxed. This "startle effect" is even more pronounced with strangers. I've read about stranger anxiety, so I expected it at about this age, but is Diana's response something more than run-of-the-mill stranger anxiety?

A: It could be. Diana may be experiencing what has been called the *looming effect.* When people approach an infant too quickly, the baby may feel threatened. She may perceive the person not as a person at all but as a fast-moving blur that is looming headlong in her direction. She may expect not a cuddle but a crash, not hugs but harm.

Your intuition about moving slowly toward Diana is right on the mark. Your approach can be modified for strangers. Instead of their directly approaching Diana, ask them to stand back until she has seen them and expresses an interest. Then they can proceed— as an "invited" guest.

These tactics, by the way, should only be necessary for another three to four months. With normal growth and development, the looming effect and stranger anxiety are quickly left behind.

Fear of Bathtub

Q: Jacob, our 9-month-old, has developed a new wrinkle. All of a sudden he's afraid of the bathtub. I don't get it. He's been playing in the bathtub without difficulty for a couple of months. There are no other problems.

Any ideas?

A: Such momentary regressions are not uncommon at this age. For example, some 8- and 9-month-olds become afraid of the vacuum cleaner, or they become terrified to climb down from a chair. It's part of the developmental landscape for these children.

Jacob's fears might be related to the fact that at about this age he probably can pull himself up to a standing position. This is thrilling, but it's also frightening. For the first time, for example, Jacob may be aware of the fear of falling. So if he has a tendency to stand up in the tub, you may be witnessing a fear of falling more than, say, a fear of water.

I suggest that you observe Jacob closely. Try to identify the source of his fear with precision. Then help him to confront it gently. For example, if he *is* afraid of standing in the tub, pick him up in your arms and stand him up. Make a game of it: Up. Down. Splash. Up. Down. Splash. But be sure to stop and reassure him if he panics.

Perpetual Motion Machine

Q: Dorie, our 9-month-old, is a little perpetual motion machine. She's always on the go. Her favorite direction is *up*; she just loves to climb and to crawl up the stairs. I think her mind must be in perpetual motion too. She's so easily bored. Nothing seems to hold her attention for very long. Is this behavior normal?

A: Yes. The typical 9-month-old is a real go-go artist. I bet Dorie gets into some strange predicaments. I observed one $9\frac{1}{2}$-month-old recently who managed to pull some drawers out of an end table and climb right up. Of course, like Dorie, he panicked at the prospect of getting back down.

Baby-proofing is certainly in order. But be sure to provide Dorie with opportunities to crawl and climb.

Dorie's attention span also sounds par for the nine-month course. I'm not surprised that she's easily bored. On the other hand, her memory for recent events should be developing. For example, she should be able to keep a series of items in mind, and she may even remember an event from the previous day.

Here are some other things Dorie should be able to do:

- Imitate speech sounds

- May say Mama or Dada

- Play pat-a-cake

- Pull herself to stand

Keep in mind, however, that developmental charts always express a range of accomplishments and that children develop at different paces. Dorie sounds right on schedule to me. If you're still worried, why not ask your pediatrician for some basic developmental screening tests? That should put your mind at ease.

Head Banging

Q: Our 10-month-old son has the habit of banging his head against the crib, the playpen, and even against the wall. Is he just trying to get attention?

A: Head banging is not unusual during infancy. It is often accompanied by rhythmic, rocking movements of the entire body. Head banging usually begins in the last half of the first year of life and disappears spontaneously at around the age of 2. Interestingly, it tends to get more severe as an infant moves from one developmental milestone to another as from sitting to standing or from crawling to walking. And it is twice as common among boys.

What causes head banging? No one really knows for sure. It is probably a habit that develops as a way of relieving tension. Some children develop the habit as a last resort if they do not have ready access to Mom's soothing when they become frustrated. Be sure that you respond to your baby by cuddling him whenever he appears irritable. You might also make a mental note of the kind of situations that give him most trouble, that result in head banging. Try to anticipate his habitual reaction. Pick him up before he starts banging his head.

Your own insight about attention seeking may be quite accurate. I'm always impressed by the intuition of mothers. Ask yourself: Why would he turn to such extremely negative attempts at attention getting? Is he not getting enough attention on the positive side of life? If not, make a special effort to praise and reward him for all the little things he does each day on the positive side of the ledger. Such an approach will pay big dividends in the long run.

While you are attempting these interventions, it would be a good idea, of course, to place some padding on the crib and the playpen. Try to protect your baby, in any way you can, from hurting himself. Some infants become such violent head bangers that they suffer head injuries. Severe cases may actually require more drastic action—like a pint-sized football helmet for the little guy.

If the problem worsens, I would definitely recommend a consultation with your pediatrician. And, yes, some head banging is symptomatic of serious psychiatric illness, but this diagnosis is much less likely if, as with your son, it begins in infancy and stands as a solitary symptom.

Constant Crying

Q: We need help. Brian, our 10-month-old, cries all the time. I can't even leave his room for five minutes without the tears. We even lost a baby-sitter because of this behavior.

A: There are two ways to approach this problem. First, let's look at it through Brian's eyes. He has certain basic needs: nurturance, protection, stimulation, and the confidence that he can trust you to provide these things in reasonable doses. Are his needs being met? It's also important to realize that, at 10 months, Brian will approach you now more often than you approach him. The average 10-month-old may approach you as often as six to eight times an hour. This is part of his newfound sensory and motor abilities. He wants to do things. He wants to make things happen.

So be sure to provide him with suitable outlets for his energy. Baby-proof the house, and let him go. You might also consider a walker for him.

Now let's look at this problem through your eyes. You may be unprepared for Brian's transition from a relatively passive infant to a demanding, curious little guy. This stage doesn't last long, but it's among the most difficult and crucial developmental stages of them all. The key is to be available to provide what Brian needs, but to be reasonable. Some of Brian's tears may simply be a game with him, his way of getting attention. You don't have to respond each and every time he cries. In fact, if you do, you may be just inviting more of the same. Be reasonable. After all, you have needs too.

Mama, Dada

Q: Our oldest children all said their first words at about 9 months of age, but our youngest, aged 11 months, John, hasn't uttered a word yet. He seems to be normal in all other respects. Should I be worried?

A: Not necessarily. There is a range of normal. And children proceed at different speeds along the various paths of development. For example, some infants may beat the charts on one line of development, such as language, but be a little pokey on another, such as sitting or walking.

As far as language is concerned, you can use these basic guidelines for the range of normal development:

1. Multiple-vowel sounds at 7 months

2. Singsong sounds like *mama* and *dada* at about 10 months

3. Two or three words besides mama and dada at 1 year

4. Vocabulary of about ten words at $1\frac{1}{2}$ years

5. Simple sentences of three words at 2 years

Keep working with John. Talk to him. That's how he'll pick up the correct cues. He may be a slow starter who will move quickly in his language development once he gets going. Be sure, of course, that his hearing is normal; this is a frequently overlooked cause of language disturbance. Otherwise, watch my guidelines and give him a little more time.

Toilet Training

Q: My son is 11 months old. When should I start toilet training?

A: The greatest danger is to start too early—before a child (1) can understand the process, (2) communicate verbally with you about it, and (3) control himself physiologically. Why? Children who are trained too early become confused. Sure, you occasionally hear about a child who is trained in one day or who "trained himself," but many of these children learn toilet training simply on a reflex basis: Potty equals excretion. It happens magically and largely out of their conscious control. They really haven't learned a thing. On the other hand, those children who do not "produce" by reflex can become very frustrated: Mom seems to want something from them, but they're not sure just what it's all about.

A child too young to comprehend toilet training is also vulnerable to power struggles. Mom wants, the child struggles, mom wants, and the child retains. Who's in control? Toilet training, after all, is really about *control*. Toilet training goes far beyond the simple matter of toileting. It is an important step on *the child's part* toward controlling his own body. If, instead, Mom uses it as a means to control the child, we have the makings of a classic stand-off. Conflict develops, and such children can themselves grow up to be controlling, rigid, and obstinate.

Why does a child become toilet-trained anyway? Because he doesn't like to mess in his diapers? No way. Messiness is not the answer. A child gives up the ease and joy of messing because Mother wants him to do it another way. And Mother's *love* is much more important to him than anything else in the world. So use this love wisely. Wait until your son can communicate verbally enough with you so that you can coach him and express your love. Wait until he has enough physiological control of his abdominal and anal musculature to work consciously with you as a team in the effort. Sufficient physical control is usually present by about 18 months or so. Praise his efforts, but do not become forceful or controlling. Be upbeat, hopeful, but, by all means, be patient. Beware pressures from friends and well-intended relatives to "break" him before a certain age. And, finally, beware books that prescribe magical formulas for toilet training in twenty-four hours or less.

A Toy for a Tot

Q: My sister is planning a birthday party for her daughter, who will be 1 year old next month. I've got a problem. I'm single, 26 years old, and have been away from children for several years. What type of toy should I choose as a gift?

A: One-year-olds love toys that can be hit and that reward with a sound. Also, toys that can be pushed and pulled and make noises are great favorites. The 1-year-old is beginning to utilize motor skills and, therefore, benefits from toys that allow her to develop coordination and to achieve some control and mastery over her little world.

Be prepared, though; she will become bored easily. She may end up playing with the wrapping or the box instead of your carefully selected gift!

Mental Retardation

Q: My sister-in-law's 1-year-old son has just been diagnosed as mentally retarded. She is taking it very hard. How can I help?

A: You can help your sister-in-law, your nephew, and the entire family by being supportive and understanding and realistic. One of ten Americans has a mentally retarded person in the family. Mental retardation strikes all socioeconomic classes, all religions, all nationalities. It can strike without warning as the 250 known causes account for only 25 percent of all cases. We have a great deal to learn about mental retardation.

One thing, however, is certain, and I'm sure that your family is aware of this truth: The retarded are just as human as the rest of us. Unfortunately, there remains too much prejudice in our society against these individuals. This prejudice, by its nature, is ill-founded. Most people do not realize, for example, that mental retardation comes in many "sizes and shapes," many degrees of disability. The vast majority of mentally retarded children fall into the "mildly retarded" range and are able, with patient love and teaching, to adapt marvelously and function in our society. As a matter of fact, 75 percent of all mentally retarded people can become self-supporting. Furthermore, some youngsters, while they may be slow in developing motor and social skills and may be handicapped in some aspects of intelligence, are actually capable of becoming quite accomplished in some particular skill.

You can share this hopeful information with your sister-in-law. I respect your interest in reaching out to her—and to your nephew.

Family Day Care

Q: Our daughter, Diane, is now 13 months old. I've spent these delightful months with her, but because of financial reasons, I'm going to have to return to work. The trouble is day care. I just can't find anything. One of my friends, though, has told me about a woman who runs a family day care; she takes children into her own home. What do you think of this arrangement?

A: Family day care goes by many names, but it isn't new. In fact the Census Bureau has reported that over 45 percent of all children under 6 whose mothers work are cared for in someone else's home.

You'll hear some experts say that this arrangement is better because it is less institutional or more homelike than day-care centers. My own observation, however, is that there's nothing magic in the idea. Any day-care program is as good as the people running it.

Parents should carefully check out the facility, the program, and the people. Visit the home and observe the interaction between children and staff. Is the psychological atmosphere warm and nurturing? What is the ratio of children to staff? For toddlers I recommend no more than three children per caretaker.

Diane, as an infant, will need special care. Be sure the caretakers are well prepared to look after her. Stop in occasionally, if you can, to check up on things.

Angry Baby?

Q: I'm frustrated. Tina, our 13-month-old, has a lot of trouble keeping her food down. I've taken her to our pediatrician several times. He's done a number of tests—all of which have been negative. Now he says that maybe Tina is just angry at me. Is this a cop out? How can an infant be angry? What am I doing wrong?

A: New research in the field of infant development suggests that babies can indeed experience emotions, such as anger.

In one case a pediatrician determined that an infant felt pain whenever his mother placed a spoon in his mouth. He reacted by spitting up his food or averting his head whenever Mom tried to feed him. Like yourself, perhaps, the mother felt that her child was rejecting *her* when, in fact, he was only doing what comes naturally—protecting himself. Because, however, his mother did not read his signals correctly and redoubled her efforts to feed him, he got angry: Feeding time became a contest, a struggle. Baby was angry. Mom was frustrated. Only after the doctor carefully observed the situation was the puzzle solved.

What are you doing wrong? Maybe nothing. Maybe you're just misinterpreting Tina's communication. The worst thing you could do is take it personally. My advice: Talk it over again with the pediatrician. Ask him to observe you feeding Tina. You may well discover the answer you're looking for.

Pinch Him Back?

Q: I'm a first-time mother. My son, Robert, is 13 months old. He's constantly trying to bite, scratch, and pull my hair. Is this typical behavior? How should I handle it? Should I say "no" firmly, or should I pinch him back?

A: Robert's behavior is not so unusual for a 13-month-old. He can't help himself, but you can. Pinch him back? No way. Children learn what they live, and Robert, at 13 months, is surely a good imitator. Pinching him back is not the solution.

The average 13-month-old is learning how to get parental attention to help him accomplish things. This attention getting is not a bad thing as long as it's on the positive side of life. Your basic plan, therefore, should be to ignore Robert's negative efforts. Next time he bites, scratches, or pulls your hair, simply pick him up, tell him that you will not allow him to hurt you, and place him in his playpen for five or ten minutes. He'll get the idea.

On the other hand, I hope you are responding adequately to Robert's positive attempts to engage you. Remember: Some activities that are great fun for him these days may be a bit of a nuisance to you. Favorite pastimes of many thirteen-monthers include a game we might call *putting things back*; that is, they love to empty Mommy's purse, then put everything back, etc. If Robert discovers this game or others like it, try to keep your good humor. Good humor will get you a lot further than pinching any day.

Siblingese

Q: My baby, Dirk, is 14 months old. I have two older children, aged 9 and 12. They just love their little brother and are a wonderful help to me. I've noticed that they've gotten into the habit of using baby talk with Dirk and that they've started talking that way with each other too. Any cause for alarm?

A: No. In fact, I give them high marks for their communication skills and sensitivity toward their baby brother. Interestingly, older siblings tend to be more natural in talking with infants than some parents. It's because they are closer to babies developmentally and they tend to spend a lot of time with them.

Your older ones are probably just having some fun when they baby-talk to each other. Such regression is to be expected. In some ways, of course, they're jealous of the baby, and their imitation may be a form of unconscious identification with him. But do not interpret these psychological explanations to them. Let them have their fun. They'll get over it.

Strong Attachment to Day Care

Q: Mary is 15 months old. I fretted about placing her in day care, but I finally took the plunge because I simply had to get back to work. I think I was more anxious than she was. I reassured her of my love again and again. And again. Well, the big day finally arrived. I was sure she'd panic at the door and cling to me—but she handled it like a trooper. In fact, she's formed a strong attachment to her caretaker, Mrs. W., and I must admit—I'm a little jealous. I feel so expendable all of a sudden. In fact, I'd like to quit my job. I don't want to be replaced as a mother. Comments?

A: The "guilt" over returning to work is natural for most mothers. In fact, it's a healthy sign of your love and devotion. This guilt, of course, is lessened if the decision is forced by financial necessity. Mary's lack of separation anxiety is not necessarily a bad sign at all, especially if she's had significant previous experience with you being away from her. She may have learned to trust that you'd return and everything would be right in her world.

As Mary grows, she'll make attachments to various people. Later she'll identify with the mannerisms and values of important adults in her life, such as teachers. This is a sign of growth and development.

So don't worry about your daughter's interest in Mrs. W., but make your time with Mary special. Make it count. And, above all, don't let your own guilt get in the way of being a good mother; don't try to compensate by pampering Mary. Be a mother first, last, and always.

Childhood Influence on Personality

Q: Our daughter, Bonnie, is 17 months old. Is it true that her basic personality will be 100 percent formed by the time she's 6 years old?

A: No. While the influence of the first 5 or 6 years of life is absolutely crucial in the formation of such things as trust or mistrust, optimism or pessimism, self-esteem, frustration tolerance, and many other vital psychological factors, Bonnie, like the rest of us, will have many other opportunities to grow and develop during her life. Adolescence, for example, is a period of significant change for many people. And even adult life holds out the prospect of continued personality growth. But remember: Your own influence over your daughter's development will be greatest in her early years.

Stages of Play

Q: Marshall, our 18-month-old, is an only child. I'm anxious to introduce him to other children so he can learn to share and relate. I realize it's probably too early to expect much sharing from him now, but when should I plan to enroll him in a play group?

A: Children go through several distinct stages of play activity before they are truly capable of the give-and-take of cooperative play:

Stage One: Solitary Play. This is the self-absorbed play of the infant. It is first directed toward fascination with his own body parts and then with objects around him.

Stage Two: Observation. By 18 months many infants become quite interested in the play of others. They look—but they don't touch. They're checking it out.

Stage Three: Parallel Play. Two-year-olds typically engage in what to the casual observer may look like true interactive play—but it isn't. The early toddler may appear to play "with," but he mostly plays "along." He's still too self-absorbed and possessive, for example, to share toys and attention.

Stage Four: Cooperative Play. The highest form of play is true cooperation with peers. Some youngsters develop this ability fairly well by 3 or 4 years of age—others have a tough time doing it consistently for several years. It is a test of a child's capacity to tolerate frustrations, to empathize, and to relate to another youngster.

Fear of Water

Q: Devon, our 18-month-old, has recently developed a fear of water. She won't even let me wash her face. What's causing this fear? How should I handle it?

A: Fear of water, of course, is not unusual among infants. It commonly begins at around 18 to 24 months of age. One of the reasons is that children often begin potty training at this time. If, for example, Devon fears the flushing of the toilet, she may generalize to a fear of water. Like other 18-month-olds she may believe that the flushed water in the toilet bowl is stealing away something valuable from her.

There are other explanations for the fear of water too. Devon, at 18 months, very much wants to be in control of things. She may feel intimidated and out of control in the tub. Then, again, she may have been legitimately frightened by water recently; don't overlook this possibility.

What to do? Be gentle. Try some sponge baths for a few days. At first you might use the sink, then the tub. Gradually reintroduce Devon to her baths. Remember: The longer you delay the baths, the tougher it's going to be to get Devon back in the bathing habit.

Mouthwash Dangers

Q: Anna, our 18-month-old, is pretty active, but I try to stay one jump ahead of her. I have the house well baby-proofed. Imagine my surprise recently when one of my girlfriends visited. She let out a gasp when she saw a bottle of mouthwash on the bathroom counter. "This stuff is dangerous," she said; "put it away." I did it—but I wonder. Is she correct?

A: Yes. You wouldn't dream of leaving an open can of beer or a glass of wine on the bathroom counter, but you might be surprised to learn that mouthwash often contains as much (or more) alcohol as beer or wine. In fact, there are reports in the pediatric literature of toddlers ingesting mouthwash. I know of at least one death.

Mouthwash. Add it to your child-proofing checklist.

Fingerprinting of Children?

Q: Our local police department has offered to fingerprint children as a way to curb child snatching and abduction. It sounds grisly to me. Our children are aged $1\frac{1}{2}$, 4, 7, and 8. Should we have them fingerprinted?

A: I doubt that fingerprinting will have a dramatic impact on the number of missing children, but it would certainly aid in identification. There are about 100,000 children reported missing every year. About 75,000 are runaways; the others are either snatched by estranged parents or abducted by strangers. Sadly, about 3000 unidentified children are buried every year.

The painful agony of the parents of missing children is enormous—and it never ends.

Fingerprinting is not very accurate under the age of 2; footprints are much more reliable. Most hospitals have gotten out of this procedure although there are some efforts under way now to reinstitute the practice.

Should you have your children fingerprinted? It is obviously a personal decision, but I'm not very enthusiastic about it at this time.

Mommy's Side of the Bed

Q: We have three children aged $1\frac{1}{2}$, 3, and 5. From time to time they have bad dreams or can't fall asleep or have a tummy ache—and they crawl into bed with my husband and me. They always choose my side of the bed. My girlfriend says that she read somewhere that this means the kids are insecure and they perceive trouble in the marriage. Is this correct?

A: It's very hard to generalize, but since most parents (over 80 percent) do allow their children into the marital bed, some Stanford University researchers have investigated this question. They found that one out of three children who habitually snuggle in bed with their parents have a strong preference for one side—Mom's. Is it a sign of perceived problems in the marriage? The researchers found no support for your girlfriend's theory.

Unwed Father

Q: I'm an unwed father. About two years ago I accepted the invitation to impregnate a local woman who wanted to become a single, unwed mother. She said: "No problem. I'll raise the baby. He'll have my name. You don't have to worry about a thing." I didn't worry at first—but now I do. I want to see the baby—but she won't let me. She says I promised to "keep out of it." I guess I did, but I didn't know at the time that I'd feel fatherly about the baby. What happens now?

A: She said "no problem," but she was wrong from the start. Your situation, unfortunately, is not unique. There have been several recent suits brought by both unwed mothers and unwed fathers.

Besides legal advice you need someone who will listen to your side of the story, to accept your feelings, and to help you resolve your conflicts. Be aware that you may be in for some hindsight moralizing by some people—but that won't help you now.

A support group in Washington, D.C., Free Men, may be able to offer some help. Some members have been through experiences like yours; they're among the few experts in this basically uncharted no-man's-land.

Will My Son Become Gay?

Q: I'm a single mother with a 19-month-old son. With the absence of a male figure in his life, does he have a greater risk of becoming a homosexual?

A: I know of no research which documents that single mothers tend to raise homosexual sons. The greatest danger is for you to fear that there's something wrong with *you* because you're a single mother. Relax. One in five American children live in one-parent families. Raise your son naturally: plenty of love, good communication, and reasonable discipline. With such a formula he should grow up to be a happy adult.

Net over the Crib?

Q: Bernadette, our 19-month-old, doesn't like to stay in her crib at night. It started with her throwing the stuffed animals onto the floor. Now she climbs down herself. This morning, in fact, I found her sleeping *under* the crib. My neighbor suggested putting one of those nets over the crib so she can't climb out. What do you think?

A: It shouldn't be necessary. But I'm a little worried, as I'm sure you are, about Bernadette falling and hurting herself during one of her nocturnal climbing expeditions. Why not get a step ahead of her? I'd suggest placing a mattress on the floor and letting her sleep on it. Eventually, of course, she'll graduate to a full-fledged bed.

Bernadette sounds like an active, adventuresome little girl. The net would probably work, but it might stifle her natural curiosity and drive toward more independence. My net advice: no net.

Parallel Play

Q: My 20-month-old daughter, Jo Ann, loves to visit her cousin, Hillary, who is 22 months old. Yet when they get together, nothing seems to happen. Am I expecting too much? Am I forcing the girls toward friendship before they are ready for it?

A: Yes and no. Most toddlers are really attracted to peers, but, of course, they lack the developmental skills to engage in anything remotely resembling a shared, mutual relationship. Their form of interaction is often called *parallel play*; that is, they play together— alone.

For example, they may briefly eye each other, then retreat to opposite sides of the room, each engaging in the same kind of activity but as soloists, not true playmates.

My advice? Peer relatedness is a very crucial task of childhood. Recent research suggests that even toddlers, such as Jo Ann and Hillary, can learn lessons from the clumsy first attempts at friendship. By all means continue the visits. Gently and gradually coach the girls toward sharing and cooperation. With your help they'll be ready for some cooperative play by the age of 3, if not earlier.

Toddler Tussles

Q: Two of my girlfriends and I have formed a play group for our children, aged 20, 24, and 26 months. We've spent a good bit of time discussing the ground rules, activities, scheduling, and so forth, but we're still divided on how to handle conflict between the children. Is it healthier to let them solve their own problems, or should we jump in right away to snuff out problems?

A: I hope you've discovered that most interactions between the three youngsters are positive. There should be more laughing than crying, more smiles than snarls.

Nevertheless, conflict is sure to raise its head with some predictable regularity. I would suggest an *active intervention* approach—but not for the purpose of snuffing out or solving the toddlers' problems for them. Instead, try to model appropriate behavior for them, teach them alternatives, for example, to taking toys from each other. Give them a positive experience with sharing and mutual interaction. Don't be too quick, however, to come to the rescue unless you witness aggression. Such misbehavior should be stopped immediately. If it continues, you might serve the offender with a five-minute time-out from the group. Then be sure to do some teaching on his return to the fun.

Mom Speaks German

Q: Gerhardt is 21 months old. My girlfriend says that he's stupid because he only knows about ten words. She says the average 2-year-old has a vocabulary of 200 words. I'm worried. When I'm alone with him, I only speak German. Am I harming him?

A: *Nein.* First let me correct your girlfriend. The average 21-month-old has a vocabulary of 20, not 200, words. I presume you are referring to a vocabulary of ten *English* words. How many *German* words does Gerhardt know? Add the two languages together for a truer picture of his vocabulary.

Children who are raised bilingually sometimes start slower in each language, but they tend to catch up down the line.

Don't let your girlfriend scare you. You're doing what comes naturally. If Gerhardt is showing suitable progress in both languages and if he's exhibiting proper development in other areas—motor, learning, social, and emotional—there's nothing to worry about.

Growing a Bigger Brain

Q: My husband is obsessed with intelligence. He wants our son, Jeremy, who's 22 months old to be a brain. Last week he brought home some flash cards to teach Jeremy Latin! My husband says that he's reviewed the research on brain development: If you pack a lot of facts into a child's head, he'll develop a bigger brain—and grow up to be superintelligent. Is this true?

A: There is some research on laboratory animals, mostly rats, showing that increased sensory stimulation causes their brains to grow larger than if they are understimulated. From here, however, to documenting that flash cards and other teaching devices cause the human brain to grow more rapidly, and that this growth results in superior intelligence, is a giant leap into the unknown. Your husband is speculating.

Success in the intellectual arena is a combination of intelligence and motivation. And, I should point out, intelligence is certainly not measured solely by the number of facts in a person's head. Jeremy needs factual knowledge, sure, but he'll also have to learn *how* to think, problem-solve, and conceptualize and to communicate his knowledge to other people. And he'll have to be healthy: socially, emotionally, and physically.

I'm a little concerned about your husband's obsession. If he loves Jeremy only for the intellectual giant that he wants, will he be able to love Jeremy if he turns out to have other skills or interests?

No!

Q: Patrick, our 2-year-old, was such an easygoing baby. Now all he seems to say is "no." What's happening?

A: Welcome to the "terrible 2s." The bad news is that Patrick has entered a stage of development where he will become controlling and oppositional. The good news is that it's normal and that it probably won't last too long.

Why is *no* the favorite word of so many 2-year-olds? First of all, these toddlers hear "no" so often from their parents that repeating it themselves comes naturally. It is no wonder that 2-year-olds are the recipient of so much parental *no* saying; because of their newly acquired motor skills and their natural drive toward inquisitiveness, they seem to be into everything. But at some point children wish to identify with Mom and Dad. Like Patrick, they may turn the tables and start saying "no" themselves.

Secondly, the word *no* has certain powerful and magical attractions to most 2-year-olds. These youngsters wish to control themselves, their world, and the people in it. Their "No!" is a childish attempt to exercise control over events and people that are largely out of their control. Their "No!" is also a statement of autonomy: "If I can control, I am independent."

So you see, Patrick's *no* saying is an important developmental organizer. Give him some slack, some successes, but do not relinquish control. He *wishes* he could exert his *no*s on you, but the maternal "yes" must still prevail most of the time.

Do vs. Don't

Q: I'm a single mother. I have two children, aged 2 and 4. The other day it occurred to me that I'm always telling them *not* to do something: Don't do this; don't do that. I must seem very negative to them, right?

A: Right. But don't be too hard on yourself. You've got your hands full. After all, there's nothing quite like an active 2-year-old or 4-year-old to bring out the negatives in any parent.

Yet you're absolutely on target about an important principle. The best way to teach discipline to children is to accentuate the positive. It's much more effective to reward them for good behavior than to scold or punish them when they misbehave. Similarly, it's much more effective if you tell what to do rather than what *not* to do. So, yes, emphasize *do* over *don't*.

There will be times, of course, when you'll have to preface your remarks with a "don't." When you do it, be sure you're very specific. It's not very effective, for example, to tell a young child: "Don't be naughty." Instead, tell him exactly what it is you want him to avoid.

Toddler Aggression

Q: He was a wonderful baby: soft, cuddly, passive. Now our Rudy, aged 2, is a little terror. He's so aggressive. He hits, throws things, bites, and spits. I've read a lot of books, and I realize that toddlers do get a little rambunctious, but this seems extreme. Do we have a problem here?

A: Could be. It's all a matter of degree and how you handle Rudy's behavior.

First of all, you're quite right. The 2-year-old plays a totally different ball game than the passive infant. He's easily frustrated and tends to strike out—not because he's vicious, but because he lacks any other means to express his irritation.

Some tips:

1. *Observe:* Try to identify the times, places, and situations that frustrate Rudy. Most youngsters, for example, get cranky when they're tired. Others are especially vulnerable to peer or sibling competition. Once you've identified Rudy's special weaknesses, try to intervene *before he throws a tantrum.*

2. *Expectations:* Do not accept Rudy's behavior. When he gets out of control, let him know by word and action that you will not allow him to injure anyone—including himself. If necessary, pick him up and take him to his room for a brief time-out.

3. *Accept words and feelings:* It's not too early to begin to teach Rudy that it's okay to feel angry and to use angry (but not abusive) words. You will not, however, accept aggressive behavior.

Two-Year-Old Terror

Q: I can't go anywhere with my 2-year-old daughter without a disaster. Recently, she bit my thigh and screamed when I insisted that she not take a toy away from another child. This is too much for me. I truly hope you can help me.

A: While such things as temper tantrums and an attitude of "I want what I want when I want it" are common among many 2-year-olds, I get very concerned when I see a child taking direct aim on a parent. Allowing your daughter to abuse you is not only bad for you— it's bad for her too.

I would urge you to try and build a positive atmosphere into the relationship. Reward her for positive behavior. Ignore all but the most flagrant negative behavior. Do not allow her to abuse you. Take charge by giving her a time-out (sitting by herself); even pick her up bodily if that's what it takes. Parents must be in charge of these situations—not 2-year-olds.

If you do not see improvement in one month, ask your pediatrician to refer you to a child psychiatrist for a consultation. From the tone of your letter I sense a bit of desperation. Help is available. Take advantage of it. Don't despair.

Climbing Out of the Crib

Q: Brian, my 2-year-old, has learned a new trick: climbing out of the crib. As soon as I put him back, he's up again. We go through this ritual two or three times every night. It seems like a game to him, but it's a nightmare for me. Last week I put twin beds in his room; now we both sleep in there. Any more suggestions?

A: Children frequently have trouble staying in bed at this age. Brian is driven to explore, and he wants to practice his new motor skills. And, yes, there is some game playing here too. Seen through the eyes of a 2-year-old, Brian would never want to be separated from his favorite toy—you.

Some tips:

1. Two-year-olds love bedtime rituals. Try a consistent sequence of bath, reading to him, etc. Take it slow. Try to "bring him down" from his fast-paced day.

2. Move back to your own room immediately because the longer you delay, the tougher it will be to ever regain your privacy.

3. If Brian still gets up at night, you might tie his door shut with an old nylon stocking or some elastic material. In this way he'll be able to open the door slightly and won't feel "locked up."

4. The best news of all is that the "terrible 2s" don't last forever.

Bedtime Battle

Q: Lawrence is 25 months old, and we have a problem. We've never established a bedtime for him. Rather than forcing him to go to bed on our schedule, my husband and I have just kind of let him decide when he's tired enough to go up to his room. Well, I bet you've already guessed what's happening. Lawrence is starting to outlast us at night. It's ridiculous. We sit there, nodding and drowsing while he plays on the floor! Then when either of us tries to interrupt his play to take him to bed, he lets out a wail you wouldn't believe. Were we wrong in the first place? What now?

A: Yes. You were wrong in the first place. Bedtime must be established by parents. After all, no infant or toddler ever really *wants* to go to bed. Lawrence wants to be where the action is—with Mommy and Daddy. Don't feel badly about "forcing" Lawrence to go to bed. He may be relieved...and you will be too. The wail? It's to be expected. Tune it out. It's to bed, to bed...gently but firmly.

What Is a Good Day Care?

Q: I will have to return to work soon. I am looking for a good day-care center for my 2-year-old daughter, Caryl. My question: How do I know if a center is good?

A: The best evidence, of course, would be the specific recommendation of a trusted friend and a personal visit by you and Caryl. On such a visit you'll want to check out both the physical environment and the psychological environment. How does the staff interact with the children? Is there an atmosphere of trust, warmth, spontaneity, and good humor? Pay special attention to how your own daughter relates to the staff and the children.

Another important factor is the staff to child ratio. For toddlers such as your daughter, I advise no more than three children per caretaker. Also, it works best if the other children are about the same age as Caryl.

Be sure to talk to other parents whose children attend the program. The center director should be pleased to provide you with a list of names. If not, beware.

Finally, after you've decided to place Caryl in the center, be sure to drop in for unannounced visits. Caryl will be delighted— and you'll keep the staff on their toes in the event you have any doubts about them.

Day Care after Divorce

Q: My husband and I were divorced two weeks ago. I'm going to have to return to work before too long. Would it be better for my children, aged 2 and 3, if I went right out and got a job immediately or should I wait a couple of months?

A: If you have the option, I'd suggest that you put off the job for several weeks. The worst time to place children into day care is immediately following some traumatic event, such as a divorce or separation.

At ages of 2 and 3, your children are vulnerable to fears of abandonment at this time. They need reassurance that you are not going to leave them. Take it slow. Gradually introduce the idea of day care.

Effects of Divorce

Q: My children are 2 and $3\frac{1}{2}$ years old. I divorced their father six months ago. The divorce doesn't really seem to have affected them very much at all; they never did have much contact with their father. But what about the future? Will they be damaged or stigmatized as "children of divorce"?

A: The long-term effects of divorce are not easy to gauge. We know, however, that about a third of the children of divorce suffer psychological symptoms such as depression for up to ten years after the event.

Studies of adults who were themselves children of divorce are also instructive. For one thing, they are more likely than others to be divorced. They also tend to be less satisfied with their lives.

My review of the literature, however, leads to one inescapable conclusion: The jury is still out. There are some contradictory findings, and you have to consider that today's children will be less stigmatized by divorce than, say, today's middle-aged population since the current divorce rate is so much higher than it was twenty or thirty years ago.

My advice: Be the best mother you can be. That's the best protection you can possibly give your children.

Parents Without Partners

Q: I'm 26, a recently divorced mother of two girls, aged 2 and 4. I'm struggling to put my life back in shape. One of my girlfriends suggested I attend meetings of the group called Parents Without Partners. What do you think?

A: Parents Without Partners (PWP) is a 27-year-old self-help organization for single parents. It's been around even longer than you have. And in that time it's helped a great many men and women— and indirectly their children too. PWP has almost 1000 chapters all around the country; they're usually listed in the local telephone directory. PWP isn't for everyone, of course, but you won't know unless you check it out. Why not give a call?

Baby Comedian?

Q: Peter, our 2-year-old, is a real comedian. Or at least his mother and I *think* he is. He makes funny faces. He mimics people. He teases the other kids. He really keeps us all in stitches. Is this really the beginning of a true sense of humor?

A: Peter may be a very funny little guy, and while it's premature to say that he has cultivated a true sense of humor, he may be on his way to becoming something of a comedian.

The earliest precursors of humor can be seen in 2-year-olds. Peter's funny faces and mimicking, for example, are forms of primitive humor. Teasing is another early sign of humor. Other things to watch for:

1. *Incongruity:* The child who learns to get laughs by, for example, incongruously putting a piece of bread in his ear is using this device.

2. *Accidents:* The child who pretends to fall is playing off an "accident" as humor.

Do you recognize these devices as typical slapstick humor? That's what they are. That's why slapstick is considered primitive humor; it appeals to the child in all of us.

If you wish to encourage Peter's attempts at comedy, by all means laugh at his efforts. Then help him develop a higher form of humor as he learns more verbal skills. Words and the juxtaposition of ideas are the next rungs of the comedy ladder.

Is My Toddler Hyperactive?

Q: Sunny, my 2-year-old daughter, never stops. It's go, go, go—morning, noon, and night. I think she's hyperactive or something. What should I do?

A: The diagnosis of true hyperactivity (or *attention deficit disorder* as it's now called) is not easy in a 2-year-old. The reason is obvious: Toddlers, by nature, are go-go types. I would need more history and some direct observation of Sunny in order to make a diagnosis. Therefore, I suggest that you confer with your pediatrician.

In the meantime, consider these factors:

1. The incidence of ADD is somewhat lower among girls than boys.

2. If Sunny has achieved her major motor milestones (crawling, walking, talking, etc.) normally, she is less likely to be hyperactive.

3. If your pregnancy, labor, and delivery were uneventful, there is less chance of ADD.

Breath-Holding Spells

Q: We're terrified. Shawnee, our 2-year-old, has learned how to hold her breath whenever she wants something. Last night, she did it until she passed out. We rushed her to the emergency room but she was fine by the time we got there, and the doctors said there wouldn't be any brain damage or anything. This morning she tried it again when I tried to leave her with her sitter. I ended up staying home, but where does this lead? I can't stay at her side twenty-four hours a day, but this is precisely what she seems to demand.

A: Breath holding is a form of temper tantrum. It is not uncommon among 2-year-olds (you've heard about the "terrible 2s," I'm sure), and it will go away—if you handle it correctly.

Two-year-olds are amazingly willful creatures. Developmentally, they are out to control their little worlds. How else can you explain the strength and determination necessary to overcome the body's automatic regulation of something as vital as breathing? These spells, however, will not damage Shawnee's brain, and there is little evidence to suggest that they will lead to seizures. So relax.

Relax and think. The worst thing that can happen is for you to habitually give in to Shawnee whenever she holds or threatens to hold her breath. This will put you squarely at her mercy. It is a form of emotional blackmail. It is a setup for how to raise a spoiled child. You, not Shawnee, must remain in control.

How to do it? Try ignoring her threats and even the breath holding itself. This may take some courage, but it will pay dividends. When Shawnee figures out that you mean business, that she cannot get her own way through intimidation, she will stop the behavior. Then *you* will be able to breathe a lot easier.

Thumb-Sucking

Q: Our 2-year-old sucks his thumb. He has had this habit since about 3 or 4 months of age. Is this a sign of insecurity? When we try to get him to stop, it only seems to get worse. What should we do?

A: If children are going to develop this habit, it generally begins at the age of 3 to 4 months. Your son was right on schedule. He probably began by continuing to suck his thumb right after feeding and is now habitually doing it during the day when he's tense or fatigued—and at night as he lulls himself to sleep.

Infants have an innate drive to suck during what is called the oral stage of development. Some little ones, however, persist in the habit as a device to ease tension and to soothe themselves. In the absence of other conflicts or problems, thumb-sucking is not symptomatic of unhappiness, insecurity, or maladjustment.

Many parents are frustrated in their efforts to curb thumb-sucking. They overreact and take it too seriously because they are led to believe by friends and relatives that something must be wrong with a child who sucks his thumb. Techniques such as forcibly pulling your boy's thumb out of his mouth whenever you find it there, painting his thumb with a foul-tasting concoction, or putting mittens on him will only make him more tense and precipitate more sucking.

My advice to you is:

1. Relax. If you do not make a fuss about it, the habit almost certainly will disappear by the age of 4 or 5.

2. Try to observe your boy closely. In what type of situations does he tend to suck his thumb? Make a list.

3. Then try to anticipate his thumb-sucking; that is, if it occurs when he's hungry, try feeding him a little earlier; if it is associated with fatigue, insist on a nap.

4. If you take his thumb out of his mouth, do it gently while skillfully diverting his attention to yourself. Ultimately we want him to learn to use you and your husband as his "pacifiers."

Preschool Benefits

Q: Please help my girlfriend and me settle an argument. She says that preschool doesn't really give children an educational head start, that it's valuable mostly as a "socialization device." I say that while preschool certainly helps youngsters learn how to get along with each other, its major benefit is academic. Cindy, my girlfriend, is not planning to send her son (now 2 years old) to nursery school because of her beliefs. I say she'll be harming his future academic development. Who's right?

A: You are—probably. Most children benefit from a preschool experience, but they benefit in different ways and in different degrees. I can't predict how a specific youngster might benefit without knowing more about him.

You might tell your girlfriend about the latest follow-up study of a group of children who participated in Head Start programs back in the sixties. These children entered the program at the age of 3; they're now 19. They have fared much better than a matched group of youngsters who did not participate in the preschool program. For example, 67 percent graduated from high school versus 49 percent of the control group. And twice as many of the preschool youngsters have gone on to college.

There's some other interesting data, too, recently released by the High-Scope Educational Research Foundation. Teenage pregnancy was cut in half among the preschool group, and 20 percent fewer had experienced trouble with the law. So clearly there are both academic and social rewards. Keep in mind, though, that the study group was limited to black youngsters from poverty-level families. As with any research study, you have to be careful about generalizing results and conclusions.

Fear of Potty?

Q: We have a toilet-training problem with my daughter who recently turned 2. She'll often call her father or me to take her to the potty, but once she gets there, she starts screaming. We switched from the potty chair to a baby seat that fits over the toilet, but the same thing happens. Any help will be appreciated.

A: Your daughter's behavior is not so unusual. She's exhibiting the typical *ambivalence* of a 2-year-old: She wants to comply with your wishes for toilet training—yet she also wants to retain control over her bodily functions. The best approach, of course, is to avoid a power struggle. Be positive. If she screams, take her off the potty seat. Such ambivalence is usually a stage that quickly passes.

Another possibility, of course, is fear. Sometimes we adults forget how frightening a potty or toilet may be to a toddler: Will I fall in? Will I be flushed away? The best antidote here is to demonstrate the inner workings of the toilet to your daughter.

Finally, don't forget that screaming on the potty can be a symptom of constipation or urinary tract infection. If in doubt, consult your pediatrician.

Toilet-Training Tactics

Q: We're having a heck of a time with toilet training. I try to be cheerful and positive, but Bobbie, our 25-month-old, just isn't getting the message. So my husband, Jerry, punishes her; nothing drastic, he just scolds her for "not going potty." Aren't we confusing her?

A: Yes. Keep it positive. Tactics of encouragement and praise work. Punishment doesn't. By the way, there's no magic age by which a child should become toilet-trained, so don't be pressured. Bobbie may not be ready yet.

What can you do? Keep the potty on the floor where she can use it herself. Play dolls with her, and allow her to assume the role of the Mommy who is teaching the doll how to use the potty. Maintain your gentle expectations that Bobbie, too, should use the potty. Praise her when she succeeds. The best formula is to keep it positive. When accidents happen, you can voice mild disapproval but don't punish Bobbie; instead, make it a learning experience for her. Give her the opportunity to correct her mistake by allowing her to change her own pants—with some help, if necessary, from Mom and Dad.

Afraid of the Dark

Q: Francis, our 26-month-old, is afraid of the dark. It's a battle every night when we put him to bed. First it's a hug and kiss. Then he has to have a night-light. Then the door has to be open just the right amount. Then he calls my wife and me back to place his shoes on top of the dresser. Last night (you won't believe this) he couldn't fall asleep until we put a box of cookies on his window sill. We've humored him along so far, but this is getting ridiculous. Are we correct in going along with his bedtime demands, or should we draw the line and see what happens?

A: Draw the line. Why? If you don't, there is no telling where Francis's rituals will lead you. Yes, rituals. In an effort to cope with his fear of the dark, Francis is developing some obsessive-compulsive rituals.

These rituals have a magic quality for him. He's not sure what he fears, but he believes that if he does things in just the right way, he can tame the monsters that lay in wait for him. We know, however, that these monsters are of his own making; they're products of his own unconscious.

Keep in mind also that Francis may be indulging in some stalling tactics here too. He may, on another level, be playing a game with you and your wife.

So make sure his basic needs are met (a hug, a trip to the bathroom, a night-light, etc.), but then be firm. Draw the line. What will happen? Francis may become anxious. You can reassure him that everything will be okay, but better to let him confront the unpleasant feeling than to go on ritualistically defending against it. If the anxiety is too much for him, if Francis panics, or if he develops nightmares, you should consult a child psychiatrist.

Can He Feed Himself?

Q: My son Jackie is 27 months old. He's very determined to feed himself. In the process, however, he spills milk and dumps cereal all over the place. I know this is the way he learns and that I have to put up with a certain amount of messiness. But my question is this: How much can I really expect of him at his age?

A: Two-year-olds are in the business of discovery and control. Jackie, therefore, is driven to discover the pleasure of self-feeding and the sense of mastering and control that accompanies it.

At 26 months of age, Jackie should be able to use a spoon—almost. That is, he ought to get *most* of the food into his mouth. He ought to be able to lift his cup, drink from it, and set it down—without spilling too much milk. And he should be able to use a fork too, although he'll be awkward with it. I hope these tips help. Don't expect more than he can handle. And, yes, a "certain amount of messiness" is to be expected from Jackie for the next several months.

Boy Play vs. Girl Play

Q: I guess our two children are very traditional. Our $2\frac{1}{2}$-year-old daughter, Kris, likes to play dolls. Our 4-year-old son, Jimmy, is always shooting monsters or something. My husband and I recall that we engaged in the same kind of play when we were kids. We thought today's children were different. Any comments?

A: There *is* more freedom today for boys and girls to experiment with new forms of play. Boys, for example, are more free to play with dolls, girls to play cops and robbers. This is a good thing. But, interestingly enough, play preferences of children, as you observe in Kris and Jimmy, have remained quite traditional.

In one study conducted at Brandeis University, researchers observed forty-five children at a day-care center. They found that preschool boys spent 24 percent of their time in fantasy play such as aliens and monsters. The girls didn't play these games at all. The researchers found, instead, that the girls' play was much more cooperative and gentle, while the boys thrived on games of conflict with clearly identifiable good guys and bad guys.

Sounds like Kris and Jimmy fit the norm. Make sure, though, that they're given opportunities to develop themselves fully through their play. A little well-controlled aggression would not be a bad thing for Kris. Some sensitivity and nurturing experience would not be bad for Jimmy.

Delayed Speech

Q: Our $2\frac{1}{2}$-year-old, Monica, is a beautiful child. She's normal in all respects—except one. She still hasn't spoken her first words. Should we be concerned?

A: Yes. When a child has not uttered her first words by the age of 2, we consider there to be a definite delay in speech development. This doesn't necessarily mean that Monica is in for big problems, but you should certainly seek consultation with your pediatrician. He may then refer you for further studies such as neurologic, psychiatric—or he may recommend a speech pathologist.

There are many causes of delayed speech:

1. *Hearing loss:* This cause is often overlooked. It may be subtle, particularly when a youngster's hearing loss is limited to certain frequencies.

2. *Family delay:* Is there a family history of late talkers? If so, Monica's problem may be due to genetic factors. Such a delay only rarely lasts beyond 3 years of age.

3. *Central nervous system:* Various brain defects can cause language lag. One of the primary signs of mental retardation is speech delay. But don't be alarmed. Monica's problems may not be so serious.

There are other, less common causes that probably do not apply in your situation, but I'll list them for the sake of completeness:

4. *Autism:* This complex condition is characterized by language delay.

5. *Maternal deprivation:* Since children learn language primarily by mimicking their primary caretakers, maternal deprivation (due to depression, neglect, etc.) is another cause.

6. *Bilingual families:* Children who are raised in a bilingual environment from birth usually are delayed somewhat in both languages.

Me Do It Myself

Q: Dawn, our oldest child, is $2\frac{1}{2}$ years old. Her favorite saying is "Me do it myself." At first I was pleased to hear it because I want her to become independent. But when I let her try things herself, she balks and wants me to do it! What should I do?

A: Welcome to the terrible 2s. Dawn, like her 2-year-old counterparts, is a creature of extremes. In her struggle to exert control over a world that she doesn't understand, she may insist on doing it herself, yet in the next breath she may want to control *you* by making you take care of it for her. Don't worry. The best news is that she'll grow out of it in about six months or so. In the meantime, I suggest you err on the side of encouraging independence. Don't do for Dawn what you believe she can do for herself. But be careful. Don't expect too much of her either. Frustration and passivity are twin enemies of independence.

Three Square Meals

Q: Maria is $2\frac{1}{2}$ years old, and for her age she's fairly civilized at dinnertime. I mean she's not *too* messy. In fact, she's such a joy that I'm trying to get her into the habit of eating three square meals a day. She's resisting it though. Should I simply refuse to give her all the between-meal snacks she craves or let her go on snacking until she's ready to be fed only at mealtimes?

A: It is the rare child who will decide spontaneously to give up snacks and to eat at mealtimes. You need a plan.

I suggest that you establish a standard snack time in midmorning and midafternoon and that you eliminate snacks on demand. In this way you can begin to shape Maria's behavior gradually toward your basic three squares a day.

Yesterday, Today, Tomorrow

Q: My daughter, Kimberly, is $2\frac{1}{2}$ years old. I marvel at the changes in her from day to day. Lately, she's been asking a lot of questions about time; for example, When is yesterday? and How long until tomorrow? I try to be patient and to answer all these questions, but I don't think I'm getting through to her. Any suggestions?

A: Kimberly is right on schedule from a developmental standpoint. In fact, the awareness and perception of *time* is one of the hallmarks of the $2\frac{1}{2}$- or 3-year-old. Therefore, I'm not surprised that Kimberly's vocabulary is riddled with time-related words and that she's asking so many questions about time.

Keep in mind, though, that her ability to really comprehend the concept of time is quite limited. This is why your own thoughtful answers to her questions seem to fall on deaf ears.

Most $2\frac{1}{2}$-year-olds have a concrete notion of time; they associate it with specific events, such as time for lunch, time for bed. Their abstract knowledge of what has happened in the past and what will happen in the future is very vague.

You can help Kimberly, therefore, by making your answers and instructions as concrete as possible. And since the average $2\frac{1}{2}$-year-old can best understand something that she can see, try to appeal to her visual interest. For example, in teaching her about past and present, use a desk calendar; you could tear out yesterday's page and peek ahead at tomorrow's. Similarly, a clock with hour and minute hands, rather than a digital clock, will serve best to teach her about time.

"Is Daddy Coming?"

Q: I don't know what to say when my son Peter ($2\frac{1}{2}$ years old) asks, "Is my daddy coming today?" His father and I are divorced, but Peter doesn't know it. Sometimes weeks go by between visits. Is this inconsistent contact harmful to my son?

A: This child of divorce needs his father—as evidenced by your son's poignant question.

Yes, I'm afraid the current situation is not good for your boy. At his age he experiences his father's absence as abandonment. It feels empty and bad and lonely. Soon your son will probably conclude that Dad left because of him; that is, if only he had been a better boy, his father would never have left home. Children usually think in these simple, self-oriented terms.

It would be best if your former husband kept a reasonably consistent visiting pattern. It would certainly be in his son's best developmental interest. Talk it over with Peter's dad. He may be divorced from you, but I hope he hasn't divorced his son.

Leaving a Toddler during a Parental Vacation

Q: My husband has been invited by his company to a one-week training course in Europe. I'd like to go with him, but I'm worried about leaving our $2\frac{1}{2}$-year-old son, Matthew. My mother, who often baby-sits for us, has offered to take care of him at her home. What would you advise?

A: A one-week absence should not be harmful at your son's age, assuming that his psychological development has been reasonably problem-free up to this time. You might, however, see some regression in toilet training. You are fortunate in having a familiar, reliable baby-sitter. I would suggest, however, that your mother come over to your home during your absence. Your little one will be more comfortable in his own surroundings. One more piece of advice: Ask grandma to start spending more time with Matthew so he can become accustomed to having her around. Then—*bon voyage.*

Toddler Morality

Q: Our $2\frac{1}{2}$-year-old, Aaron, is a delight most of the time, but, on occasion, he is your typical terrible 2. Why is it, for example, that he can't get the idea that he'll be punished for emptying drawers and breaking things? I have to punish him for the same misbehavior time after time.

A: Aaron, like other toddlers, does not have a well-functioning inner voice or conscience that reminds him that a particular behavior is bad or wrong. At his stage of development his natural drive toward adventure and mischief is checked mostly by the presence of Mom and Dad. Until his conscience is formed, you function as a kind of external superego for him, a police officer at his elbow.

His behavior, therefore, is kept in check not by the prospects of feeling guilty (the weapon of the conscience) but by the real threat of punishment. Take the police officer away from his elbow, and his natural drives are off to the races.

Be careful, though, that his repetitive misbehavior is not becoming a game for him. Some youngsters learn that they get most attention from parents when they misbehave. Be sure to find opportunities to praise and encourage him for his positive efforts.

Quiz

It's so important to get a good start as a parent. Infants are wonderful, lovable—and very complicated creatures. They require some study if you're really going to be effective with them. So take the following quiz. If you answer a question incorrectly, go back to the text. Work on it. That's the spirit and commitment that will make you a parental success now—and in the future.

1. An infant should double her birth weight by:

   ☐ A. Six weeks

   ☐ B. Three months

   ☐ C. Five months

2. Babies can react to the human face at:

   ☐ A. Birth

   ☐ B. Not until 2 weeks old

   ☐ C. At about 1 month

3. True or false? Infants prefer black-and-white objects over colored objects.

4. The ability of an infant to get other people interested in him is called:

   ☐ A. Narcissism

   ☐ B. Sending power

   ☐ C. Reciprocity

5. The average 7-month-old infant should be able to (select all that apply):

   ☐ A. Transfer objects from hand to hand

   ☐ B. Sit up unaided

   ☐ C. Repeat simple vowel sounds

6. True or false? Scientists have identified three distinct types of crying as early as the first week of life: hunger, anger, and pain.

7. True or false? Developmental testing (psychological, social, and motor skills) should be a routine part of all pediatric well-baby care.

8. True or false? It's best to allow a 2-year-old to establish his own bedtime.

9. The best technique for toilet training is:

   ☐ A. Praise and encouragement
   ☐ B. A firm schedule for potty
   ☐ C. Punishment

10. True or false? Thumb-sucking at 3 to 4 months of age is usually a sign of insecurity.

11. If your $2\frac{1}{2}$-year-old hits you:

   ☐ A. Forget it. Hitting is normal at $2\frac{1}{2}$.
   ☐ B. Scold her and punish her with a time-out.
   ☐ C. Tell her to put her feelings into words, not action.

12. True or false? Child psychiatrists are able to diagnose and treat depression in infants.

13. What percentage of mentally retarded infants can actually become self-supporting adults?

   ☐ A. 10 percent
   ☐ B. 50 percent
   ☐ C. 75 percent

14. If a mother must return to work soon after the birth of her baby, the best time is:

   ☐ A. Before 3 months
   ☐ B. After 3 months

15. Two-year-olds achieve discipline largely through:

   ☐ A. An inner voice, or "conscience"

☐ B. Threat of punishment

☐ C. Promise of rewards if they're good

16. True or false? Babies do not dream.

17. True or false? Babies who are fed well will gain weight even if they are not held and cuddled.

18. How much time does the normal 2-month-old spend crying every day?

☐ A. Fifteen or twenty minutes

☐ B. Up to three hours

☐ C. Over six hours

19. By the age of 3 to 4 months what percentage of babies sleep through the night?

☐ A. 25 percent

☐ B. 70 percent

☐ C. 95 percent

20. The average 1-year-old can (select all that apply):

☐ A. Stand alone easily

☐ B. Walk

☐ C. Walk up steps unaided

☐ D. Balance briefly on one foot

21. Infants usually begin showing fear of strangers at:

☐ A. 3 months

☐ B. 6 to 8 months

☐ C. 1 year

☐ D. 2 years

22. A 10-month-old who habitually bangs his head against the crib (choose all that apply):

☐ A. May be seeking attention

☐ B. May be trying to relieve tension

☐ C. Is more likely to be a boy than a girl

☐ D. May be psychologically disturbed

23. Arrange these developmental stages of child play in the proper order:

☐ A. Observation

☐ B. Parallel play

☐ C. Solitary play

☐ D. Cooperative play

24. True or false? Sons raised by single mothers have a greater incidence of homosexuality.

25. The favorite word of most 2-year-olds is:

☐ A. Why?

☐ B. What?

☐ C. No!

☐ D. When?

26. Breath-holding spells by a 2-year-old (choose one):

☐ A. Should be ignored

☐ B. Should be punished

☐ C. Usually lead to brain damage

27. The 2-year-old who has not yet begun to talk (select all that apply):

☐ A. Is still within the range of normal

☐ B. Is definitely delayed

☐ C. May have a hearing problem

28. What percentage of children of divorce suffer some form of depression?

☐ A. 10 percent

☐ B. 33 percent

☐ C. 75 percent

☐ D. 90 percent

29. Weaning from the bottle (select one):

    ☐ A. Should be done abruptly to discourage dependence

    ☐ B. Should be done only when the infant himself gives up the bottle

    ☐ C. Should be done gradually

30. True or false? Multiple baby-sitters are much more of a problem after 3 months of age than before 3 months.

Answers

1. C	**9.** A	**17.** False	**25.** C
2. A	**10.** False	**18.** B	**26.** A
3. False	**11.** B	**19.** B	**27.** B, C
4. B	**12.** True	**20.** A, B	**28.** B
5. A, C	**13.** C	**21.** B	**29.** C
6. True	**14.** A	**22.** A, B, C, D	**30.** True
7. True	**15.** B	**23.** C, A, B, D	
8. False	**16.** False	**24.** False	

CHAPTER 3

Preschoolers (3 to 4)

Your child's development has been dramatic to this point, marked by momentous physical events such as her first word or his first tentative step. Now, however, the markers are more subtle; they're less physical, more intellectual, psychological, and social.

For example, your youngster will be able to engage in progressively more cooperative play with other children. He will be able to share and engage in the daily give-and-take demanded by play groups, nursery schools—and siblings.

Language development blossoms. He'll have an ever-expanding vocabulary, but his favorite expression will probably be "Why?"

Father's role becomes increasingly important at age 3 and 4 too. Up to this point his role and mom's have been fairly identical; both have provided basic "mothering" functions. Now dad becomes an important psychological figure in his own right: He becomes the model for male behavior. Daddy's little girl wants to grow up quickly so she can marry him. Mommy's little boy, on the other hand, may temporarily view his father as a competitor. Important patterns of sexual identity and sexual role development are being established.

It's more subtle, but it's very real. Keep in mind also that when your child has completed this stage of development and moved into the school years, your own influence will lessen, step by step and year by year, as the world of peers, teachers, and other extrafamilial influences compete for attention. So make these preschool years count.

Six Steps to Discipline

Q: My children (aged $3\frac{1}{2}$ and $4\frac{1}{2}$) are getting out of control. They just will not accept my discipline at all. I've tried just about every punishment in the book but nothing seems to work.

A: Punishment ranks very low as a teacher of discipline. You are probably missing many opportunities to teach real discipline to the children because you are jumping immediately to the "punishment solution" instead of using other, more effective techniques.

Try my six-step formula for achieving discipline without hassles:

1. *Parental example:* The most effective tool of discipline, by far, is for you to set a good parental example of self-discipline. I don't mean you have to be perfect; none of us is perfect, but try your best to set the right tone in your own home.

2. *Accentuate the positive:* Miss no opportunity to praise your children when they do things right. This is also called the art of "catching 'em when they're good." Praise and reward are better than punishment any day.

3. *Ignore the negative:* That's right. Stop and think about it. Most misbehavior of children can be safely ignored. This theory works. When negative behavior is ignored, it dies a quiet death. (But do not ignore behavior that jeopardizes health and safety or behavior that violates important family values.)

4. *Logical consequences:* Let your children learn from their own mistakes whenever possible. Remember: There does not have to be a parental solution to every problem.

5. *Contracts:* If you have identified a specific pattern of misbehavior, talk it over with your child. Explain your position. Ask for his ideas. Try to make him part of the solution. Finally, be very clear about what he can expect if the misbehavior continues. In this way you're leaving the decision up to him. If he chooses to misbehave, he chooses to lose a privilege. Put it in writing so there are no loose ends.

6. *Punishment:* Yes, there is a place for punishment, but it comes last because it is simply not as effective as the other five methods. Punishment should be consistent and "fit the crime," and you should have a graduated response plan that ranges from scolding to time-outs to restriction of privileges. Spanking comes last; its effectiveness is mostly limited to preverbal children. It should be used sparingly.

Spanking

Q: Curtis, our son, is 3 years old. My husband tends to spank him lightly when he misbehaves. I don't believe in spanking. My husband says: "If you spare the rod, you'll spoil the child." What do you think?

A: Spanking has a place in the discipline of children, but its place is limited because it is not a very effective way to teach *self*-discipline to children.

Spanking is a resort to parental power. One thing is sure about all forms of such power: Eventually you run out of it. Parents who repeatedly spank a younger child will one day have a teenager on their hands who cannot be spanked—and who has not learned self-discipline. Many of these children yearn for the day that they can retaliate, in some way, against their parents.

Spanking introduces physical and psychological pain into the parent-child relationship. It is a real "pain game." Children learn to mistrust and avoid a parent who relies primarily upon physical punishment.

Yet, the gentle spanking of a preverbal child (birth to 18 months of age) can be effective—especially in teaching the child to avoid danger such as wall sockets and traffic and hot objects.

And even the best parents sometimes spank a youngster in a fit of annoyance—after all else has failed. Children are forgiving and recover from such occasional lapses. No irreversible psychological scars will result in these cases, and your child will not grow up hating you. Such occasional spankings might even make mom or dad feel better momentarily and might put them back in control of a situation that has gotten out of hand. By the way, there is no need to apologize for these "lapses."

With these exceptions, I do not know of any situations in which spanking is actually the preferred method of punishment. There are many techniques that are not only more effective but also much less costly to the parent-child relationship. In general, it is not a good idea to get on "spanking terms" with your child.

Children Learn What They Live

Q: My 3-year-old son, John, is in a play group. John and all the other children are terrified of Joshua, another 3-year-old, who is the bully of the group. He hits, bites, screams, pushes, takes, grabs, and completely intimidates the other kids.

I happened to watch Joshua's mother yesterday when she picked him up at the play group. First she ignored him. Then she asked one of the other mothers if he had been bad. Then she criticized him in front of the other children. When he stomped his foot, she whacked him on the behind.

He hit back. Then she screamed and whacked him again, harder this time. What I'm getting at is this: Who's the bully here, Joshua or his mother? She seems as bad as he is. Which came first, Joshua's misbehavior or his mother's? How can this vicious cycle be stopped?

A: You've put your finger on an important principle of life: Children learn what they live. The child who is criticized becomes the child who blames others. But your second question is a good one too. Which comes first, Joshua's hitting or Mom's hitting? I can't be sure. But one thing I am sure about is that the Joshua-Mom relationship is mutually destructive. Someone has got to break the chain of aggression that links them so negatively. Mom is the only one of the two who could do it, but from the sound of things, I believe she's perhaps too locked in and overwhelmed to be able to change very much on her own. Therefore, Mom needs help. Believe me, consultation with a child psychiatrist *now* will save a lot of pain for everyone over the years to come.

The Child-Centered Family

Q: My husband and I have devoted our lives to our children, aged 3, 6, and 8. Their happiness is important, more important than our own. Imagine my shock, then, when my sister-in-law criticized us. She says that we could be *ruining* the kids, that we're too wrapped up in them for their own good. Doctor, please set the record straight.

A: I doubt that you're ruining the children, but you could be unwittingly hampering their development—and your own.

A child-centered family places an inordinate emphasis on the happiness of the children. Paradoxically, it can result in unhappy children. Some common symptoms are overdependence, shyness, demanding behavior, inability to make friends outside the family, and loneliness. Such a family may also be a cover-up for a problem marriage; but the problems usually come back to haunt you after the youngest child has finally left home.

Is your family child-centered? Try this true-false test:

1. You and your husband generally relate to friends and community as "parents." You are known more as the parents of Jimmy (etc.) than as Mr. and Mrs. Smith.

2. Family financial decisions usually are based on the children's needs.

3. You emphasize education to the point that you've chosen your neighborhood mostly for its good school system.

4. Most recreational events are done as a family, seldom as a couple.

5. When you're alone with your spouse, you usually talk about the children.

6. You and your spouse share few, if any, interests except the children.

7. Your basic philosophy goes something like: "Our children come first."

If you've answered *true* to four or more of these statements, your family has a strong tilt toward child-centeredness. My advice: Put some balance back into the equation. It's wiser to make your marriage your top priority. It existed before the children came on the scene, and it will still be there after they've moved on. A strong marriage makes for happy, well-adjusted children—and adults too.

Body Language

Q: Please settle a disagreement between my husband and myself. In communicating with our 3-year-old daughter, is it more important to talk her language (to use the "right words") or to use correct body language?

A: There are three basic components to conversation: the words you use, the tone you convey, and your body language. *Body language* is simply shorthand for how we communicate attitudes through our facial expression, posture, touch, movement, etc.

Controlled studies have shown that body language is, by far, the most powerful factor. As your daughter gets older, your choice of words will be more crucial, of course, but always be sure that your body language "says" what your words are conveying. Otherwise you'll be sending a mixed message.

Toddlers and Body Language

Q: I've been observing our 3-year-old, Elizabeth. Whenever she's with a group of other children her own age, she seems to smile and reach out toward them. It's astonishing. The other children, even if they're upset or crying, tend to melt. They look up, smile, and interact with her. How has she learned this "technique"? Will it continue? I hope so.

A: I hope so too.

Elizabeth's body language is no accident. She has probably learned it from you and your husband. Hubert Montagner, a French scientist, has been studying nonverbal communication among children for the past fifteen years. His findings have linked specific body language with personality type. For example, children (like Elizabeth) who are perceived by their peers as kind and pacifying tend to use actions intuitively, such as offering toys and candy, smiling, extending the hand, leaning sideways, and lightly touching other children.

Montagner's research, by the way, suggests that these are lasting traits. The 2-year-old who attaches easily to other children and pacifies them tends to become the 10-year-old with a lot of friends.

Keep up the good work.

Superbaby

Q: My sister-in-law has enrolled her 3-year-old daughter, Gaynelle, in one of those enrichment programs. It's hard to believe, but she says that the course teaches infants how to play the violin, read books, and even speak several foreign languages. Is it possible? Is it a good thing for children?

A: It is possible to teach gifted 3-year-olds an incredible array of skills. There are reports, for example, of toddlers mastering musical instruments and completing complex mathematical calculations. There is, however, a good deal of skepticism among professionals about some of these claims.

My own concern is that some parents, in their zeal to make a superbaby of their child, might overemphasize cognitive or intellectual development at the cost of emotional, social, and physical development. If this happens to Gaynelle, for example, she could turn out to be a very bright but unhappy, maladjusted little girl.

I believe that infants and toddlers should receive rich educational stimulation, but it should not be exaggerated. Furthermore, there's danger in overstimulating a child; she could become so frustrated that she'll turn off to learning completely.

The answer? Balance and good judgment. Be sure that a child receives a balance of needs, and use good judgment about how much is too much for your own youngster.

Child Care Woes

Q: I'm a working mother. I have two children, aged 3 and 4. Believe me, it's a full-time job. But I'd like to find a paying job: We need the money. My problem is child care: where to find it, how to afford it.

A: You're not alone. Financial pressures are sending more and more mothers out into the work force. A recent Census Bureau survey reports that over 50 percent of women with children under the age of 5 are employed outside the home; this is up from 41 percent in 1977.

The survey also noted that well over 1 million women like yourself *would* jump into the job market if they could afford and find reliable child care.

It might help to take a look at how the nation's 5.1 million working mothers do it:

- Enrolling their children in day-care centers, 15 percent

- Taking their little ones to someone else's home, 40 percent

- Arranging for sitters to come to their homes, 31 percent

Another interesting note is that 14 percent of the children cared for in their own homes are watched over by their fathers.

So consider the options. Talk to friends, especially women facing your own predicament. A common lament of working mothers these days is that good day care is hard to find. Since other working mothers have made the search before you, check with them. Learn from their experiences.

Language Development and Day Care

Q: Emilie, our 3-year-old, attends day care. Her language development seems much better than her older sister's was at the same age. I wonder if the reason is that Emilie gets much more verbal stimulation from her peers than her sister (no day care) did at 3 years of age.

A: It's possible, but I have my doubts. The verbal stimulation of other 3-year-olds is not nearly as formative as, let's say, the influences of day-care *adults*. If these caregivers talk to Emilie a lot and if their verbal interactions are positive and encouraging, Emilie will learn to verbalize and communicate well.

Why is Emilie developing language skills more quickly than her sister did? Let's not forget that another factor may well be—her sister. That's right. Older siblings are great influencers of language.

Talk Play

Q: Our 3-year-old, Marilyn, is very talkative. Too talkative. The thing that disturbs me most, though, is her habit of making up silly, nonsensical words. I patiently correct her, and I know that she understands, but nothing I do seems to work for very long. Should I just relax? Will she get over it?

A: Yes. Many 3-year-olds take to language as if it's a new toy. They love to play with talk. The act of making up new words, which sound nonsensical to our adult ears, is serious work for Marilyn; it is her way of gaining control over the spoken language. Last year, for example, when she was 2, she probably had a number of discreet words at her disposal. This year she is combining them into language. Now she can use most of the vowels and has a vocabulary of increasing complexity. The real test, however, is combining sounds, words, phrases, and sentences in a way that communicates her ideas.

Marilyn's "talk play" may give you fits, but it's harmless. She's developing nicely and having fun with language.

S-s-s-s-stuttering

Q: My 3-year-old son has begun to stutter when he is under stress. So far I've tried to be calm and unconcerned and even to ignore it. Do you recommend any special techniques or treatment?

A: Three cheers for a mother's intuition! You are off to an excellent start in helping your son cope with this vexing problem. You are deliberately responding in a low-key manner. This is very important as parental overconcern and anxiety only adds to the frustration for a stuttering child.

Since stuttering in 3-year-olds is usually related to stress, you might also discover what kind of situations or conflicts make him anxious. If you can anticipate these events, you might be able to steer your boy clear of them. One clue: Temporary conflicts with fathers are not uncommon for 3-year-old boys. If this is the case, provide your son with positive, "fun" experiences with Dad.

Some additional tips:

1. Look at your child when he speaks to you. Stutterers feel even more embarrassed when a would-be listener avoids eye contact.

2. Do not interrupt your child or change the subject when he stutters. Such tactics are more for the benefit of an uncomfortable listener and do not help the stutterer.

3. Do not force a child to "confront his problem" by speaking in front of you or in front of a group.

4. Speak slowly, calmly, and deliberately when responding to him. This will help your child to slow down and to relax. So-called speed stress is one of the most common causes of stuttering in children.

5. Finally, if your child's stuttering worsens considerably or does not respond to these techniques within six months, ask your pediatrician for advice. Referral to a speech pathologist and/or a child psychiatrist may be indicated.

Mommy Sharing

Q: I have a problem that is probably getting more common these days. I run a small child care center in my home. My problem is my own 3-year-old daughter, Lucy. She's jealous of the other children. I've tried scolding, ignoring, reasoning—nothing works. Any ideas?

A: You're right. This is not an uncommon problem. It's estimated that about 50 percent of all the day-care homes in this country contain at least one child of the provider.

I'm sure you're aware that many women go into the day-care business because it potentially gives them the best of two worlds:

(1) an income without leaving their home and (2) their children. Another benefit, especially for mothers with only one child, is a built-in play group for the youngster.

But there are drawbacks. Jealousy and a form of sibling rivalry constitute one of them. It's important to understand that this phenomenon is to be expected. On the other hand, you'll have to make a special effort to allow your daughter some special considerations and, above all, some privacy. Her room and her possessions, for example, should be off-limits to the other children. But be careful not to pamper her—otherwise she may expect this kind of treatment from teachers when she enters school. Yes, it calls for a delicate balancing act, but it can be done—with advantages to everyone.

3-Year-Old Rituals

Q: My 3-year-old daughter, Angela, has some annoying habits. She has a number of rituals, such as getting dressed in a precise order and saying good-night to ten dolls in an exact order before she goes to sleep. The list goes on and on. Is this normal behavior? Will she grow out of it?

A: Rituals at Angela's age are normal. The 3-year-old's clamor for *sameness* is an internal defense to contain the normal anxiety she feels about a world that seems to control her. Therefore, if she can control at least a few things in her little universe, she feels less vulnerable.

As Angela develops more coping skills, she will be able to abandon her rituals. But if these habits continue for more than six months, if they get worse, or if she becomes so preoccupied that she cannot enjoy normal conflict-free activities, consultation would be the order of the day.

Bad Habits?

Q: Kathleen, our baby, is 3 years old. Lately she's developed some bad habits, such as rocking back and forth when she's upset and twirling her hair around her fingers. Should I ignore these things? What do you suggest?

A: Relax. Kathleen may just be doing what comes naturally. Many 3- and 4-year-olds develop transient habits or rituals.

Basically, these habits are designed to absorb tension and ward off anxiety. They are defense mechanisms, similar to the coping devices of adults, such as tapping the foot or cleaning the house when you're upset about something. These habits, therefore, have a way of diverting attention, consciously and unconsciously, from anxiety-provoking thoughts and feelings.

Of Kathleen's two habits, I'm a little concerned about the rocking. This is a regressive habit, a throwback to being rocked as an infant.

My advice is this: (1) Don't make a big deal of it and (2) when Kathleen launches into one of her habits, gently divert her attention to yourself by words and actions. In this way, you'll teach her that anxiety can be discharged through relating to a trusted adult. You'll take some of the magic out of her rituals and help her grow into a child who's better able to deal with stress.

Imitation

Q: Our 3-year-old son, Barry, loves to imitate his father. I think it's cute, but my husband doesn't like it. He says that Barry is making fun of him and that he shouldn't "copy": he should be himself. What do you think?

A: Parody is beyond Barry and the world of the 3-year-old. Barry's imitation is based on love and wanting to be like Dad, the most important man in his universe. Imitation, in fact, is an important step in learning and in personality development. It should be encouraged, not snuffed out. Imitation leads to identification, a more powerful unconscious process by which Barry will acquire a number of your husband's (and your own) behaviors, beliefs, and values.

Artist in Residence?

Q: I really think we've got a budding artist here at our house. MaryJo, our 3-year-old, has a flair for drawing and painting. She's very creative with finger paints, oil pastels, and felt-tip markers. Do you have any tips for encouraging this interest?

A: The most important factor is your own continued interest in MaryJo's artistic endeavors. Be sure to provide her with the opportunities she'll need to develop her skills and with the realistic praise she'll need to fuel her interest. Here are some other tips:

1. *Be specific:* It's more effective to comment on something specific in a drawing ("Wow, look at all those circles. Were they hard to make?") than simply exclaim, "It's a beautiful picture."

2. *Collect and display:* Help MaryJo keep a collection of her work, and be sure to display some of it on the refrigerator door— or somewhere suitable.

3. *Museums:* It's not too early to expose MaryJo to the very best. She won't grasp the technical achievements of the masters, of course, but she'll learn to appreciate the important place of art throughout history and in our contemporary world.

Smart Art?

Q: Lilliana, our 3-year-old, is very artistic. She loves to draw, and she's gifted at it. For example, she can draw the human body and name the parts. She can draw almost anything she sees for more than a few seconds. What does this mean? Is it a sign of intelligence?

A: For years psychologists have tended to relate the artistic ability of children with intelligence. For example, several standard psychological tests are based, at least in part, on drawing ability: the Stanford-Benet, the Goodenough-Harris, and the Bender, to name a few.

Recent studies, however, cast doubt on these assumptions. Hermelin and O'Connor, London researchers, studied two groups of children matched for IQ. One group was composed of artistically gifted youngsters. The other group was not artistic. The researchers found that although the artistic group scored higher on the standard drawing tests, the reason was not due to higher basic *intelligence*, per se, but rather to a greater ability to remember visual cues. They excelled, therefore, at what we call visual memory.

Seems that Lilliana also has superb visual memory. Like the children tested in London, she simply does not forget the visual images of the things around her. But intelligence is composed of many factors: auditory recall, reasoning, mathematical ability, abstract thinking, etc. When Lilliana goes to school and is tested for intelligence, she will score high on subtests that rely on visual memory. How she fares on the other factors remains to be seen.

In the meantime, relax. Help Lilliana build on her marvelous skills. It's a gift she can draw upon forever.

IQ and Parental Attitude

Q: We want to give Donna, our 3-year-old, all the advantages. What can we specifically do to help her develop a high IQ?

A: First let me say that sometimes we put too much emphasis on intelligence test scores. Remember: A child's happiness in life depends on a complex mix of biological and environmental factors, some of which you can influence, some of which you can't. Some youngsters, including a number of truly gifted children, simply don't test well; they may have average IQs but be whizzes at math, virtuosos in music, and so forth. In other words, don't enslave Donna to the tyranny of test results.

Yet, in answer to your question, researchers have found that high IQs do tend to relate to the following parental behaviors:

1. Encouraging the child to verbally express himself

2. Pride in school achievement

3. Setting a good model for intellectual and academic achievement

4. Providing a solid model for effective communication, vocabulary, and language skills

I hope Donna grows up smart—and happy too.

Fussy Eater

Q: Andrea, our 3-year-old, is a fussy eater. She picks at her food, hates chicken, hates any food colored yellow, doesn't like milk, thinks that vegetables are yucky. Get the idea?

The thing that stumps me is that when she was a baby, she ate everything that was offered her. It's only been in the last year or so that she's gotten so darn finicky. Any ideas?

A: Many children go through stages of eating preferences that are related to their general stage of physical and emotional development. Infants, for example, should be expected to trust their parents completely. This also means that infants, by and large, accept whatever food is given them. As a child gets a bit older, her taste buds develop more acutely and some preferences and dislikes emerge. The color of the food may also be a factor.

I'm not too surprised that Andrea's problems started about a year ago. As you know, the 2-year-old wants to be in control. Some "2s," like Andrea, may choose to battle for control at the dinner table. As a child gains more control over other parts of her life, however, the need to fight over food generally lessens.

Something else to look forward to: nursery school. Andrea's eating habits will be influenced by her peer group.

In the meantime, don't go overboard. Keep the dinner table atmosphere relaxed, warm, positive. Watch the nutritional bottom line: Is Andrea healthy and growing properly? If you're not sure, consult with your pediatrician. If her health record and growth chart are on target, you can give Andrea some slack.

TV Close-Up

Q: Our youngest child, Roger (aged 3), insists upon sitting right on top of the television whenever he watches it. I don't think there's anything wrong with his vision. Why do kids do this?

A: Some youngsters, especially infants and toddlers, simply thrill at seeing their own reflections in the TV screen. It holds a magical fascination for them. Other children cozy up to the tube because it makes them feel more intimate or involved with the characters on the screen. And, of course, children with vision problems are "TV close-ups" too.

Still other youngsters nuzzle up to the tube simply to block out all visual references. They try to absorb themselves totally in the on-screen experience. These youngsters could use a dose of reality. Better to nuzzle up to Mom and Dad, for example, to keep things in perspective. Television, after all, should not be allowed to become a force that's bigger than life.

Vision problems *caused* by TV? Not really. But, all things considered, it's not a habit to encourage.

Jane Fonda Workout

Q: I'm a physical fitness freak. I jog at least 5 miles every day, follow a healthy diet, and work out regularly. Lately, I've been doing the Jane Fonda workout. Is there any problem if my 3-year-old daughter does it with me?

A: Not at all. As long as she doesn't push her little body beyond its capabilities. I'm sure she wants to identify with you and to go through all the workout motions. You're setting a good example. The best time to introduce good exercise practices is in the early, formative years.

It's sad but true that most American children are not physically fit. Data released by the public school testing programs show that no more than 15 percent of our youngsters are in good condition based on international standards. In fact, a study by the Center for Parenting, UCLA Extension, showed that 86 percent of first-graders were unable to pass a minimum physical fitness test. I bet your daughter will pass her test one day with flying colors, thanks to you and Jane.

The Emergency Room

Q: Two weeks ago, our 3-year-old, Crystal, fell and cut her forehead. There was blood everywhere, and we rushed her, in a panic, to our local emergency room. Crystal was shrieking, and my husband was shaking so violently he could hardly drive. But when we finally got to the emergency room, we had the rudest shock of all: The doctors and nurses wouldn't let us go in with Crystal for the suturing. She cried even more, and we felt completely helpless. Fortunately, it all turned out fine. You can hardly see the scar now, but we're still upset about the way the hospital handled the matter. What is your opinion?

A: Crystal's facial scar may be small, but her emergency may have left an emotional scar on the entire family. It's very unfortunate.

Every emergency room I've ever known has allowed (and encouraged) parents to assist in the reassurance and restraint of their children during suturing. It's good practice from a surgical standpoint since children usually respond well to the presence of their parents and suturing, especially of the face, goes better if a child is absolutely motionless. It's good practice from a psychological standpoint, too, since children should experience their parents as available, concerned, and helpful.

So what happened here? I can think of a couple of possibilities: The charge nurse or the physician may have decided that you and your husband were too upset yourselves to be helpful. If so, they exercised clinical judgment and excluded you from the treatment room. They may have been wrong, and maybe they should have gently told you this, but remember that although emergency rooms are usually staffed by very compassionate people, true emergencies sometimes don't leave much time for niceties.

On the other hand, your hospital's policies may, in fact, prohibit patients' being accompanied into treatment rooms. I doubt it, but why not check? A letter or call to the hospital administrator should get the answer.

The Spoiled-Brat Image of the Only Child

Q: Our daughter, Melanie, is 3 years old. My husband and I are happy with her and with the idea of having a single child. But we've heard that the only child tends to grow up to be a spoiled brat. For Melanie's sake, should we plan to give her a brother or a sister?

A: Only children have been getting a bum rap for years. It has long been assumed that they grow up to be self-centered, lonely, socially awkward, and, yes, spoiled brats.

Recent research, however, is casting a new light on these youngsters. A study based on 400,000 high school students begun in 1960, for example, compared only children with two-child families. Only children were found to be smarter, more creative, and more ambitious. They appeared more cultured, mature, and socially sensitive, although they were less outgoing.

Only children tend to grow up faster because they are generally more adult-oriented. Yet such closeness to mom and dad can be a double-edged sword. In families where marital conflict predominates, only children tend to get pulled right into the heat of marital spats. And if their parents separate or divorce, they tend to be hit harder than other children since mom and dad are literally their entire familial world.

Another thing to consider is that although Melanie is perfectly content now in her cozy little world with you and your husband, I can predict that there will be times when she wishes that she had a brother or a sister: when she gets to know the siblings of school friends; when she enters adolescence and longs for a brother to protect her or a sister with whom to share secrets; when she's an adult and feels the loneliness of a "generation of one." How will *you* feel at those times?

The answer? Many parents today are choosing to have only one child. The reasons are largely financial or career-related. In the final analysis, however, the decision about whether or not to have another child should be based less on what's good for Melanie than on what's best for you and your husband. If the two of you can sustain a solid marriage, Melanie's chances for success and happiness are good whether she's an only child—or the oldest of many more to come.

Second Generation of Abuse?

Q: My former husband was a child abuser. I have custody of our 3-year-old, Tommy, and his father is barred by the courts from any contact with him. That's the good news. But I'm worried. Tommy is very aggressive toward other children. He hits and screams and has to be in control at all times. Has he been permanently damaged by his father? What should I do?

A: We know from our studies of adults who abuse children that they were very frequently victims of abuse themselves when they were children. But how early does it begin? A new study at the University of California is directed at this important question. Researchers found that toddlers (aged 1 to 3) who were abuse victims consistently (over 50 percent of the time) responded to crying playmates with fear, threats, or physical abuse. On the other hand, a comparison group of nonabused toddlers typically responded with concern, sympathy, and sensitivity. In fact, this group demonstrated a very low (6 percent) incidence of aggression toward playmates.

So you see, the habit of abuse can start very early. It doesn't lie dormant only to erupt when the victim becomes a parent.

Tommy, therefore, is at risk. He's already showing some disturbing symptoms. I definitely suggest that you consult with a child psychiatrist.

The scars do not have to be permanent. The time to excise them is now.

Is Anger Contagious?

Q: My sister has two children, aged $3\frac{1}{2}$ and $5\frac{1}{2}$. She and her husband are having a lot of problems. Their arguments are loud, bitter, and frequent. I've noticed lately that my nephew ($3\frac{1}{2}$) is more aggressive and demanding. His sister ($5\frac{1}{2}$) doesn't seem to be bothered as much by all the fighting. My question: Is anger contagious?

A: As a rule, children learn what they live. If they're raised in an angry environment, they learn anger. Some youngsters, like your nephew, may express their rage directly in their behavior. Other youngsters, perhaps like your niece, tend to repress their anger; they wear their problems on the inside.

Researchers at the National Institute of Mental Health have studied this issue. They found that children exposed to verbal arguments are much more likely to push, kick, and hit their playmates afterward. On the other hand, when they were subjected to warm, nurturing situations, they were only slightly less aggressive than they were before the experiment. What does this imply? That anger is a more powerful conditioner than warmth and encouragement—and that it apparently is more "contagious."

Following in Daddy's Footsteps?

Q: Stevie is only 3 years old, but I can see it happening already. I'm afraid he's going to be just like his Daddy. Let me explain: My former husband was placed in a juvenile center when he was 12 years old because he was so aggressive and uncontrollable. I'm afraid he never grew out of it. He used to beat me until, finally, I went to the police. I'm safe now, but Stevie's behavior scares me. I think he has his father's temper. He screams and kicks until he gets his way—which he usually does since I always end up giving in to him. I'm afraid he's following in his Daddy's footsteps. Help!

A: Aggressive children, unless they receive therapy, do tend to grow into aggressive adults. Your former husband apparently is a prime example.

As a child psychiatrist I can also confirm that the earliest signs of behavior problems can often be observed as early as 3 years of age. So your concerns about Stevie are right on the mark.

How much of this is inherited? It's hard to say. Children certainly inherit something of their basic temperament from their parents. Their ability to tolerate frustration and the tendency to discharge their tension, rather than keep it inside, can also have some genetic roots. But there's an important environmental matter here too, and you can do something about it.

You clearly identify Stevie with his father. My hunch is that you are unconsciously reacting to Stevie in the same way you reacted to his father. You're scared of him. You allow him to terrorize you. You give in to him. Stevie, of course, then learns that aggression works. He's developing a repertoire of misbehavior designed to get him what he wants, when he wants it. And you are going to be the target of his nastiness.

Don't let it happen. For Stevie's sake and yours, I urge you to consult *now* with a child psychiatrist.

Should My Husband Grow a Beard?

Q: My husband would like to grow a beard. It's fine with me, but I'm afraid of the effect on our 3-year-old daughter and 5-year-old son. What do you think?

A: I'm aware of only one study that has addressed this subject. The general conclusion was that beards do, indeed, frighten children.

Over 200 youngsters (aged 3 to 7) were asked to look at a series of drawings of a man's face. These drawings were identical except that one face was clean-shaven, one had sideburns and a simple brush mustache, one had slightly longer sideburns and a drooping mustache, and one had a mustache and a full beard.

A large majority of the children chose the clean-shaven face as belonging to the "nice man" and the bearded face as belonging to the "scary man."

Keep in mind, of course, that these children were not reacting to the presence of a beard on the face of their own father. That's a powerful distinction.

In my own work with children in various hospital and university settings, I have encountered one other problem: Beards hide facial responses from children; they remove an important visual clue as to what the adult is feeling. These clues are important to youngsters. I had one professor, for example, who insisted that male staffers had to be clean-shaven and that female staffers were required to wear their hair pulled back from their faces. While the professor's reaction might be considered a bit excessive, he certainly drove home his point.

But why not ask your own children? They'll probably be better guides for you in this particular matter than the research data and even my old professor.

Father Divorces Child

Q: My former husband and I have been divorced for three years. No problem—it was a terrible marriage. But I didn't expect Jim to "divorce" our 3-year-old daughter. He sees her only once or twice a year. Comments?

A: It's sad but true. Most divorces break the bonds between children and their noncustodial parent. For example, a University of Pennsylvania study of over 1000 children revealed that only 17 percent had regular, weekly contact with their noncustodial parent—which, in today's divorce climate, is usually the father.

You might be interested to know, however, that in those less common divorces where fathers have custody, the noncustodial mother is more than twice as likely to keep in touch with her children.

Talk to Jim. Whatever your differences with him, it is in your daughter's best interests to have some form of reliable contact with him (assuming, of course, that such contact would be good for her—and from the tone of your question, I assume you believe it would be).

Make sure that your little girl understands that it's Daddy's problem, that *she* hasn't done anything wrong to keep Daddy away.

Bringing Father into the Act

Q: I have no complaints about my husband. He really wants to be a good father, and he helps a lot with the children, aged 3 and 5. The only puzzle is that the boys don't seem to appreciate it. For example, if both of us are sitting in the den, the boys come straight to me with their problems. If they're in another part of the house, they call out for Mommy, never Daddy. So far my husband doesn't seem to mind too much, but I'm afraid he's going to get turned off. What can I do?

A: First, let me applaud your husband. The father who actively participates in the raising of his children is doing them a real favor. He's also doing you a favor. And, most important, he's doing himself a favor too.

But what's happening here? The key may be in the age and sex of your children. Boys are often competitive toward their fathers at the ages of 3 and 5. They view Dad as something of a rival for Mom's attention. Don't worry. This phase will pass. In the meantime, you can help by discouraging the boys' exclusive preference for you. Help bring Daddy back into the act. Your own active efforts plus time and patience should do the trick.

Good Guy vs. Bad Guy

Q: We have two children, aged 3 and 5. I'm a stay-at-home mother, and I love it except for the fact that most of the disciplining falls on my shoulders. The most frustrating part of it is that my husband, John, has a very laid-back, permissive attitude. I'm the one who punishes; he's the one who always says "yes." The children obviously see their father as a hero, and I'm the wicked witch of the west. I don't like it. What can I do?

A: I don't like it either. You and your husband are falling into the well-known trap of *good guy versus bad guy.* It's troublesome now, but if it's allowed to continue, it could become very dangerous to your family life.

Since you're the on-site disciplinarian, you often have to set limits on the children, to say "no." The youngsters need this form of discipline, but they also need a father who knows how to say "no."

What can you do? The key, of course, is your husband—not the children. Kids, after all, will be kids. They want what they want when they want it. They'll go to the parent who will give in to them. As long as your husband insists on being the "good guy," the children will tend to favor him over you. This could lead to a permanent disruption and sabotage of your efforts to discipline the children. It could also lead, obviously, to serious friction between you and your husband.

Why does John find it so hard to cooperate in the disciplining of the children? That's the crucial question. There are many possible answers. Some of the more common ones include:

1. Lack of knowledge of the youngsters' real needs

2. Fear of loss of love if he says "no"

3. Marital conflict that is being played out through his undermining of your relationship with the children

Whatever the reason, the time to have a serious talk with John is *now.* The two of you must act together. While the two of you can't possibly agree on everything about raising the children, you should surely share a basic set of values and you must support each other. You need a teammate, not an adversary; start building that team *now*—for the sake of your children—and your marriage.

Broken Promises

Q: My husband is famous for breaking promises to our children, aged 3, 5, and 8. I know he loves them. That's why he promises them things like gifts or outings or special time with them. But when it comes time to deliver—no Daddy. The kids, of course, don't forget his promises, and they remind him, but he kind of shrugs it off. I know this is damaging to the children. What should I do?

A: The first step is to try and understand the situation. Just why does your husband feel he has to make promises that he can't deliver? I wonder if he also does this to you?

Talk it over with him calmly. Don't put him on the defensive like, I bet, the children do after he's disappointed them. You might show him this page. I want him to know that habitually broken promises lead to suspicion and mistrust and, also, that your children may well identify with him as they grow older. Some day *they* may be the ones *promising* him that they'll do their homework, mow the lawn, wash Dad's car. He won't like it anymore than they like it now.

Also, you can help by taking some of the heat off Dad. Don't let the kids pressure him. Maybe they badger him too much and his promises are unconsciously designed to get them off his back.

Finally, tell your husband not to promise something he can't deliver. It's far better to say "no" and give a brief explanation than to say "yes" and disappoint a child.

Shaping Up the Family

Q: I am busy, busy, busy. I'm the mother of three children, aged 3, 5, and 8. My husband is helpful and supportive, but our family life is going down the tubes. I want to shape it up before it's too late. I've made a list of our problems, and I want to draw a plan of attack for each problem. Is this a good way to get rolling?

A: Yes. Go for it. But don't jump to the attack all by yourself. At the very least you should enlist your husband's cooperation for the campaign. Have him draw up a list too. Then compare it to yours. Discuss the lists. This could be a very illuminating experience.

It might help to compare your final list with the top ten causes of family stress as recently compiled by researcher Dolores Curran:

1. Financial worries

2. Problems with children's behavior

3. Not enough time alone with spouse

4. Poor sharing of family responsibilities

5. Poor communication with children

6. Not enough time for yourself

7. Guilt over not accomplishing more

8. Unsatisfactory relationship (including sex) with spouse

9. Not enough family playtime

10. Overscheduled family calendar

Is Shyness Inherited?

Q: I'm shy. My husband's shy. Our son (aged 3) is shy too. What I want to know is this: Is shyness inherited?

A: Up to now the prevailing wisdom has been that shyness is largely a factor of environmental influences—that it is not transmitted genetically like, say, your hair color or the shape of your face.

Some researchers at the University of Colorado, however, have uncovered some evidence that shyness may be genetic—at least to some extent. These psychologists surveyed adoptive children, their adoptive parents, and their biological mothers. Interestingly, the shy children tended to have shy *biological* mothers.

On the other hand, there were also some strong environmental influences too. For example, parents who reported active social lives tended to have sociable children, while parents who tended to avoid the social scene had reclusive, shy children.

Is shyness inherited? Well, we haven't isolated a "shyness" gene yet, and in my opinion, behavioral factors are still the strongest determinant. If you'd like to help your son overcome his shyness, you should start by trying to become more sociable yourself. Children do tend to identify with the behavior of their parents.

Pet Theories

Q: My husband and I think we ought to buy a puppy for our children, aged 3, 5, and 6. We just think they're missing something if they don't have a pet. Don't you agree?

A: Yes—but.

Yes, the experience of having a dog, a cat, a rabbit, a hamster, or even a goldfish can enhance a child's development. How? By providing an opportunity to care for a defenseless creature, the child assumes the role of protector. He also has a chance to develop a sense of mastery, an important building block in his life. And let's not forget that pets provide companionship and that they're fun.

You might be interested to know that a recent survey by the Pets Are Wonderful Council discovered that 94 percent of a group of Fortune 500 executives had grown up with a pet in the family.

But, let's face it, most of the dirty work is going to fall to Mom and Dad—at least until your children are a bit older. So if you and your husband are ready for it, a trip to the local pet shop is a good idea.

Picky Parent or Picky Child?

Q: Donna, our $3\frac{1}{2}$-year-old, may be the world's pickiest eater. And I try so hard to give her a balanced diet. I've tried everything— punishment, rewards, even bribes! Nothing works. Any ideas?

A: You might learn something from a recent Canadian study of seventy-five families. Researchers found that parents who try hardest to force their children to eat a balanced diet tend to have the pickiest children. The study, however, could not conclude whether the worried parents made their children picky or the picky youngsters created harried parents. But one thing is sure. If you get too worked up about Donna's diet, you'll hand her a very potent lever to manipulate you. So relax. Remember: Even the worst eaters in the Canadian study were very healthy.

Is Grandma the Problem?

Q: Lawrence, our 3-year-old, throws a temper tantrum whenever I pick him up at his Grandmother's house. He kicks and screams. Usually I just snatch him up bodily and march him off to the car. Sometimes I whack him on his bottom a couple of times. At this point Grandma starts acting very sympathetically toward him. She tells him that he can come back tomorrow or that she'll call him later on the phone or that she'll bake some brownies for him. I'm beginning to think that Grandma, not Lawrence, is the problem. What do you think?

A: Yes, Grandma has the leading role in this drama, but the two supporting actors, you and Lawrence, are playing your parts too.

Lawrence, as a 3-year-old, wants to control his little world. He also operates on the basis of the *pleasure principle:* He wants what he wants when he wants it. He is the innocent victim in this real-life soap opera. You, as Lawrence's mother and ultimate limit setter, are stepping into the villain's role, the bad guy of the piece.

Grandma, the heroine, probably assumes that she's acting out of love for Lawrence, but of course she's undercutting his development by "rewarding" him for misbehavior. She has allied herself with his impulses, his pleasure principle, while she should side with you on the side of the reality principle: You have to go home at the end of day; Mom's in charge.

I guess I'm being invited in as a director to save the play. It needs a rewrite job, or it'll never make Broadway. Lawrence will be Lawrence, that's for sure. But I don't like you as the villain at all. In fact, if we can write Grandma's good guy out of the script altogether, your character would change automatically.

Talk to Grandma. Lawrence needs her—not to feed his misbehavior but to help him grow into a self-disciplined individual. You need her, too, not as a heroine to your villain—but as a true costar... heroines both for a better Lawrence.

Nightmares

Q: My $3\frac{1}{2}$-year-old son has been having nightmares for the past few months. He wakes up crying once or twice a week. These bad dreams are usually about monsters. I know that this kind of thing is relatively normal during his stage of development, but is there anything that I should do to help?

A: You are quite correct when you suggest that nightmares "go with the territory" for the normal $3\frac{1}{2}$-year-old boy. Even the themes (monsters, being chased by animals, etc.) are predictable. In psychoanalytic terms your son is in the oedipal phase of development. In symbolic terms the monsters represent his father with whom he is momentarily competing for your favor. I know that, as a knowledgeable mother, you won't let this little bit of theory alarm you. Such reactions are normal for boys from about age 3 to 5. The nightmares, however, should not last more than a few months. They may reappear sporadically throughout childhood, of course, in the face of stress and conflicts.

A few guidelines:

1. Reassure your son that dreams are not real. (This may sound silly, but $3\frac{1}{2}$-year-olds need this kind of reassurance from time to time.)

2. Your husband should also reassure your son about the dreams.

3. Do not attempt to "interpret" the dreams. Such interventions are fine in psychotherapy but not in parenting.

4. Your husband should expect some competition from your son. He should allow it to run its course. It would also be a good idea

for your husband to structure some "fun" (noncompetitive) time with your boy.

5. Your little guy very much wants to be Mommy's little man. He may try to impress you with his strength, his dexterity, his skills. He may even bring you bouquets of flowers or dandelions. It's wonderful! Accept his offerings, and praise him for his efforts. When he gushes, "I want to marry you, Mommy," you will be justifiably thrilled. A kindly answer would be: "Yes, I love you very much too. But I'm married to Daddy. You *wish* you could marry me. I'll always be your Mommy, and I'll always love you." Such an answer is both loving and realistic.

6. While your son may need some reassurance from Mom and Dad when he wakes up at night, resist his efforts to spend the rest of the night in the marital bed. It is a bad habit to initiate, particularly at his stage of psychological development.

A Girl Who Eats Crayons

Q: My 3-year-old daughter, Karen, likes to eat crayons. I know that the habit is not healthy from a physical standpoint, but are there any psychological dangers?

A: Karen's problem is called *pica*, the habitual ingestion of non-edible substances. Child psychiatrists generally do not become too alarmed about the symptom unless it persists beyond the age of 3. After this time it can sometimes indicate an emotional disorder.

Although crayons may be preferred by such children, it is not unusual to hear of youngsters who eat such unappetizing things as laundry starch, plaster, dirt, strings, and cigarette butts.

My first concern is with Karen's physical health. Be sure your pediatrician knows about her habit. Anemia and lead poisoning, for example, may go undetected in such children unless the pediatrician is alerted.

Treatment of pica is usually a team effort by the pediatrician and the child psychiatrist. Your pediatrician would be the best judge of whether Karen's habit is mild and something she can be expected to outgrow or whether she needs a psychiatric evaluation at this time.

Illegitimate

Q: My 3-year-old son, Dennis, is illegitimate, and it doesn't bother me a bit. I could have had an abortion; I could have even forced his father to marry me; but neither of these solutions was for me. I considered adoption, but I just couldn't do it. I mean, after all, he's *mine*. But now I realize that I didn't ever stop to consider *him* at all, and I'm having second thoughts. I mean: I've worked it out, but what about Dennis? Will the stigma of illegitimacy be a problem for him?

A: Most researchers seem to agree that the stigma of illegitimacy just isn't what it used to be. Dennis's future will depend more on your own attitude and ability to be a good parent to him than on the specter of his out-of-wedlock birth.

One UCLA researcher who has traced the lives of fifty children like Dennis from birth to age 10 suggests that factors such as the mother's income, social support system, and mental health are key variables.

My best advice: Do the very best job of mothering you can do. Avoid very close interdependence with Dennis; keep a sense of balance in your life. Give him the opportunity to have adult male role models. And I'm pleased that you've moved beyond your own concerns to now consider Dennis in the family equation. After all, 1 plus 1 equals 3 in this matter: you, Dennis, and the two of you as a family unit.

Parental Nudity

Q: A couple of our friends insist that my husband and I are old-fashioned because we do not practice nudity in front of our children, aged 3 and 5. Is it better for the sexual development of children if they frequently see their parents nude?

A: There are all degrees of parental nudity. Most children, for example, experience their first vision of the adult body when they happen to see (often by accident) Mom or Dad undressing or entering the shower. There is no harm at all in such an encounter. Young children usually develop little more than a passing anatomical interest in such events. Even the undifferentiated "sexual" arousal of the 3- to 5-year-old boy or girl is brief and fleeting and does not result in serious psychological problems because in these innocent and chance situations, children do not associate sexual arousal or physical intimacy with Mom's or Dad's body.

In later development, however, youngsters may well experience sexual arousal when viewing a naked parent. This is where problems can occur. Persistent parental nudity can be devastating to a preteen or teenager. Such youngsters may be bombarded by sexual stimuli from a parent at a stage in their development when they should be moving from parental relationships to peer relationships. Children who develop strong or conflicting sexual attraction to a parent may have difficulty in making the switch to peers of the opposite sex.

A parent who practices nudity at home and believes that he or she is being completely natural and free of hang-ups about sex may, unknowingly, contribute to sexual conflicts in a son or daughter. After all, every boy and girl develops a bit differently, and there are many sexual matters that are outside of parental control and parental awareness. Furthermore, it is unwise to assume that parental nudity, in itself, is a teacher of good sexual development. Sexual education includes the example of the marital relationship as a model of how men and women live together. It includes core family values such as love, fidelity, intimacy, privacy, and religion.

Parental nudity, in final analysis, can be a two-edged sword. Parents who practice it should be very sensitive to the changing developmental needs of their children and should be very careful about not being erotic or sexually provocative toward their children.

On the other hand, we all know that excessive parental squeamishness about the body and being seen by children can produce sexual inhibitions too.

The answer? Steer a middle course. Accept the body and sexual development as a very natural part of life. Understand that excessive and inappropriate nudity can be as problematic as repressive parental avoidance of nudity and sexual communications. Know your own youngster and his or her ever-changing development needs.

Many Gifts vs. One Gift

Q: My wife and I have an annual disagreement about Christmas gifts for our children, aged 3, 7, 8, and 10. She comes from the quantity school: Give them lots of little gifts. I come from the quality school: Take the money, and buy each of them one very nice gift. What do you suggest?

A: This is a common disagreement, and there are no easy answers. Young children, of course, are impressed by quantity over quality any time since they don't really appreciate the cost and value of things. The trouble is that you may simply succeed in overwhelming and overstimulating them. How many parents have looked on, dismayed, as a 5-year-old, after opening all the gifts, spends the rest of the day playing with the wrapping and the boxes!

Teenagers also like quantity, but they're much more appreciative of a few well-chosen quality gifts. From a practical standpoint, of course, most of their gifts cost more and you can afford fewer of them, anyway.

Obviously, I'm trying to give you a developmental perspective on your dilemma. I hope you can apply it and work out some kind of compromise.

Whatever you do, try to keep alive the spirit of Christmas. Put the emphasis on giving, not receiving. Your children, therefore, should plan to give—and only hope to get.

Should Kids Believe in Santa Claus?

Q: My husband believes that we should tell Lori, our 3-year-old daughter, that Santa Claus isn't real. He says she'll learn the truth eventually: Why "perpetuate a myth"? Is there any harm in letting her believe in Santa Claus?

A: No. There is no harm in letting children believe in Santa Claus—as long as they want to or need to believe. Most youngsters learn the truth about Santa by the age of 6. Either they pick it up from TV, from their older siblings, or from friends or they figure it out for themselves. Their reaction, for the most part, is mixed: the joy of discovery and a sense of disappointment.

It's interesting that many children actually pretend to believe for a year or two after their big discovery—for the sake of Mom and Dad. In a way this is a gift from them to you.

When Lori finally figures it all out, you might acknowledge that Santa is not a real person but that he is a real symbol of the spirit of Christmas: Peace on earth and goodwill to all men.

Protection against Sexual Abuse

Q: Our 4-year-old daughter attends a preschool. We've educated her about sexual abuse, especially in the school setting. I guess all those magazine articles and TV shows have had a real impact on us. Are there any additional steps you would suggest?

A: Try this list of five safeguards:

1. *Educate your child:* Talk to your child about "good touch" and "bad touch." Also, you might try a game called "what if." Ask your child "what if" someone, even a familiar and trusted adult, touches her in the wrong place ("bad touch"). What would she do? Teach your child that it's okay to say "no" to an adult. And that it's okay to tell Mommy and Daddy what happened.

2. *Visit the facility:* I'm not talking about a preadmission visit but about periodic, unannounced visits. This is one of your best bets.

3. *Investigate:* Check the school out. Talk to other parents.

4. *Be alert:* Watch for the danger signs such as physical symptoms, poor appetite, insomnia, nightmares, extremes of behavior, and preoccupation with sexual questions or masturbation.

5. *Listen:* Yes, listen to your child. Ask questions about what she did today. There should be no secrets. Listen to what she says... and to what she doesn't say.

Single Mothers and Child Abuse

Q: I'm the divorced mother of two boys, aged 4 and 5. The oldest boy, Tommy, is a real discipline problem, and I must admit that I've been losing my cool with him lately. Last night, for example, I smacked him in the face. I hate myself for doing it. I'm afraid I'm becoming a child abuser. How can I get help before it's too late?

A: I've suspected for a long time that the higher level of stress in single-parent families results in a relatively higher level of family violence. A report by the American Humane Association certainly makes the point: Some 43 percent of all cases of child abuse reviewed in its study occurred in female-parent households even though these households represented only 14 percent of all households nationally. By contrast, 50 percent of all the cases were from two-parent families, which totaled 83 percent of all households.

I hasten to point out, however, that some reviewers of this particular research study think that it's overstated. They do not believe that mothers are much more likely than fathers to abuse their children. They argue, for example, that since mothers, like yourself, are much more likely than fathers to call for help, they are simply identified more often in some research studies.

I, therefore, respect you for admitting a potential problem. What to do? Contact a local chapter of Parents Anonymous, or consult with a child psychiatrist, who should be able to help you with Tommy and your reaction to him.

Mother's Fault?

Q: Why do I feel so guilty? I mean, every time something goes wrong in the life of Rachel (aged 4), I assume it's my fault.

A: Mother guilt is a well-known syndrome. I'm glad you're trying to shake loose from it. Many explanations have been offered. Here are a few to try on for size:

1. Identification with a perfectionist or guilt-laden mother.

2. Grandiose belief that you actually can control every facet of your child's destiny.

3. Lack of self-esteem and vicarious identification with the child who must be perfect in order to enhance the mother's own self-worth.

4. Hostility toward the child; that is, "Look how badly you make me feel when you fail. Where did I go wrong?" Guilt, in this case, is a two-edged sword. Both mother and child suffer.

There are, of course, many variations on these themes and other factors, too, that apply to individual cases.

Guilt, however, is not all bad. If you feel guilty, you care.

To be without guilt is to be without a conscience.

But excessive guilt or inappropriate guilt is a problem. It's not good for you—or for Rachel. Think it through. Find the answers. Then—go easier on yourself...and don't feel guilty about it either.

Fearful Children

Q: My $4\frac{1}{2}$-year-old niece, Janie, is afraid of everything. So is her mother. Isn't this the cause?

A: It's not that simple, but yes, fearful children tend to "catch" many of their symptoms from Mom and Dad. Fearful children also tend to be overprotected children.

Interestingly, however, this type of child has a good chance of changing over the years. Why? Mothers often tend to relax with time, and if they do, their children become much less fearful of the world around them. Better, though, if Janie's Mom could start relaxing right now.

Playing with Fear

Q: Our 4-year-old, Melanie, is afraid of monsters. Lately we've noticed her playing monster with her dolls: A monster doll invades the dollhouse and is beaten up by all the baby dolls. It seems very healthy to me. Is it?

A: Yes. Children use play for many things. The conquering of fear and the resolution of normal developmental conflict are legitimate uses of play.

Since your daughter has discovered this route on her own, there is no need for you to actively encourage it. Just relax, and let Melanie slay her own monsters. I'd worry only if she became pre-occupied with this monster in the dollhouse drama.

Fear of Dogs

Q: My husband and I are both dog lovers. We've been married five years and have always had one or more dogs. Imagine our grief when our 4-year-old daughter, Michelle, developed an intense fear of Sport, our English sheepdog. We got rid of Sport, Michelle has been cured of her panic, but someday we'd like to get another dog. We think it would actually be good for Michelle to have her own dog. What do you think?

A: Most childhood fears of animals are based on one or more un-fortunate episodes of real or perceived danger. It is probable, for example, that Sport may have frightened Michelle in some way. I stress this aspect because it would be unrealistic to view Michelle's fear as some sort of deeply rooted psychological conflict unless her fear has spread, unrealistically, to other dogs, other animals, going outside where animals may be hiding, etc. This brand of unrealis-tic fear is called a *phobia* and requires psychiatric intervention.

Let's assume that Michelle's fear of Sport was just a garden va-riety "fear." What to do? I tend to agree that having a pet is healthy for a youngster. Yet you seem to be sensitive. You know better than pushing another dog on Michelle too soon. Why not start with something tame like a turtle or hamster and then work your way back to a dog? In the meantime try to desensitize Michelle's fear of Sport by giving her positive experiences with dogs via pictures, TV, movies, and watching you pet and handle the neighbors' dogs. Don't push too hard. Let her guide you about when to visit the pet shops to bring home Sport II.

Fear of the Doctor

Q: My 4-year-old son is deathly afraid of his pediatrician. What can I do to help?

A: It is normal for children to have some apprehension about a visit to the doctor's office. After all, nobody looks forward to things like tongue blades and injections. You can help by preparing your son before you visit the pediatrician. Try to explain what the doctor is likely to do, etc. But do not guarantee that he will not "get a shot." Agree that injections and some other exams do hurt. It also helps, of course, to be present during the examination and treatment for physical closeness and moral support.

Four-year-old boys (and girls too) often experience other fears of a developmental nature. As they are becoming more aware of their bodies and of sexual differences, a trip to the pediatrician complete with disrobing and probing of the body can take on complex undertones. The good news is that most pediatricians are prepared to deal with this phenomenon and most children grow out of it.

Fear of Mustache

Q: I'm the divorced mother of a 4-year-old daughter, Shelly. Recently I've been dating a very nice guy named Taylor. He's very sweet to Shelly. She seems to like him a lot—except for one thing: his mustache. It scares her. She won't kiss him. She won't hug him. My questions:

1. Do you think the mustache fear is for real or is Shelly using it as an excuse for something deeper?

2. Will she get over it?

3. Should Taylor shave it off?

A: I like the way you've formulated your questions. It's clear that you've done a lot of thinking about this matter.

In general, children tend to mistrust mustached men. Why? Stereotype is one reason. Movie and TV villains are so often bearded that kids equate facial hair with evil. Another reason, however, is that large mustaches often hide the facial expressions of men, and children, who are so attuned to body language, have a tough time reading reactions. It can, therefore, be confusing or frustrating for them. They don't like cover-ups of this sort.

Shelly, of course, may simply resent Taylor's intrusion into her life. It's not uncommon. Maybe she wants Mommy all to herself. Ask her about it. Encourage her to express herself. Accept her feelings. Reassure her of your love.

If, on the other hand, Shelly does not resent Taylor and his role in your house, we might be dealing with a simple case of what might be called "mustacheitis." As she gets to know the man behind the mustache better, she'll get over it.

Shave it off? Not necessary. If Taylor's as attached to his mustache as I am to mine, he'll find it hard to do anyway. Hold the razor as a last resort.

Fear of the Dark

Q: Our 4-year-old, Robert, insists on sleeping with the light on. So far we've gone along with it, but aren't we establishing a bad habit? I mean, if he needs the light every night, how will he ever get over it?

A: Like most children, Robert will probably just grow out of it. As you probably know, it is not unusual for children at the ages of 3 to 5 to want a light at bedtime. Developmentally, these children (especially boys) are dealing with some unconscious fears that often take the form of bad dreams or nightmares. A bedroom lamp can shed some light on their hidden world as well as brighten their room.

Listen to what Robert is saying to you. He's afraid. Listen, reassure, empathize. Parents are the best lights that children ever had to guide them through the darker paths of growing up.

We Want a Girl

Q: We have two lovely sons, aged 4 and 7. Although we're very satisfied with our family just the way it is, my husband and I both feel "incomplete." We really want a daughter to round out the family, to make it complete. Of course, there's no way to guarantee a girl. So I have two questions: (1) Is wanting a girl the correct motivation to have a child? (2) Would I be cheating the baby if it turned out to be another boy?

A: I really salute your thoughtfulness about this important question. Too many couples go right ahead without giving it much thought.

Wanting a child of a different sex is a very common motivation for having another baby, but it's not the best motivation. The best motivation is simply wanting a child. Here are some other issues to consider:

1. The health of your marriage

2. Financial considerations

3. The impact of a new baby on your two sons

4. Loving the baby regardless of its sex

Think it over. I know you will.

Television Violence

Q: I've been concerned for some time about all the violence that my three children (aged 4, 6, and 8) witness on television. How dangerous is it to their development?

A: The National Institute of Mental Health recently issued a report on television and child behavior. The study was conducted over a two-year period and reviewed hundreds of previous experiments and research findings that have been released over the past ten years. The conclusion was clear: There is now conclusive evidence that excessive violence on television causes aggressive behavior in children.

Such TV-inspired aggression can be observed in children as young as 3 or 4. Furthermore, it has been documented that the more television children watch, the more accepting they are of aggressive behavior; they become numbed and accustomed to atrocity and violence.

On the other hand, I must stress that television can also be a potent positive force in child development. Who can deny that millions of youngsters have gotten a head start on the alphabet, on spelling, on math, and on learning about the world around them from the marvelously entertaining but thoroughly educational programs that are produced especially for children?

What is a parent to do? Tame that would-be monster called television. Exert some control over what the youngsters watch and how often they watch it. As one network executive has remarked: "It's all there, good and bad. All you have to do is flip the dial."

You might wish to write for a free booklet that gives some additional tips: "Children and Television, A Primer for Parents." Send a postcard to: TV, The Boys Town Center, Boys Town, NE 68010.

Cartoon Violence

Q: Saturday mornings at our home are like Saturday mornings in millions of other homes: cartoons, cartoons, and more cartoons.

I've never paid much attention to them—until last Saturday. I took some time to sit down with Lucy (aged 4) and Laura (aged $5\frac{1}{2}$) and watch their cartoons with them. I was shocked. The violence. I couldn't believe it. Any comments?

A: You didn't let the slapstick and the canned laughter fool you. Cartoons *do* tend to rely on violence and aggression to keep their young viewers hooked.

In one study it was determined that Saturday morning cartoons average twenty-seven violent acts per hour. And if that doesn't get your attention, here's what another review by the American Academy of Child Psychiatry has concluded:

1. By the time the average child reaches 16, he has witnessed 200,000 acts of violence and 50,000 attempted murders on the tube.

2. Children's television programming is six times as violent as adult television.

I'm glad that you took the time to watch the cartoons with Lucy and Laura. All parents should know what their children are viewing on the TV. Watch, learn, and control—that's my formula.

Witness to Violence

Q: Last week I took Justin, my 4-year-old son, to a local sporting event. When we were leaving the stadium, some teenagers got into a nasty fight. One of the boys broke a bottle over the head of another boy. There was blood everywhere. Since then Justin talks about it all the time. He can't get it out of his mind. How can I help?

A: Try to keep calm and reassure Justin that most teenagers are not violent. Also, reassure him that you will protect him. He will respond more to your own reaction than to the memory of blood and flying glass. If you present the picture of confidence and safety, Justin will learn to be confident and safe. If you overreact with fear, Justin may acquire some unrealistic fears. But do not deny the obvious. The incident was frightening. He must have been pretty scared. Help him express himself. Also help Justin develop the good judgment to avoid situations where he may become the victim of violence.

Finally, help him learn the difference between anger and violence. Everyone gets upset or mad or angry sometimes. That's okay as long as the feelings are expressed in *words*. But it's not okay to put those feelings into violence.

Quiet Time

Q: My girlfriend has three children, aged 4, 6, and 8. She uses a technique called *quiet time,* in which each of the kids goes to a secluded part of the house each day to read or play or rest—by himself. I wonder about this approach. Is it a very good idea—or is it a form of punishment?

A: It's a very good idea if it's used appropriately. All children, including infants, need some quiet time during the day; a time away from all the stimulation of people, TV, sights, and sounds. Quiet time not only serves to protect the nervous system from overstimulation but also teaches a child the pleasure of silence and solitude. If you begin this practice early in life, for example, you'll help your youngster develop a tolerance for being alone with his own thoughts each day; this can be good exercise for later study skills and academic pursuits.

Is it punitive? No. Maybe you're confusing quiet time with a disciplinary technique called *time-out*. The time-out technique is a sophisticated version of "go to your room," and it's used in response to a youngster's violation of a family rule. Quiet time, on the other hand, should be a regular, daily feature of family life like bathing, eating, or sleeping. It's not a punishment at all.

The Silent Treatment

Q: My girlfriend, Angie, has just remarried. Her husband, Bob, is a great guy, but he isn't used to children; Angie has two: a boy, aged 4, and a girl, aged 5. Bob's idea of punishment is to give them the *silent* treatment. He'll go for two or three days sometimes without speaking to them. He expects Angie to go along with him. She doesn't like it, but she's caught in the middle. I think it's a bad idea. What do you think?

A: Bob's solution is bad for the children, and it's bound to disrupt his marriage too.

Children do need discipline. On occasion, they might be sent to their rooms for a brief time-out of fifteen or twenty minutes. At other times, a restriction of privileges is in order. But to cut them off from parental communication breeds loneliness, anger, resentment, and, ultimately, revenge.

Bob needs a crash course in how to raise children.

Winning by Whining

Q: Ruth, our 4-year-old, is a problem. She whines and whines and whines—until she gets what she wants. What should we do?

A: Ruth has learned that whining pays. What should you do? Establish new rules. Show her that whining does not pay. Do not give her what she wants. Sure, she'll escalate her whining at first and make it hard for you. Why not? It's always worked before.

Tough it out. Ruth's whining can be cured if you cure yourself of the habit of rewarding it.

A Bossy Child

Q: Roseanne, the oldest of our three children, is 4 years old. She's always been very "bossy" toward her younger sisters, but now we notice this trait in her relationships with other children outside our home. She's a very bright little girl, but we're afraid that her bossiness is going to make it hard for her to make friends. How can we help her?

A: Oldest children have a tendency to be bossy—and unpopular. You are very perceptive to recognize that Roseanne is developing an undesirable trait that could stick to her for a long time. It is important to teach her how to win the cooperation of other children, to win them over to her side—not to berate them into submission.

From a developmental standpoint Roseanne is at the stage where early conscience formation (the internal voice of right and wrong, good and bad, do and don't) occurs. Therefore, we'd expect her to be a little officious. Some children, for example, experiment with their conscience a bit by externalizing it: Before using it to control their own behavior, they use it to control other people. Such children sometimes become the *neighborhood superego:* the child who is the keeper of the rules for all the games, the arbitrator of all kiddie disputes. While such a step may be momentarily necessary to Roseanne's development, it will not win her many popularity contests at home or at school.

Emphasize the values of cooperation and sharing and tolerance. Make sure that she has plenty of opportunity for genuinely cooperative play, that she is required to live by the rules of other children at least as often as she imposes her own rules. Since her younger sisters may have some trouble, at this stage, in offering much of a counterweight to Roseanne's tendency to be the boss, it would be wise to create opportunities for her to participate in group activities with select friends and even with children who are one or two years older. Such experiences might assist Roseanne in developing skills in getting along with other children.

Careful, though, not to stifle what could become bona fide leadership qualities. You're not trying to make Roseanne into a follower. You're just trying to help her become a better, more acceptable leader. After all, even the best leaders have to know how to follow sometimes.

Should I Bite My Son?

Q: My 4-year-old son, Paul, has a painful habit: He bites other children whenever he fails to get his own way. It's getting to be quite a problem. Many kids refuse to play with him. My girlfriend says I should spank him or even bite him back. What do you think?

A: This form of oral aggression on the part of a 4-year-old is cause for alarm. Although many children use biting to express displeasure in the first two years of life, they quickly give up the habit through the normal course of discipline and social learning.

At the age of 4 Paul should be less aggressive toward other children; when he's upset, he should be able to express his anger in more appropriate ways.

As far as your own reaction is concerned, my advice is this: Do not meet fire with fire. If you spank him, you teach him more pain and resentment. If you bite him, you teach him that you can sink to his own primitive level. This would be even more frightening for Paul; he needs you to be in charge, to take control, not to match his violence with a counterattack of your own.

Instead, try this technique: If you see Paul biting another child, immediately pick him up, scold him, and give him a time-out; for example, remove him to some solitary corner of the house for fifteen minutes. When the time is up, go to him and try some role playing: Reconstruct the episode, and teach him alternative ways that he might have handled himself. Finally, encourage him to rejoin his playmate, to apologize, and to return to their play.

It is important that you actively intervene and get this problem solved. Paul must learn to contain and channel his natural aggression into socially acceptable behavior. He must learn the joys of friendship and cooperative play. If he gets branded as a bully, he's going to have loads of trouble at school, and ultimately he's going to feel mighty lonely unless, of course, he gravitates to the company of other bullies. This scenario is common to many youngsters who grow up into antisocial teenagers. Don't let it happen to Paul.

Only Child as Movie Queen

Q: Lydia, our $4\frac{1}{2}$-year-old, is an only child. She's always gotten our individual attention, of course, but now her kindergarten teacher tells me that Lydia expects special treatment at school too: She acts like a "movie queen," expecting adulation from her fans. It's embarrassing for us, and I know it's bad for Lydia. What can we do?

A: Only children are often stars at home, but as you're finding out, stardom can boomerang out there in the real world.

Your best bet is to give Lydia plenty of opportunity to relate to other children, especially peers or older children who will not be star-struck by her would-be celebrity. Also be sure to maintain firm but reasonable discipline and teach her a realistic appraisal of her strengths and weaknesses; when you get right down to it, I'm sure Lydia is pretty much like other children—none is perfect.

On the other hand, you might be interested to know that many only children do grow up to be bona fide stars. Among them are Carol Channing, Sammy Davis, Jr., Marilyn Monroe, Robert De-Niro, and Al Pacino.

It's a long shot, but even if Lydia finds her name in lights someday, she'll be better served by less ego—and more humility.

Potty Chair Pullback

Q: I am 21 and have a 4-year-old son. I was a single mother until recently when we moved in with my boyfriend. My son, Matthew, seemed well adjusted until two weeks ago when he started messing his pants. I was shocked. He's been potty-trained for about two years. We try to praise Matt and to pay attention to him. It doesn't work. What more can we do?

A: Matthew's symptom is not unusual. Many youngsters under the age of 5 will temporarily regress from toilet training in the face of significant change or stress in their life.

The move from his familiar surroundings was certainly a change. The introduction of a full-time competitor, your boyfriend, is another change—and a stress too.

While it's important for you to keep things positive and encouraging and it's important for your boyfriend to befriend Matt, don't forget that Matt's major stress is his perceived loss of his special and exclusive relationship with you. Therefore, don't force your boyfriend on him at this time. Try to spend some special time with him—and try to make the toilet training your own responsibility just as it was when Matt first learned to use the potty.

You should be able to turn the problem around in a few weeks.

Mom out of the Picture?

Q: Our 4-year-old, Blane, loves to make drawings of the family. Recently I've noticed that she's been leaving me out of the drawings and placing herself close to her father. It's amazing: This is just the way she's been acting lately. What's going on?

A: Blane's behavior sounds pretty typical for a 4-year-old girl. She's in the throes of a family romance with Daddy. She wants to be his little girl—and she may, temporarily, view you as a competitor for Daddy's attention.

Blane's drawings simply reflect her own underlying wishes: If Mom is not in the picture, she could have Daddy all to herself. Don't be alarmed. As you may know, most children go through a phase of competition with the same-sex parent for the attention of the opposite-sex parent. It's part of normal development.

But don't sit idly by while Blane competes with you. Remind her, for example, that she left you out of the picture; you might even acknowledge that "sometimes you wish you could have Daddy all to yourself." But I wouldn't advise anything more analytic.

Your husband should accept Blane's efforts to woo him—neither encouraging them too much nor ignoring them. He should, as always, be sure that Blane knows, though, that he and Mommy are a team.

Caught Having Sex

Q: He caught us in the act. Our 4-year-old son, Jimbo, barged right into our bedroom last night while my husband and I were making love. He looked at us, and we looked at him. Finally, my husband mumbled something like: "Mommy and Daddy are busy," and Jimbo returned to his room. The next morning at breakfast I told him matter-of-factly that Mommy and Daddy love each other and we like to hold each other close in our bed. I also stressed that we like to have privacy for this and that he should knock before entering our room. Was I making too big a deal out of it?

A: No. You handled it beautifully.

For many years it's been theorized that children viewing adult sex (Freud's "primal scene") were prone to develop psychological conflicts. This is not necessarily so at all. Certainly a one-time peek does not a neurosis make.

Be aware, though, that Jimbo, as a 4-year-old, has lots of sexual curiosity. He may well have been attracted to your bedroom with some vague notion that there was something exciting and private going on between Mommy and Daddy. Also keep in mind that young children often misinterpret what they see and what they hear as aggressive or violent. That's why I'm so pleased with your explanation—you and your husband love each other.

One question: Does your bedroom door have a lock? Sounds like you could use one. Jimbo's curiosity will continue. Better not facilitate another "accidental" intrusion.

The Role of Grandparents

Q: We have two children, 4 and 8 years of age. My wife and I are both close to our own parents and want them to have every opportunity to be grandparents to the children. What do you think is the major contribution(s) that grandparents can make?

A: Researchers have agreed on four basic roles of grandparents:

1. *Teacher:* Grandparents excel at teaching personal and practical wisdom.

2. *Buffer:* Grandparents can be the ones to smooth out problems in the family. It's sometimes said that the reason grandparents and grandchildren get along so well together is that they have a common enemy!

3. *Historian:* Grandparents are the best people to pass along family traditions and a sense of family roots.

4. *Role model:* Most of today's children will be grandparents themselves for twenty or thirty years of their lives. Their models for grandparenting will be their own grandparents.

What to Tell the Sitter?

Q: We have two girls, aged 4 and 7. They've never had a baby-sitter except for their grandmother. We've recently moved, and I'll have to start using sitters. Is there some kind of checklist I can use to provide the sitter with information?

A: The most important "check" is on the reliability of the baby-sitter herself. Be sure to request references. And, by all means, have the sitter come to the house about a half-hour before you leave so she can meet the girls and chat privately with you.
    You might also try this checklist:

1. Outline the duties exactly. It helps to put it in writing.

2. Provide an emergency phone number where you, or a trusted adult, can be reached.

3. Be sure to brief the sitter on any special habits or routines the girls may have—especially concerning eating preferences, play preferences, and bedtime rituals.

4. What is likely to upset each of the girls? How should the baby-sitter respond? What should she do? What should she not do?

5. If the girls require discipline, how should the sitter react?

Remember the sitter is there to take care of the girls and she's there for your peace of mind too.

Call the Baby-Sitter "Mommy"?

Q: Ellen, my 4-year-old, has had the same baby-sitter for the past year. She spends a lot of time with the sitter: about nine hours each weekday. Lately Ellen has been referring to the sitter as "Mommy." The sitter likes it, and I thought it was kind of cute, but my husband says it's a bad idea. What do you think?

A: I agree with your husband. You, and only you, are Ellen's mother. When a child habitually refers to someone as "Mommy," there may be a lot more at stake than just a name.

Normal psychological development usually requires the mother to be a child's *primary object*, the major source of nurturance, protection, and stimulation—the one to whom the child bonds and from whom the child learns trust, love, and values.

Be careful. Ellen may be telling you something. Are you in danger of losing your primary role with her?

The answer, by the way, is not to fire the baby-sitter—that could be dangerous to Ellen. The answer is to increase and enhance your influence while putting your baby-sitter's role back into perspective—Mom's helper.

Psychology of Colors

Q: My daughter, Linda, is 4 years old. Next month I plan to repaint her room. I've been reading about how colors affect people in certain ways. It's very interesting. For example, Linda's favorite color is red, and that's what she wants for her room. I know that red is a hot color, and I think that a bedroom should be more peaceful. Blue maybe. What do you think?

A: Many researchers believe that color can definitely affect moods and feelings. Interior designers have known this intuitively for years. Now industrial psychologists are attempting to make a science out of it.

You're right, of course, about red being a hot color. Children who are attracted to red tend, in the opinion of researchers, to be industrious and energetic. They are curious, inquisitive, and a bit tempestuous and impulsive too.

Blue, on the other hand, represents tranquillity and a search for inner harmony. Yes, it is a more peaceful color.

But what about Linda's room? I know of no research that addresses your question specifically. And, remember, there are all sorts of individual variations to the rules of colors. Why not allow Linda red as an accent color and use blue as the basic color?

Bedtime vs. Sleep Time

Q: A nightly battle, that's what it is. We put our 4-year-old, Robin, to bed and go back downstairs. Ten minutes later she's standing in front of us, complaining that she can't sleep. We take her back to bed, and (you guessed it) the whole process repeats itself. And repeats itself. And repeats itself. Help.

A: Let's distinguish between bedtime and sleep time. Bedtime is something you control. Sleep time is something that Robin controls.

So my advice is, first of all, select a reasonable bedtime. Then insist that Robin remains in her room. You can't demand that she falls asleep as soon as she goes to her room, but you can insist that she stays there. By the way, be sure to make this a pleasant experience for everyone. Be sure that Robin has toys and other diversions. Let her know that while you are in charge of bedtime, she can be in charge of her own sleep time. Try it. It works.

Go to Bed!

Q: We have a problem with Louis, our 4-year-old. He refuses to go to bed at night. He puts up a real fuss and succeeds in upsetting both my husband and me. In the past I've punished him by making him go to bed. Is he getting even with me now?

A: Could be that ol' Louis believes that turnabout is indeed fair play. Because the act of going to sleep should be kept calm and free of conflicts, I usually counsel against making go to bed a punishment. A brief time-out in his room or elsewhere would be more effective.

In this case, however, there could be another explanation. At his stage of development Louis has a natural curiosity about what goes on between Mom and Dad after he goes off to bed at night.

In either case, a gentle but firm insistence at bedtime is the rule. If necessary, carry him to his room to show him you mean business. He'll get the message.

"I Want to Sleep in Your Bed, Mommy and Daddy"

Q: Phillip, our 4-year-old son, slept with us for one week while we had house guests because we needed his room for our friends. Our friends have gone back to Chicago, but Phillip doesn't want to leave our bed. We take him to his room every night at bedtime, but, sooner or later, he shows up at our door and crawls in with us. What should we do?

A: Be firm. The longer you wait to draw the line at the threshold of your bedroom, the harder it will be to get Phillip back into his own room.

But who can blame Phillip? A 4-year-old has his world defined by Mommy and Daddy. If it was up to him, he'd be with you twenty-four hours a day. The closeness and warmth of the parental bed, of course, is a special attraction.

From a developmental standpoint Phillip is probably drawn more to you than to your husband at this particular stage of his life. He wants to be your "little man." He may even see Daddy as something of a competitor for your love and attention. Getting between the two of you in bed, therefore, solves several problems for him. Sure, this last piece of information is a bit theoretical, but one thing, I bet, is factual: A 4-year-old in the bed can't be doing a lot of good for your marital relationship—another good reason to gently but firmly return Phillip to his own room whenever he comes calling. It will be good for him—and for you too!

Night Terrors

Q: Our pediatrician says that our son Jason, aged 4, is having night terrors. I've heard of nightmares. What are night terrors? Are they just severe nightmares?

A: Not at all. Night terrors are completely different monsters of the night than nightmares.

Night terrors occur in about 2 to 3 percent of all children. If Jason's experiences are typical, they are indeed terrifying to behold. Usually the child suddenly awakes screaming from a very deep sleep. He may call for help or shout incomprehensible words while staring blank-eyed into space. When he is approached by a parent, he is completely unaware of anyone trying to help him. In fact, he may get up from bed and sleepwalk. In the morning he will have absolutely no memory of what happened.

Night terrors are generally considered to be due to an immaturity of the central nervous system. The best thing about them is that they are infrequent and that children almost always grow out of them in a few years.

The usual attempts at reassurance that work wonders with nightmares ("The monsters are not real," etc.) will not get you very far with Jason. His terrors are not based on bad dreams that he can tell you about in the morning. If there is a gap of wakefulness between night terror and falling back to sleep, comfort him gently and naturally; do not attempt to get him to talk about it. If he is sleepwalking, you might secure his room and his door so he won't hurt himself.

Medication for the treatment of night terrors is sometimes successful, but physicians prefer to reserve it for only the most severe cases because of possible side effects.

Prejudice at Age 4?

Q: My 4-year-old daughter, Collette, attends a private preschool. There are several black children in the school and three black teachers too. Last night Collette told me that she "hates black people." She couldn't give a real reason: only because they're black. I explained that people are people, that God makes people in different colors, but color doesn't make people bad. Collette doesn't understand. Should I drop the subject until it comes up again? How could a 4-year-old be so prejudiced? We have never taught her these ideas.

A: Collette is too young to be labeled as prejudiced. Yet the dynamics of her reaction are very similar to prejudice in adults: an unjustified and unreasonable generalization and projection of negative feelings or qualities onto an entire class of individuals. You see, adult prejudice really is an infantile reaction after all.

Collette may be imitating the behavior of older children or even of something she's seen on television. She may also be testing your own reaction to her statement. Congratulations for letting her know exactly where you stand.

The time to instill basic values, of course, is now—in early development. After a day or two of cooling off, I would suggest a subtle approach, using yourself as the model. Without preaching or moralizing just let it be clear through your behavior that blacks (and other minorities) are good people. Collette will take her cues from what you say about blacks, how you react to them—not in theory but in real life.

Child Snatching

Q: I'm desperate. My former husband snuck into town last week and snatched my 4-year-old daughter on her way home from kindergarten. He called the next day to tell me "not to worry" and that Kerry really wants to live with him. My lawyer says that although I have legal custody, there isn't much we can do immediately; we have to go to court in my husband's home state. In the meantime, I'm a wreck and I'm worried to death about my daughter.

A: My heart goes out to you. Unfortunately, child snatching is much more common than most people realize: over 100,000 cases per year in the United States. Why? As long as children are made pawns in an ongoing postmarital conflict and as long as child snatching so frequently goes unpunished, it will persist.

What are the dangers for Kerry? If you legitimately fear for her physical safety, contact the local Child Protective Services immediately. Otherwise, your best strategy, in your daughter's interest, is to work things out with your husband so that you can, at least, talk to Kerry by phone. She is probably bewildered and frightened. She may have been told that you do not love her anymore and that you have sent her away. It is crucial that you reassure her of your love as soon as possible and in any way that you can do it; for example, you might try to enlist the aid of a trusted in-law or a mutual friend.

I hope your attorney has told you that your husband's state conforms to the Uniform Child Custody Jurisdiction Act; for example, it respects custody orders issued in other states. In fact, over forty states have adopted this act, with some variations. Keep in mind, though, that the legal wheels may grind slowly. The goal in the meantime must be to make contact with Kerry, reassure her, and make every effort to neutralize the psychological trauma. Keep a lifeline open until she is safely back with you.

My Son Kisses Boys

Q: My 4-year-old son, Edward, kisses boys. I mean he only kisses boys. He refuses to kiss little girls. What can I do? Is this an early sign of homosexuality?

A: Take it easy: A kiss is still just a kiss! Edward is probably not developing into a homosexual. Such development is complex and goes far beyond the innocent "homosocial" smooching of a toddler.

But what's going on here? You say that Edward "refuses" to kiss girls. I interpret this to mean that you may be pushing him, perhaps out of your fear of homosexuality, to kiss girls. Edward's problem may be that he finds more reward in being oppositional to you. Think about it. What happens when he kisses boys? Do you get bent out of shape? Do you punish him? I bet you do. Paradoxically, your punishment may be encouraging, not discouraging, the behavior. Similarly, Edward may get a kick out of refusing to kiss girls—precisely because that's what Mom wants.

Try ignoring Edward's kisses. If he's doing it to get a reaction from you, the behavior will cease after a few weeks. By the same

token, do not urge him to kiss girls either. Give Edward time—
he's got plenty of it. The fundamental things will apply...as time
goes by.

Handicapped Children at Risk for Abuse

Q: Our 4-year-old son, James, is moderately retarded. We recently
heard a report on the radio that handicapped children are more
likely to be abused by parents than normal children. We don't understand.

A: Strictly from a statistical standpoint, handicapped children are
more at risk for abuse than are other children. But every child,
including James, is a special case. Don't let statistics scare you.

Let me explain. There are four basic ingredients in the equation, according to a paper presented to the American Academy for
Cerebral Palsy and Developmental Medicine:

1. Parents who were themselves abused as children are more
apt to abuse their own children.

2. A handicapped child with special needs usually puts a degree of strain upon the best of parents.

3. When parents face severe financial strain, as is the case for
many people today, tensions of all kinds are potentially more ex-
plosive.

4. A number of handicapped children, unfortunately, learn that
the surest way to get parental attention is through misbehavior,
nagging, or making demands.

I suggest that you analyze this equation. How much applies to
your own family? I'm sure you realize that the vast majority of parents love their retarded children, protect them, and nurture them.
Abuse is not common. I'd add one more tip, though, for all parents of retarded children: Learn as much as you can about your
youngster's condition and your role as a parent. An excellent way
to do this is to join a local parents' group. You might wish to write:

Association for Retarded Citizens, 2709 Avenue E. East, P.O. Box 6109, Arlington, TX 76011.

A Retarded Sister

Q: Our 4-year-old daughter, Marta, is retarded. We've been told that our older children will suffer if we keep her at home rather than sending her to an institution. Is there any truth to this prediction?

A: A researcher at the University of Texas has studied this problem extensively. She compared twenty-eight families with a mentally retarded child with twenty-four families having only normal children. The result? There were no differences in the mental health of the older children.

The key is to treat Marta naturally and to educate your older children about her condition. Although Marta may require some extraordinary attention at times, be sure that there's still plenty of Mom and Dad to go around for the other youngsters. In this way you'll avoid their resentment and the guilt that often follows close behind.

Breaking Away

Q: I guess I've become too attached to our youngest daughter, 4-year-old Penny. The fact is that I've never really been away from her. She cries even if I try to go to the store without her. My husband and I are arguing about it now. Jack says that it's not good for Penny or for me, and he thinks that my "obsession" with Penny is interfering with our marriage. He wants the two of us to go away for a weekend—without the children. I know he's right. But how can I do it? Should I just hire a baby-sitter or what?

A: Jack is probably correct, but let's not leap at solutions immediately. First, I'd suggest that you examine the reasons for your deep attachment to Penny. I take it that you were not so overinvolved with your older children. What has changed?

Some parents tend to become preoccupied with a youngest child in order to unconsciously prolong what they know will be the last infancy in the family; it's a way of holding onto a stage of parenthood, just as some *children* resist growing up into a next stage of development.

Another common dynamic in these situations is a mother who is herself a youngest child. There can be a tendency to become overidentified with the baby, even making an unconscious effort to do for her what you feel you may have missed as a child.

Third, Jack has raised the issue of your marriage. Think carefully. Are you hiding from Jack behind Penny? He evidently thinks so. If it's true, the real problem may be in the marriage, not in the child.

Examine these common factors and any others that may come to mind. Try to resolve any conflicts that you may have about your own life or about your marriage. Then design a careful step-by-step game plan to gradually wean yourself from Penny. Hiring a strange baby-sitter for a weekend at this stage would be too precipitous and traumatic for a needy, dependent 4-year-old. Start with short trips to the store. Introduce a trustworthy baby-sitter slowly: first while you're in the house, then for a few hours. Build up to the weekend. Breaking away will probably be painful for you too, but, yes, it is in everyone's best interest.

Take a Child to a Funeral?

Q: When my brother-in-law died last month, I decided not to take my 4-year-old daughter to the funeral. I didn't think she'd understand, and I wanted to protect her from all the grief. Now I'm having second thoughts. She keeps asking when Uncle Jim is going to visit. Would it have helped her to grasp the meaning of death better if she had attended the funeral?

A: No. Children do not really comprehend the real meaning of death, the finality of life, until about the age of 8. Until that time their limited intellectual ability does not allow them to comprehend abstract concepts like death. They tend to think of death in very concrete terms; they understand it as temporary, like going to sleep or taking a brief vacation. Much of their own experience encourages these misperceptions: They learn of Christ rising from the dead and they see TV heroes bouncing back from "death" as they return in next week's program or on another channel.

It is not uncommon for 4- and 5-year-olds who do attend funerals to ask when the corpse is going to "get out of the box." This simple question is both a defensive wish that everything will go back to the way it was and a profound indicator of the limits of their comprehension.

The decision about whether to take young children to a funeral often turns on the tradition of the family. You can help your daughter by following these tips:

1. Tell the truth.

2. Use the word *death*, even though she cannot fully understand it yet. Ease her into a gradual understanding over a period of time. Use examples such as dead leaves falling from trees or a pet's death.

3. Do not hide your grief. Share your feelings.

4. Anticipate that your daughter's greatest worry is that *you* might die and abandon her. Reassure her.

A Child's First Halloween

Q: We have just moved to the United States from South America. We have a 4-year-old son. My husband and I went to college on the west coast, so we know all about American holidays. Our son is very timid, and we're afraid that he will be frightened by the trick-or-treaters this year. How can we help him?

A: First let me congratulate you for thinking ahead. So many problems can be avoided when parents anticipate them.

Our lighthearted holiday of Halloween had its beginnings as a Celtic celebration, All Hallows Eve, that supposedly marked the night that spirits came back to haunt the living. The Celts lit fires to ward off the evil spirits and put out food to placate them. Over the centuries the holiday has evolved into our now familiar night of trick or treat—Halloween.

This interesting evolution explains why Halloween, to this day, is laden with ghosts and goblins, witches and warlocks. It also explains why so many of the children will come to your door on Halloween night outfitted in costumes that might frighten your son.

A few tips:

1. Explain the holiday to him in words that he will understand.

2. Take him to a store, and show him the costumes.

3. Buy a couple of masks, and at home, teach him that a real human face lurks behind even the most grotesque-looking facade. To do this you can try a variation of peekaboo.

4. When trick-or-treaters come to your home, be sure to ask them to unmask after they have received their treats. "See, they're nice boys and girls" could be your response.

5. Finally, you might try a little trick or treating with your son. There's nothing like a few pieces of candy to convince a 4-year-old that Halloween is a good deal.

Covering Up an Adoption

Q: My husband and I are from Europe. We moved to the United States three years ago with our adopted daughter, Vivian, who is now $4\frac{1}{2}$ years old. Our family and our friends in Europe know that Vivian is adopted, but no one in this country knows about it. We would like to keep it a secret from Viv and from everyone else, but we're not sure. We notice that most Americans are fairly "open" about adoption. What do you advise?

A: As Vivian grows older, the chances for a successful cover-up will grow slimmer each year. Children inevitably learn the truth—sometimes in a shocking and traumatic manner. That is why most adoptive parents are counseled to be open with their youngsters. Better, for example, that Vivian learns the truth from you rather than in a letter hidden in a drawer, from a European visitor who might "slip," from a little cousin who might spill the secret out of childish spite, or even from a birth certificate or other legal record when, in later years, Vivian herself applies for a passport or a marriage license. You see, there are a thousand and one ways for children to discover the truth about their origins.

But is the truth so bad? I think not. Adoptive parents are motivated by the highest human values. In fact, when adoption is a secret, it tends to become a bit sinister. When the child finally learns the truth, she may feel not only that she has been cheated but that the truth must be so horrible that it has had to be hidden from her. This is why late discovery can be so injurious.

Vivian is not too young to be told. You could even do it today— together with your husband. Don't make a big deal out of it. Vivian is not ready to grasp the full significance anyway. By all means use the word *adoption*—it is not a dirty word. At $4\frac{1}{2}$, Vivian can probably understand that she "came from another lady's tummy." If she asks why the other lady did not keep her, explain that the other lady loved her very much but that it was not possible for her to be the Mommy, that you and your husband saw her, loved her, and picked her out specially to be your own little girl.

Over a period of years Vivian will gradually come into a fuller knowledge of her adoption and will have specific questions for you. It will be a growth process for her and for you.

Don't forget that adoptive parents may need some help too. The best resource is other adoptive parents. Contact some adoption agencies in your city, and ask to be put in touch with other adoptive mothers and fathers. They're always ready to assist. That's the American way. Welcome to our country!

Explaining Adoption to a Child

Q: Our 4-year-old daughter is adopted. We've been advised to be very natural with her about the adoption, and we've told her that she is adopted. So far, no problems except she really doesn't seem to understand. Any comments?

A: Your daughter will grow into an understanding of what it means to be adopted. At this stage of her development you should not expect her to understand very much about the whole idea. She'll be interested in pregnancy and "where babies come from" and may briefly comprehend that she came from "another woman's tummy," but even this startling piece of new information won't have much of an impact.

It's generally not until the age of 6 or 7 that most children can really grasp the concept of adoption. At that time you should be prepared for questions like: "Why didn't my mommy keep me?" and "Are you going to put me up for adoption if I'm bad?"

Be natural about the adoption, but do not clobber your daughter with information. For example, too much reassurance by parents who are trying to be up-front and natural can be interpreted by children as defensive; that is, "If it's so natural to be adopted, why does Mom talk about it all the time?"

Fathers of Divorce

Q: My husband and I were divorced three months ago. We have two children, aged 4 and 5. I have been given custody. Jim has been a good father, and I really want him to continue to be involved in the lives of the kids. The problem is that he hasn't been around at all since the divorce. He's called to tell me that he loves the children and misses them but that he's "too messed up" right now to be with them. Is this a bad sign? Does it mean he'll continue to distance himself from the children?

A: The signs are not good. Without knowing very much about Jim's situation, it is still easy to empathize with him—and with you. This is a rough time for both of you as you struggle to put your lives back together again.

It is also a very tough time for the children. Ages 4 and 5 tend to be among the most difficult developmental periods to experience divorce. Your idea to involve Jim with the children appears to be sound. The divorce is not their fault. He'll always be their father. They need him in many ways.

Some recent research conducted at Yale University asked the question: What are the predictors of continued involvement by divorced fathers? There are three important factors:

1. Fathers who stay involved during the first year of divorce tend to *stay* involved.

2. Men who have felt comfortable and competent as fathers before divorce continue fathering their children after divorce.

3. If former wives cooperate in visitation plans, the chances of involvement are much higher.

We know where Jim fits on factor number one. He's not making a good start. Where does he fit on the other factors?

Whatever the answer, you should have a frank talk with your former husband. Remember: The longer he stays away, the less likely it is that your children will ever see very much of him.

Former Husband's Live-in Girlfriend

Q: My former husband and I have been divorced for three years. I have custody of our children (aged 4 and 5). They visit their father for two weeks every Christmas. The visits have gone pretty well, but I'm very concerned about the next one. I've just learned that my husband's girlfriend has moved in with him. I don't think it's the proper environment for young children. They're impressionable. Their morals are at stake. Should I get a lawyer so I can eliminate the visitation altogether. Should I call Bob (my "ex")? Should I tell the children? What should I do?

A: Bob's new lifestyle is a sign of the times. You may not like it, but it's his life. On the other hand, I certainly appreciate your concern for the children; it's a legitimate worry.

Your first step is to call Bob. Maybe he's already thought about it. Some fathers in these situations ask their friends to move out temporarily; others take great care to avoid intimacy in the presence of the children and to even use separate rooms during the visit.

It's a matter of values and sensitivity.

Some men opt to be "natural and open" and refuse to make accommodations. They reason that the children will get used to it. They do, of course, but there can be some pain in the interim. If

Bob won't budge, therefore, ask him to be very sensitive to the youngsters. Their biggest fear, at ages 4 and 5, will be that Daddy might stop loving them if he has a new friend. Be sure that Bob reassures them of his love. And alert him that his friend should not attempt to "mother" the children. She can be their friend, but they already have a mommy back home.

Single Father

Q: My son, Bob (aged 36), is trying to raise his two children, Caroline (aged 4) and Peter (aged 6). I admire him and wish I could help, but he won't hear of it. He says he's got to do it his way. I'm afraid, though, that he's just trying to prove something to his ex-wife, who gave up the kids so she could become a swinger. Any advice?

A: Bob is not alone. Whatever their motivation, more and more men are stepping into the role of single fathers. Check these statistics: In 1970 single fathers headed up 1.3 percent of all U.S. families; in 1980 it was 2.2 percent; and in 1984 the figure was 2.8 percent—more than double the 1970 figure. But it's not easy—especially if a man, like Bob, spurns help. I do not, however, suggest that you try to force yourself on your son. He may resent it—for now.

The Stepchild Factor

Q: My fiancé and I are getting married next month. It's the second marriage for both of us. I have two children, aged 4 and 6. Frank also has two children, aged 11 and 13. I'm worried about the potential problems we're going to face in trying to blend two families together. The closer the marriage date comes, the more frightened I get. Any advice?

A: I don't want to add to your fright, but, first, let's take a hard look at an inescapable fact. The toughest marriage to hold together is a second marriage where each partner brings children to the union. This is the conclusion of two sociologists who surveyed over 1500 families. They found that 17 percent of these marriages end up in divorce within three years. Compare these figures to a 10 percent divorce rate within three years for remarriages without children and a 6 percent rate for first-time marriages.

What's the problem? The children. Most of the divorcing couples surveyed indicated that they just couldn't handle the stepchildren, that, in effect, they were divorcing the *kids* more than they were divorcing their spouse.

Forewarned is forearmed. If you and Frank are aware of these factors, you can plan now to confront any problems that arise. Things to consider:

1. Your respective roles in discipline

2. The roles of your ex-spouses and of the youngsters' grandparents

3. The basic values of your new family

4. How each of you will be addressed by the other's children

Some don'ts:

1. Don't try to treat all the children equally—treat them fairly according to their needs.

2. Don't play favorites.

3. Don't allow the children to "split" you and Frank by forcing you to take sides.

4. Don't be too quick to have a baby (the so-called mutual child); concentrate on stabilizing your current family first.

Your concern is natural and even a good sign in my opinion. That's good medicine for any marriage. Best wishes.

The Successful Stepfamily

Q: Nobody's promising me a rose garden, and I don't expect one. But I'm getting married in three months to a woman who has three children (aged 4, 7, and 9) by a previous marriage. We've talked about it a lot, and we're preparing ourselves and the children for our new roles. My question is a general one: What are the factors that predict success or failure for stepparents?

A: From a statistical standpoint there are several factors:

1. *Age:* Women under 40 are more successful as stepmothers, but age doesn't appear to be a factor for men.

2. *Children:* The younger the children, the greater your chances for success. The toughest challenge, as you might guess, is teenagers.

3. *Income:* Interestingly, research has shown that lower-income stepparents fare better than upper-income stepparents. I believe it may be due to the fact that there's more forced sharing of responsibility and a sense of "being together against the world" in lower-income families.

4. *Former spouses:* The attitude of your fiancée's former husband is going to be a crucial factor. He can make things rough (by encouraging the kids, for example, to defy you), or he can make things easier for you. If at all possible, I suggest you get together with him before the wedding; however you cut it, the two of you are now part of each other's life.

Stepparent-to-Be

Q: I'm 32 years old, and I've never been married. Next month I'm getting married to Alex, the man of my dreams. Alex is divorced and has custody of his two children: Polly (aged 4) and Rachel (aged 6). The wife-to-be part of this doesn't scare me a bit, but the stepparent-to-be part sure does. I'd appreciate any help you can offer.

A: You'll be joining a mighty big club when you become a stepparent. Did you know, for example, that one out of every five Americans becomes a stepparent sometime during their adult lives? In addition, one out of seven children is a stepchild; that's 18 million children. So you see, the stepfamily is very common. It's an accepted form of family life today. Here are some tips:

1. *Anticipate problems:* Sit down and talk to Alex. Where will the problems arise? Plan ahead.

2. *Your role:* Define your role. What will the girls call you? They have a "Mom," so don't expect them to view you as their mother. One solution is: "Mum."

3. *Discipline:* Polly and Rachel are young enough for you to take a direct role in discipline, but don't expect them to obey you automatically. You'll have to win their cooperation patiently.

4. *The girls' mother:* I suggest a meeting with Alex's ex-wife. She'll be a silent partner to your household whether you like it or not. Approach her in the best interests of the girls. Tell her that you're not out to replace her at all. You'd like to cooperate with her.

5. *Your marriage:* Your marriage comes first. The children may, at some point, become jealous of you. They may try to drive a wedge between you and Alex. Talk about it in advance. Make sure Alex's top priority is you. In the long run this will not only be best for you and him—it will be best for the girls too.

When to Start Kindergarten

Q: Our daughter, Roberta, is 4 years old. She goes to a half-day nursery school and has some trouble keeping up with the other children, physically and socially. She's not retarded or anything. She was a premie, and she's just always been about six to eight months behind on everything, that is, talking, walking.

Roberta will qualify, by age, to go into kindergarten next fall, but I'm not sure. Should we send her or should we hold her back for a year?

A: A sensible question—and one that could affect Roberta's entire life.

As a child psychiatrist, I'm much more concerned about a youngster's developmental age than I am about chronological age.

I would urge you to actively pursue a definitive answer to your question. Start with Roberta's current teachers; what do they think? Consult your pediatrician. Talk to the kindergarten people. You might even obtain some independent testing to determine Roberta's academic, social, emotional, and physical readiness.

I don't have enough information to give you my own definitive answer, but from what you've said, I would lean toward keeping Roberta back for a year. For her it could truly be a gift of time.

The Boy Who Ignores His Teacher

Q: Our 4-year-old son, Jamie, has been attending nursery school for the past several weeks. He seems to look forward to going. We've never had any trouble with his attendance. He gets along fine with the other children, but there's one problem: He refuses to speak to his teacher, whom we've found to be a very nice woman. What's going on? Is this a case of school phobia?

A: First of all, it is a good sign that Jamie's actual attendance is not a problem. Some youngsters do exhibit signs of school phobia on entrance to nursery school. These youngsters usually do not fear school at all—they are anxious about leaving Mom behind at home. Clinically, we refer to this phenomenon as *separation anxiety*.

Jamie is not suffering from separation anxiety. He is, however, having some difficulty in accepting someone other than Mom as an adult authority figure in his life. I wonder if he has had much experience with adult women in his life. Has he, for example, had trouble with baby-sitters? Has he had an opportunity to relate to grandmothers, aunts, your female friends and neighbors? If not, it would be a good idea to build such opportunities into his life.

Jamie apparently is "checking out" his teacher. Is she reliable? Is she trustworthy? I'm pleased that you've spoken to her and that you are positive about her. It would help, of course, for you to be very supportive of her in your little talks with Jamie.

Another very strong possibility, particularly given Jamie's stage of psychological development, is that he views his teacher as your competitor. At this point in his life Jamie wants nothing more than to be Mom's little man. He wants you to be almost exclusively devoted to him. He may be faced with an unconscious dilemma: "If I accept my teacher, will Mom feel betrayed and will I lose Mom's love?" But don't let me scare you with this psychodynamic interpretation. It is actually one of the garden variety conflicts of normal development. Jamie will get over it. You might help him by taking him to school a few times and spending a couple of minutes chatting with his teacher in his presence. Jamie will see, firsthand, that his teacher has your blessing and that there can be a place for both of you in his young life.

Masturbation

Q: Our 4-year-old son spends a lot of time "playing with himself." We know that a certain amount of this is normal, but where do we draw the line? And how do we draw it—especially when he does it in public?

A: Yes, a certain amount of genital masturbation at the age of 4 is to be expected from boys and from girls too. It is part of their growing awareness not only of their bodies but of their emotions. Most masturbation, therefore, is simply self-soothing at this age.

On the other hand, some of what may pass for masturbation may not be masturbation at all. The child who clutches his or her genitals repeatedly throughout the day may do so more out of anxiety rather than for pleasure. In such cases there are usually other signs of distress to alert a parent: nightmares, fears or phobias, rituals, and so forth. These children may, at times, require the consultation of a child psychiatrist.

I hope your son falls into the first category: developmentally normal masturbation. How to respond? Most parents today are aware that children should not be fed horror stories about what will happen to them if they "play with themselves." Similarly, masturbation should not be encouraged either overtly or covertly (the school of thought of "I don't care if you do it as long as you do it in private") since such tactics put parents on the side of a child's darker impulses and against his developing conscience.

You should seek refuge, therefore, between these two extremes. Gentle, nonpunitive disapproval is a wise course of action. Try to divert your son's attention tactfully to something interesting and wholesome if you catch him "in the act." In that way you can actually aid his psychological maturation. You will be teaching him how to channel a strong, natural drive into some other form of gratification. This ability—*sublimation*—is a hallmark of good child development.

Imaginary Playmates

Q: Following my marital separation, my youngest daughter, Shelly (aged 4), created an imaginary companion that she calls "Janet." Whenever she gets upset, she withdraws into intense conversations with her invisible friend. Most of the time Janet seems to help her, but I'm worried. Is this a phase? Is she ill? Should I humor her along, or should I insist that Janet does not exist? I would deeply appreciate your advice.

A: Imaginary playmates are not so unusual. They are generally seen at the ages of 2 to 4 and again at 9 to 10 years of age. They are often invented as a defense against loneliness or as a creative way of coping with some form of childhood conflict.

The transient use of an imaginary companion is not generally a symptom of serious psychotic illness. As a matter of fact, there is ample evidence that children who invent such invisible playmates are themselves quite gifted and creative. In a study of approximately seventy-five 3- and 4-year-olds with imaginary companions, Yale researchers found these youngsters to differ considerably from other children: They were more expressive; they smiled more; they showed a greater ability to concentrate; they were seldom bored; they were more cooperative; and they were less aggressive.

Nevertheless, I appreciate your concern. I would be worried too, but only if Shelly has completely abandoned the real world for a fantasy world and only if she cannot also utilize warm, human relationships to assist her in coping with the loss of her father.

As long as she generally prefers *you* to Janet and is faring well in other areas of her life, there is little cause for alarm.

I suggest that you empathize with her and humor her along a bit—but do not engage in conversations, etc., with her make-believe confidant. Stand firmly, but gently, for reality: "No, honey, I do not see Janet. You wish she was real but it sure helps sometimes to have a pretend friend just like her, doesn't it?"

Seek opportunities to talk directly with Shelly of her feelings about the separation. Help her work through this difficult time of her life in the real world. With time she will leave Janet behind— in the perplexing but always wonderful world of childhood fantasy.

Bye-Bye Easter Bunny?

Q: When Beth, my 4-year-old, recently asked at the dinner table about when the Easter bunny will come this year, her sister Peggy (aged 8) started scoffing. I managed to shut her up just before she blurted out the news that the Easter bunny isn't for real. Should I tell Beth myself? I know it's not a big deal, but it's important to me.

A: It's important to Beth too. Most children learn the truth about those fabled fantasies such as Santa Claus, the tooth fairy, and, yes, the Easter bunny from older siblings or from savvy playmates. It's kind of a rite of passage.

You can be sure that Peggy has already spilled the beans to Beth—probably right after dinner. So what should you do?

Have a talk with Beth—listen to her carefully. Try to learn, indirectly, what she knows. Ask if she has questions, but don't answer questions she isn't asking. She probably wishes that the Easter bunny was real. Empathize with her. You can always reassure her that while "he's not real, he's the symbol of giving and joy at Easter" and that Beth can count on his presence this year just as in years past.

Quiz

Try your hand at these questions about preschoolers, 3- and 4-year-olds. Pretty soon it's off to kindergarten and first grade, which means that your child will gradually slip from the rather exclusive influence you've had over her for the past few years. Make this time count. Get informed. Stay involved.

1. Imaginary playmates (choose one):

   ☐ A. Are usually signs of mental illness

     ☐ B.   Are often associated with gifted children

     ☐ C.   Are rare among all children

2. Among the disadvantages of too much TV for children are (choose as many as apply):

     ☐ A.   Influencing children to violent behavior

     ☐ B.   Boredom, passivity

     ☐ C.   Isolation from family and friends

3. True or false? The 4-year-old who likes to play monsters may actually be engaging in healthy psychological work.

4. If you notice your 4-year-old son or daughter masturbating, you should:

     ☐ A.   Warn them that it will cause them to lose their eyesight

     ☐ B.   Tell them it's okay

     ☐ C.   Matter-of-factly divert their attention to something else

5. The child suffering from school phobia:

     ☐ A.   Should be allowed to stay home for a couple of days

     ☐ B.   Must be firmly but gently forced to go to school

     ☐ C.   Just wants attention

6. Four-year-olds:

     ☐ A.   Cannot share toys

     ☐ B.   Are capable only of parallel play

     ☐ C.   Should be capable of some genuine cooperative play

7. Fear of visiting the pediatrician on the part of a 4-year-old boy is likely to be due to:

     ☐ A.   Fear of pain

     ☐ B.   Fear of being separated from mother

     ☐ C.   Sexual fears

8. True or false? Night terrors are basically the same as nightmares except they're more violent in content.

9. The age at which most children can really comprehend the finality of death is:

☐ A. 3
☐ B. 5
☐ C. 8

10. When asked "How is an automobile like an airplane," most 4-year-olds will answer:

☐ A. They're not alike at all.
☐ B. They both have wheels.
☐ C. They are both means of transportation.

11. True or false? Handicapped children are at great risk for abuse.

12. Which of the following is *not* a proper role for grandparents?

☐ A. Historian
☐ B. Role model
☐ C. Teacher
☐ D. Disciplinarian
☐ E. Buffer

13. Which of the following is the best predictor of whether a divorced father will remain involved with his children?

☐ A. How soon he remarries
☐ B. His relationship with his ex-wife
☐ C. The amount of visitation in the first postdivorce year

14. In the face of stress (birth of a sibling, parental conflict, etc.) a common symptom among 4-year-olds is (select one):

☐ A. Facial tics
☐ B. Temporary loss of toilet training
☐ C. Sadness
☐ D. Vomiting

15. In recognizing 3- and 4-year-olds for good behavior:

☐ A. Allow them to earn "points" toward future rewards

☐ B. Remind them that you expect them to keep it up

☐ C. Give them immediate rewards

16. Arrange these six basic techniques of discipline in proper order based on their relative effectiveness:

☐ A. Ignore the negative

☐ B. Contracts

☐ C. Punishment

☐ D. Accentuate the positive

☐ E. Parental example

☐ F. Logical consequence

17. True or false? Fearful children tend to have fearful parents.

18. Which of the following is *not* a positive indicator for a successful stepfamily?

☐ A. All children under the age of 6

☐ B. Stepmother under the age of 40

☐ C. High income

19. Sexual abuse of young girls (select all that apply):

☐ A. Is less common than rape of adult women

☐ B. Twenty-five percent are victims before they reach the age of 13

☐ C. Is four times more common than rape of adult women

20. True or false? A new stepparent should not expect to be called "Mom" or "Dad."

Answers

1. B	6. C	11. True	16. E, D, A,
2. A, B, C	7. C	12. D	F, B, C
3. True	8. False	13. C	17. True
4. C	9. C	14. B	18. C
5. B	10. B	15. C	19. B, C
			20. True

CHAPTER 4

School-Age Children (5 to 10)

School bells. School bells. They herald the onset of what is sometimes called the *latency years*. At this point your child has developed sufficient psychological strengths to keep his inherent drives in check, or latent, most of the time. It's no accident, therefore, that formal education begins at this time.

These are usually the golden years of childhood. Every state has a capitol, basic mathematics is dutifully absorbed, and friendships form in the neighborhood, in the school, or on the Little League team.

But these are also the years when behavioral or psychological problems are generally first noticed. Why? The child who did not properly accomplish the developmental tasks of infancy, the toddler phase, or the preschool years enters school at a disadvantage. He may only be running on three or four cylinders instead of six or eight. The behavioral and performance stress of school may precipitate problems that up to now may not have been obvious. Teachers are often the first to recognize the boys and girls who are not coping since they are in a good position to compare them to their peers.

If your child does develop some difficulties, don't despair and don't feel guilty. Instead, become informed and seek consultation if it's indicated. The questions asked by parents in this chapter cover the entire range of normal and abnormal behavior. They should be good guideposts for what to expect.

187

Off to Kindergarten

Q: Adam, our oldest, will soon be starting kindergarten, and I'm a little worried about it. Last year he had some trouble leaving the house a few times to go to nursery school. This summer we had to bring him back early from a trip to his grandparents because he was homesick. Do you have any recommendations?

A: Sounds like Adam suffers from a touch of separation anxiety. He finds it tough to separate from Mom. But don't despair. First, realize that Adam will take his cues from you. If you appear apprehensive about him or about kindergarten, he'll feel insecure also. Therefore, take a bright, optimistic outlook on his new adventure. Second, if Adam will be walking or taking the bus, try to practice the route with him a few times; even bring along a few of his new classmates if you can round them up. Third, check with other mothers to learn something about the first-day "rituals" at Adam's school. If it is customary for mothers to accompany their children, then do so; otherwise, simply plan to give him a positive send-off, a big hug at your front door, and a happy "See you after school!" Be positive and upbeat. Don't mention how much you will miss him while he's at school. Adam could misinterpret such a remark. To him it could be a cue that you really prefer for him to stay home.

For children like Adam, who are potentially "school phobic," it is generally *not* a good idea for mothers to prolong the separation process by walking them to the door of the classroom unless all the other mothers are doing it. And it is not a good idea to volunteer as a teacher's helper during the first week of school either. Such a maneuver usually makes it even tougher on the child (and the mother) to make a clean break.

Finally, if Adam has any difficulty with returning to school on day 2, do whatever you have to do to get him there. If you can get him over the hump of the first few days, you will probably be able to avoid a lot of future hassles.

Kindergarten Flunk Out

Q: I've heard everything now. My brother's little girl, Tanya (aged 5), has just flunked kindergarten. And that's not all. Her parents are all for it. They say she wasn't "ready" to move on to first grade in a prestigious private school. They favor holding her back until her chances are better for the ritzy school.

A: Sounds like Tanya's being redshirted. And if it's merely to improve her chances for a place on the academic fast track, there's something wrong here.

On the other hand, if Tanya's academic or developmental readiness is lagging, then holding her back could certainly be in her best interests.

Educators are increasingly concerned about early school readiness. They know the importance of children getting off to a good start. In Los Angeles, 1712 kindergarteners were flunked in a recent year. In Minneapolis, 200 children were placed in a special repeat year of kindergarten after having failed a basic screening test on numbers, colors, and the alphabet.

What kind of tests was Tanya given? What is the objective data? I hope it's more than just her supposed inability to be accepted to the first grade of her parents' choice.

Music Lessons

Q: Our 5-year-old, Amanda, really seems to have an aptitude for music. My wife and I would like to get her started on learning an instrument, but our friends all say that she's too young. What do you advise?

A: Music teachers generally prefer to wait until the fourth grade before beginning instrumental instruction. Why? Because most children do not have enough strength and fine motor coordination until this time. Their fingers, for example, must be long enough to reach strings or keys, strong enough to press them down, and dexterous enough to move quickly to the next note. There are other reasons as well. Reading music requires a certain level of cognitive skill: the recognition of symbols. And, most importantly, the music student must have enough self-discipline and frustration tolerance to make it through all the squeaky notes and missed beats of early learning. These skills are generally acquired first in the school classroom and in the traditional student-teacher relationship.

Does Amanda, at 5, meet these criteria? If not, you may be well advised to postpone formal lessons and to find other ways of fostering her interest in music (singing, listening, record collecting, etc.) until she's ready for the piano or violin or trumpet. If, on the other hand, Amanda is really pushing you for lessons and you believe there is a reasonably good chance of success, be sure to select a teacher who has skills in relating to children.

Is My Daughter Gifted?

Q: Christy, my 5-year-old, is very bright. I'd like to enroll her in a special program for gifted children. How do I know if she's truly "gifted"?

A: Children are generally considered to be gifted if their IQ is above 130. You could certainly have Christy tested by a psychologist to learn her intelligence quotient.

These IQ tests, however, are only part of the story, in my opinion. Some children test well; others do not. Some children have high IQs but do not have the energy, or the motivation, to use their ability; they are only potentially gifted.

Therefore, in determining whether or not Christy is truly gifted, consider these factors:

1. *Curiosity:* Does Christy exhibit a high level of interest in the world around her? Does she ask questions? Does she seek answers on her own?

2. *Language skills:* Most gifted children have advanced vocabularies. They speak in adult-sounding sentences. They use adverbs. They like word games and are perfectly at home with books.

3. *Logic:* Gifted children tend to grasp ideas and abstract concepts at an early age. For example, they understand the meanings of proverbs, such as "Every cloud contains a silver lining." And they comprehend *similarities*. Ask Christy this question: "Why is

an airplane like an automobile?" Many children would say that they are not alike at all. Most children answer concretely: "They both have wheels." The truly gifted 5-year-old might answer: "They are both means of transportation."

For further information about the gifted child, write to Institute on the Gifted and Talented, 316 West Second Street, Los Angeles, CA 90012.

Miss Manners

Q: My sister-in-law has really done it this time. She's enrolled my 5-year-old niece in an etiquette class. Poor little Debbie. They have her sipping tea and using the correct silverware and all that jazz. Last week when I visited the house, they made her come to the table and demonstrate her good manners. "Show Aunt Mary the soup spoon." It almost made me vomit.

A: This is more of a comment than a question. You obviously have very strong feelings about this matter. While I'm sure you're concerned about Debbie, I also detect some resentment toward your sister. Could Debbie, then, be the pawn in some unresolved competition between the two of you? If so, it's too bad. On the other hand, Debbie's enrollment in an etiquette class at the age of 5 probably does say more about her parents than it does about her. The greatest danger here is that the etiquette class may be just one example of Mom and Dad's need to accomplish "success" through their daughter.

All parents, of course, have aspirations for their children; this is natural and it's fine as long as parents' needs do not conflict with children's needs.

Etiquette class for a 5-year-old? Debbie, I'm sure, would prefer finger paints to finger bowls. She should certainly be taught some good manners at home, but I tend to agree with you that Debbie is being pushed a bit too far. One last note: I have nothing against formal manners and etiquette classes. A better time, though, would be at the age of 9 or 10.

Discord vs. Divorce

Q: My marriage has been very rocky for the past three years. My husband and I are at each other's throat a lot of the time. Many of our spats occur right in front of our children, aged 5 and 9. I know that it's probably not a good idea to stay married "for the sake of the children," but I also know that divorce can be very bad for children too. Please help me. Are children harmed more by a bad marriage or by divorce?

A: Constant exposure to fights between mom and dad obviously injures children in many ways. One of my patients, a 14-year-old, described it to me once as "growing up in a combat zone." There are no noncombatants in these husband-wife wars. Inevitably, the children become targets in the marital cross fire.

Your question has been studied by researchers in London. In a study of 2775 children it was found that ongoing domestic strife produced much more tension and maladjustment in the youngsters than did separation, divorce, or even parental desertion. The major problems included aggression, poor school performance, and depression.

I am not suggesting, however, that divorce should be the solution to your dilemma. If there is any chance of working things out with your husband, all of you would be better off for it. If he'll agree to marital therapy, great. Otherwise try therapy on your own, and use it to help you examine the situation and plan thoughtfully for the future.

Divorce: How to Tell the Children?

Q: It's all over. My husband and I are getting divorced after eight years of marriage. I accept it, and, in fact, I know it's best for the both of us. My biggest worry is my children: Wendy (aged 5) and Jason (aged 8). How should I break the news to them?

A: Let's clear up a few things first. As bad as things may be in the marriage and in spite of the fact that you and your husband are divorcing each other, neither of you is divorcing Wendy and Jason. They are not only *your* children but *his* children too.

If you keep this fact in mind, the question of how *you* should

break the news becomes moot. Both of you should break the news—
together.

Boys Injured More by Divorce?

Q: I have been separated from my husband for over a year, and
we will soon be divorced. I have a daughter, aged $5\frac{1}{2}$, and a son,
aged 7. I'm worried about both of the children, but I've been told
by friends that boys are usually harmed more by divorce than girls.
Is this true? What can I do about it?

A: Most research in child psychiatry has tended to suggest that boys
have more problems following divorce than do girls. These problems range all the way from problems on the "inside" (headaches,
peptic ulcers, etc.) to problems on the "outside" (fighting, vandal-
ism, running away, etc.).

Why is this so? Some researchers believe that boys are more
vulnerable psychologically than girls, that they are inherently more
susceptible to emotional trauma of this sort. I do not see any hard
evidence for this. Instead, it may be related to the fact that children of divorce tend to live with their mothers and that boys, particularly in the early developmental years, are apt to suffer more
through loss of their male identification model, their father.

Such reactions, of course, are highly individualized and depend
on a number of factors including:

1. The age of the child

2. The quality of the father-son relationship

3. The postdivorce relationship of father and son

4. The extent to which mom is able to fill the gap, not as a "substitute father" but as a loving, reliable parent

Psychiatrists and Child Custody

Q: My husband and I are in the midst of a divorce and a custody
fight over our 5-year-old daughter. My lawyer wants me to consult

with a child psychiatrist in hopes that he will take my side in court. What should I do?

A: I appreciate your concern. Unfortunately, there are probably some conflicting strategies in this situation.

Your attorney will take an adversary role. He will do all in his power to build a case for you. Most psychiatrists, on the other hand, prefer not to be drawn into an adversary conflict but rather to evaluate the custody matter in the best interests of the child. Therefore, the psychiatrist generally prefers to consult directly to the court and to evaluate all three sides of the equation objectively: mother, father—and child. This is only possible, however, if both you and your husband agree to it.

If the psychiatrist sees only yourself and your daughter, the best she or he can say is that you are a fit mother and that the relationship is strong and healthy. Since he hasn't examined your husband, he really cannot make substantive comments about him as a father.

What should you do? Work closely with your lawyer. Follow his advice. See the psychiatrist, but view her or him as a colleague, not someone whose role will be limited to building your legal case. For example, you can ask for advice on how to help your daughter through this difficult time. You can ask about yourself too.

Summer Separation

Q: I am a divorced mother. My former husband recently moved out of the area. Therefore, this is the first summer that the children will be away from me; they'll be visiting their father for two weeks at the end of August. I have two children: Belinda, aged 5, and Eddie, aged 8. I'm especially worried about my daughter. She's so close to me. What can I do to make the trip easier for her?

A: A nice chat with Belinda would be the logical first step. How does she feel about visiting her father? How does she feel about leaving you behind? Listen to her feelings but also respond to any factual information that she may need. Some 5-year-olds, for example, may fear abandonment. If this is the case with Belinda, you can reassure her of your love, that you'll miss her, and that you'll be waiting for her return. And don't forget Eddie.

It helps to give children some "practice" at being away. If Belinda has never slept away from home, try arranging some overnight visits to family and friends.

Most children also find it comforting to take some familiar toys and objects along on the trip—including a picture of Mom. Telephone calls or perhaps some tape-recorded messages can also help plug the loneliness gap. But don't overdo it. Too much concern may telegraph fear or doubt on your part.

Which leads me to the last point. How do *you* feel about the children going off for the visit? Separation can be painful for mothers too. Be sure to plan some fun for yourself while the youngsters are away.

Christmas Visitation

Q: I have been divorced for two years. Under our custody agreement Larry, my $5\frac{1}{2}$-year-old, spends every other Christmas with his father. This is his year to stay with me for the holidays—but he's insisting on visiting his Dad; I guess he had a great time last year. Should I let him go?

A: No. You'd probably be setting a dangerous precedent. Larry must learn to live by the rules. I take it that you are the custodial parent. Larry must learn just what this means. It's in his best interest.

Why does Larry want to visit his Dad? Listen to him. Help him express himself—but do not change the rules for him.

What to Call New Stepfather?

Q: I have three children (aged 5, 8, and 9) from a previous marriage. I'm getting married soon to a man who has no children of his own. He says he wants the kids to call him "Daddy." I'm worried. I want him to feel like a father to the children, but I think they'll resent him if he insists on "Daddy." Besides, they *have* a father. Advice please.

A: Stick to your intuition. Your children can only have one father in their lives. But there *is* room for a stepfather. I generally do not recommend that stepfathers be called *Daddy*, *Dad*, or anything paternal. It can cause resentment not only from the children—but from their real Daddy as well.

Sounds like you'll have to be gentle with your husband-to-be. Help him find his niche in his new family. That, after all, is what this issue is all about.

Rejection of Stepmother?

Q: I'm 28. Last year I married a 35-year-old widower with two children, aged 6 and $7\frac{1}{2}$. I should have known something was wrong right from our very first date when the kids unfavorably compared my clothes to their mother's, but I thought I could win them over with a lot of patient understanding and love. Well, it isn't working. The children, one girl and one boy, simply don't listen to me; they avoid me. My husband tries to help, but he's frustrated too. I feel like an organ that's been transplanted into his family and that's being rejected. What can I do?

A: The role of stepmother, whether due to divorce or death, is always tough. Why? You are a constant reminder to the children of what used to be and is no more. Stepchildren are created from loss; they hurt; they're often resentful. But what can they do with those feelings? Too often they dump them onto the handiest target they can find: the stepmother. Now let's look at your side of the equation. Did you view yourself as something of a savior to these motherless children? If so, I can understand your sentiments. They're noble—but they're unrealistic. In fact, unrealistic expectations doom more stepparents than any other factor. I suggest you reassess your role. Expect some resentment. Don't expect automatic love. You'll have to earn it the hard way. The key is your husband. He's got to make your marriage his number one priority. Most second marriages, according to a recent survey, fail because of problems with stepchildren. Take action now. If you and your husband need help, don't delay a visit to a marriage or family counselor.

The Mutual Child

Q: We have a "his and hers" family. My husband has one child (aged 10) from his first marriage, and I have two children (aged 5 and 7) from my first marriage. Our little stepfamily is doing just fine. But we're about to become a "his, hers, and ours" family. I'm four months pregnant. Jack and I are thrilled. Maybe too thrilled. I'm afraid we're going to pour so much love into *our* child that we may neglect the other children. Any ideas?

A: You are about to have what is sometimes called a *mutual* child. And I salute your sensitivity. The mutual child is often projected as the symbol of a second marriage. He may become larger than life because he represents all the hopes and aspirations of the remarried couple. At worst the mutual child may become something of a "mascot."

You are also correct in being concerned about the other children. Your mutual child may threaten to displace them in a way that neither family of siblings threatened each other. After all, the baby will be the only "complete" child of the new union, and the other children, you can be sure, are acutely aware of this fact.

What to do? First talk things over with the children. Let them voice their fears. Reassure them of your love. It also helps to involve them in the plans for the new arrival. Try to avoid jealousy but realize that you can certainly expect some garden variety sibling rivalry. Finally, beware of the trap of making the baby a mascot. Treat him fairly but not preciously.

Traveling Mom

Q: We have three children: aged 5, $6\frac{1}{2}$, and $9\frac{1}{2}$. I've just taken a new job that will require me to travel from time to time. I've explained it to the kids, and they seem to accept it; actually they're happy about my career advancement. Do you have any tips that will help take the sting out of my absences?

A: Try these guidelines:

1. *You miss them:* This is elementary, but it's easy to overlook when youngsters apparently accept your traveling. Let the children know you'll miss them. Don't get dramatic about it, but do express your feelings. This will be the cue to the kids that they can share their feelings with you too.

2. *Announce in advance:* Your children are old enough to be told a few days in advance of your travel plans. Don't spring surprises.

3. *Keep them posted:* Leave a written summary of your itinerary, with phone numbers, and post it in an obvious place like on the refrigerator door. This is a concrete reminder and organizer for the youngsters.

4. *Take them along:* If it's at all possible, I suggest you take the youngsters on one of your business trips. It will relieve their anxiety. In the future they'll be able to picture what you'll be doing. It gives you a clearer psychological presence in their minds while you're away.

5. *Easy does it on return:* Some traveling parents tend to overreact with gifts and other offerings on their return. Not a good idea. Instead, try to communicate through your actions that the family is still your top priority. One tip here: Don't return so harried and frazzled that you just want to go right to bed. Remember, the children expect some special time with you. Bon voyage!

Leave the Pressure at Work?

Q: I have two children, aged 5 and 8. I went back to work about four months ago. I enjoy it even if it is pressured. Up until now I've believed that I've been able to leave the pressure back on the job, at the travel agency. But my husband says the kids are suffering. He says that Ronnie (aged 5) is getting more sore throats and colds and that Elizabeth (aged 8) is falling behind in school. "What's this got to do with my job?" I ask. My husband says, "Everything." I love my kids. I love my work. What should I do?

A: Before you conclude that your job is bad for your children, stop and examine all the issues. Start with your husband. Does he have an ax to grind? How did he feel about your going back to work in the first place? I wonder if he's digging up convenient data to fit his foregone conclusion: Mom, quit your job.

Obviously you need your husband's support, not his sabotage. Talk it over.

Then be honest with yourself. Are the children suffering? Most parents, by the way, are not aware of how many pressures they actually bring home from the workplace and of how these pressures affect their children. A recent Yale University study documented this phenomenon and found that 70 percent of all the parents interviewed didn't think their jobs hurt their children. But what did the kids say? They disagreed. They were very much aware of the job-related tensions, and it made them tense too.

So think it over. Identify the roots of the problem. Then plan a frontal attack. I'm not suggesting that you quit the travel agency; that may or may not solve your problems. And, besides, there are many solutions open to you short of quitting.

Growing Up on TV

Q: Our two children (aged 5 and 7) would spend most of their waking hours in front of the television if we allowed it. My husband and I are starting to worry. How much TV should children be allowed to watch?

A: Recent national surveys reveal that most American children are hooked on TV by the age of 3 or 4. In fact, children watch an average of almost twenty-five hours of television every week. This equals about 1300 hours in front of the tube per year—which is more time than kids spend in school!

While there are a number of valuable and educational programs and while television can be a very positive force in the lives of children, three or four hours per day (as suggested by the surveys) is excessive.

Parents, of course, must be concerned not only with how much TV is being viewed by their youngsters but also with what types of programs are being viewed.

What is the possible negative effect of television on child development? There is some evidence that aggression depicted on television can make children prone to violence. Just as important, however, is the fact that too much TV can lead to lethargy, passivity, boredom, and social withdrawal. These "indirect" effects can be crippling over a period of years. Children who glue themselves to the television screen are missing out on developmental opportunities. There is less interaction with people. Social skills are not acquired. Creativity can be blunted.

I would suggest a two-pronged approach. First, make a list of those programs that you will allow the children to watch. Second, I would suggest a basic limit of one hour per day with some flexibility to allow for movies or specials or sporting events.

Finally, it is wise to remember that most children really prefer the company of their parents to the flickering images on the screen. Kids often turn to television out of boredom or loneliness. Examine your family's lifestyle. Are the children getting enough of the real-life "Mom and Dad Show"?

Does TV Cause Nightmares?

Q: My sister-in-law has a 5-year-old son, Marcus. A few months ago she told me that he was having a lot of nightmares. Well, last week I baby-sat for him, and now I know why: too much TV violence. He watches all those monster movies and shoot-'em-ups. No wonder he has nightmares, right?

A: The negative effect of TV violence on child behavior is pretty well established, but it would not be precisely correct to say that TV "causes" nightmares. Dreaming is a physical and psychological phenomenon that exists independently of our daily experiences but is affected by them. The meaning of dreams is determined by our basic needs and conflicts. The dream expresses an unconscious wish or a method of solving a problem. The dream content, however, is always disguised; dreams are full of symbols; nothing is what it appears to be on the surface.

This is where TV violence comes in for Marcus and other children. Our basic dream themes are colored by significant events of the day. Therefore, if you see a lot of monster movies, it may be more likely that monsters will appear in your dreams—but the underlying meaning of the dreams can only be unlocked by careful analysis.

He Won't Fight Back

Q: Thomas is 5 years old. He's smart, loving, and beautiful. The only trouble is that he lets other kids pick on him all the time. He just stands there and takes it. He won't fight back. My husband and I are frustrated. We've even told him that he'll have to answer to *us* unless he starts standing up for his own rights. What else can we do?

A: Hold it! You're going to punish Thomas for allowing himself to be punished? That's a new kind of double jeopardy in my book. Not a good idea.

Children can be vicious. Yes, they tend to pick on someone who's a soft target and that may be what Thomas is. But there may be more wisdom and savvy in his passive resistance than meets the eye. I suggest you get more information. Observe Thomas in some of these incidents, if you can. Talk to his teacher. You seem to assume active retaliation is the answer. It may not be. Some youngsters learn to win over their tormentors rather than beating them at their own game. Help Thomas feel good about himself. Help him explore new ways of coping with his peers—ways that work for him. But don't punish him for *not* fighting. He's got enough enemies on his hands.

Grandma's Snack Attack

Q: Following my divorce three months ago, I moved back into my mother's home with my daughter, Carolyn (aged 5). My mother, who is very overweight, is continually stuffing Carolyn with snacks. She did it to me, too, when I was a little girl, but I was able to break the habit when I became a teenager. But it took a lot of pain and effort, believe me.

I've tried to get Grandma to stop. She won't. I've tried to get Carolyn to stop. She can't. What should I do?

A: Grandma's snack attack is obviously a way of life for her. The danger for Carolyn is both physical and psychological. If she becomes obese, her physical health, attractiveness, and self-esteem could be damaged.

You've tried to resolve the problem at its source, but you haven't had much luck. So let's take another tack. Sometimes the act of eating can substitute for missing emotional nourishment. You've been recently divorced. How is Carolyn handling it? If she's having trouble with it, she may be more vulnerable to Grandma's enticements and less responsive to your own discipline.

Focus, therefore, on Carolyn's feelings. Listen to her. Talk to her. Feed her emotionally. If that's the "food" she really needs, she'll be able to resist all those sweets and snacks.

Superstitions

Q: We have two children, aged 5 and 11. Marti, the youngest, is much more superstitious than her older brother. Is this because of the age difference or the sex difference? My girlfriend says that females are more superstitious than males. I don't believe it. We have a bet.

A: I know of no hard data suggesting that girls are more superstitious than boys. There is plenty of clinical and developmental evidence, on the other hand, that younger children tend to be more superstitious than older children. Why? The phenomenon of superstition is much closer to the magical thinking of the 3-, 4-, and 5-year-old. For these children the boundary between fantasy and the real world is often blurred. They also perceive their own thoughts as omnipotent: "If I can think it—it must be so."

Superstitions are irrational beliefs that we sometimes invoke to explain the unexplainable. Your son, at age 11, is able to explain more of the world in rational terms and, therefore, has less need to lean on magic and superstitions to bring order to his world.

Looks like you'll collect on your bet. Congratulations.

Telling Him That Grandpa Died

Q: How do I tell my 5-year-old son that his grandfather has died? I've tried to explain that Grandpa is in heaven, but Robbie insists that Grandpa is still in the hospital and will be coming home soon. It hurts. How do I gently make him understand?

A: Robbie *wishes* that Grandpa were still alive. He is using a common defense mechanism called *denial.* I applaud you for being so sensitive and for not immediately ripping Robbie's defense away from him. Children, like adults, must go through some distinct stages of mourning.

You can gently assist him through this mourning process by first acknowledging that, while Grandpa has indeed died and gone to heaven, Robbie wishes Grandpa were still here with him and the family. You wish it too, I'm sure. Do not hesitate to let your own feelings show. Encourage Robbie to express his own special feelings.

As a 5-year-old, Robbie's concept of the finality of death is limited. You might help him by reminding him about the death of a pet if there is such an event in his experience. Talking about the pet's death will allow Robbie, metaphorically, to begin working through the loss of his grandfather.

A book that sometimes helps youngsters understand death is Marjorie Rawlings's *The Yearling,* a story about a boy and his pet deer. The novel stresses the wisdom of allowing a child to share in the family's grief.

Some things to avoid:

1. Do not equate death with sleep; some children have been known to develop a fear of falling asleep.

2. Do not make up magical stories about what happened.

3. Do not force Robbie to attend the funeral.

4. Do not crush him with clinical details.

5. Do not become alarmed if Robbie expresses anger or resentment.

6. Do not become alarmed if your son regresses to some earlier behaviors for a short period.

This is a difficult time for you too. Be sure that there is someone in whom *you* can confide.

Our 5-Year-Old Wants to Die

Q: Our 5-year-old son, Alexander, has been scaring the life out of us lately. He keeps repeating that he "wants to die." What should we do? We try to pass it off and ignore it. Is this right? He seems to be doing okay in everything else. He seems happy. What should we do?

A: I appreciate your anxiety and your confusion. At age 5, Alexander is really too young to have an adultlike understanding of death, and, besides, he appears to be developing normally. Yet he's talking suicide, and as a parent, you fear that you should not take this lightly.

Although the National Office of Vital Statistics does not document suicide trends for children under 10 years of age, child psychiatrists know that suicide threats and actual attempts among children are not rare. Again, you are wise to be concerned.

What does Alexander mean by wanting to die? I suggest that you ask him directly. Most 5-year-olds, for example, have only a fantasized notion of death. They see it as temporary—like someone taking a trip and coming back home. You might use some family examples to teach him about the permanence, the pain, and the sorrow of death.

Careful though. My second question is, What is Alexander's goal in repeating this childish death wish? Is he after attention? Is he trying to injure you or your husband? Is he simply wishing to join a pet who has died—as in the case of a 6-year-old boy I recently interviewed.

Another important question: Is there any history of suicide in your family? Studies show that suicidal youths have a strong family history of suicide. And beware of accidents, the leading cause of death among children; many are camouflaged self-destructive acts.

I would urge you to reexamine Alexander's life. Is he *really* doing okay? Maybe he is by your standards, but how does *he* feel about it? In other words, assess not only his physical health, his behavior, and his mood but also his self-esteem. How does Alexander feel, deep down, about himself? It is amazing what even 5-year-olds can reveal about themselves if they are given the chance.

If you can give Alexander a clean bill of health after this informal assessment, you probably don't have anything to worry about. You'll be able to relax. Continue to listen to him, though, and to observe his development closely, but do not fuel his seeming preoccupation with death by dwelling upon it yourself. If you are left with any lingering doubts, a one-time consultation with a child psychiatrist or pediatrician may be all it takes to put you at ease.

Childhood Obesity

Q: Our pediatrician told us that Bruce, our 6-year-old, is obese. We've known that he's a little overweight, but we didn't think much about it. We figured he'd "grow" out of it. What's all the fuss?

A: Bruce's pediatrician was probably using a technical definition of overweight. The medical definition of *obesity* is 20 percent or more above the normal weight for age, height, and sex.

What's all the fuss? First of all, many children do not grow out of it. There is a marked tendency for obese children to grow into obese teenagers. And we know that 60 to 80 percent of obese teenagers will grow into obese adults.

What's all the fuss? Even moderate obesity is hazardous to your health. For example, 20 percent obesity increases mortality by 25 percent; 40 percent obesity increases it by 50 percent.

What's all the fuss? Bruce's health and his self-esteem are at stake. He needs a sensible and sensitive diet and exercise program.

Ulcers in Children?

Q: I'm shocked. I've just been told that our 5-year-old daughter, Katherine, has a peptic ulcer. I thought only adults got ulcers because they worry too much. I've always thought that Katherine was such a happy child. Should she see a child psychiatrist?

A: Not necessarily. Your pediatrician should be consulted on that question.

Peptic ulcers, by the way, are not so rare in children. The prevalence is almost 2 percent in childhood. In youngsters under the age of 6, like Katherine, the most common symptoms are vague abdominal pain and vomiting. Bleeding occurs in about a third of the cases.

Katherine's pediatrician probably made the diagnosis through a careful history, physical exam, and laboratory tests. The most common x-ray procedure in these cases is the "upper GI," a series of stomach and duodenal x-rays taken after a liquid barium compound is swallowed; this test detects about 50 to 75 percent of ulcers that may be present. Sometimes a specialist may be consulted to perform an *endoscopy,* a direct look at the stomach lining by placing a long tube down the throat and esophagus.

I'm listing these procedures because I know that Katherine, for a 5-year-old, has been through a lot. Be sure to listen to her fears. Reassure her.

The causes of peptic ulcer are multiple. The culprit is too much acid in the duodenum, the first section of the small intestine. Sometimes stress or unhappiness contributes, sometimes not. So don't rush her to a child psychiatrist without first checking with her primary physician, her pediatrician.

Hide Cancer from Him?

Q: My son has cancer. Jimmy, our beautiful 5-year-old, has cancer. He has one year to live. The doctors told us last night. My husband and I are crushed, but Jimmy doesn't know. My friends and my husband say not to tell him right away, but I think he ought to know. After all, he's going to find out anyway, right?

A: Right, but I don't recommend "telling" him now. There's time—maybe even more than the year you describe; after all, cancer survival rates are statistical projections. It's very tough to predict actual survival in a specific case.

As a 5-year-old, Jimmy's concept of illness and death is very limited. He's still a child of the moment; if he hurts *now,* that's what matters to him; if he feels okay, any discussion of future suffering will go right over his head.

Let Jimmy grow naturally into an awareness that he's seriously ill. Steer a middle course. On the one hand, you shouldn't clobber him with the facts, but neither should you pretend there's nothing wrong. Be available to him. Answer his questions when he asks them. Let him know you're prepared to face the grim facts with him—when he's ready.

I've seen some parents be a bit too eager to confront their cancer-stricken children with the "truth." You may be one of them. Why? If you must share the burden, share it with your husband and your friends. If you're worried that your sadness and your tears will give you away, don't worry. Let your feelings show. Jimmy will pick them up anyway. But lead him gently to the facts; he'll have to grow into them.

Children and Surgery

Q: Our 5-year-old son is scheduled for a tonsillectomy. How much should we prepare him for the operation?

A: A number of hospitals around the country have special prehospitalization programs for youngsters and parents. Specially trained nurses guide the families through the facility, answer questions, and familiarize the children with the hospital routine. Such programs are marvelous because they make the child less anxious and more cooperative.

When I was in family practice, before going into child psychiatry, I used to "play surgery" with such youngsters in my office. I'd let them use my stethoscope and other nonthreatening equipment as they played doctor by operating on the office teddy bear! The emotional aspects of the drama were even more important than familiarizing them with the technical items. For example, we'd discuss that "Teddy must be scared. After all, this is his first operation and Momma Bear can't come in here to the operating room with him." Most kids would coo reassurance to Teddy and even hug him—just as they would wish to be treated by their own surgeon.

If your hospital does not have a formal program, consult with your pediatrician or your boy's surgeon. You might even wish to "play surgery" yourself. It can be wonderfully empathic—and fun!

Missing Children

Q: I want to help my sister, but I don't know what to do. A year ago her 5-year-old daughter, Tina, went out to walk the dog and has never returned. My sister's life has been destroyed. She spends all her spare time searching for Tina. She'll even stop the car in the middle of the road if she sees a little girl who looks like Tina. Although all of us in the family have been devastated by Tina's disappearance, everyone except my sister has been able to get on with life. What can I do to help?

A: The anguish of a parent for a missing child is excruciating. One such mother told me, "Sometimes I think it would be better if she had died in an accident or something. At least I would know what happened to her." The pain of uncertainty, of not knowing, is a heavy cross to bear. The worry over what might have happened lurks just beneath the surface of a mother's daily thoughts. The frustration of not being able to do anything about it is agonizing.

Each year about 50,000 to 100,000 children leave home and are not heard from again. Some, of course, are snatched by a divorced noncustodial parent. Many others are simply stolen.

Until recently there was absolutely nowhere for parents to turn. Two organizations, however, have been formed to provide advice and support. They are Child Find, Inc., Box 277, New Paltz, NY 12561 (800-431-5005) and SEARCH, 560 Sylvan Ave., Englewood Cliffs, NJ 07632 (201-567-4040).

Put your sister in touch with these groups. Continue to comfort her. Encourage her to get back into the mainstream of life. If she cannot work out her grief process with this kind of support, I would definitely advise a consultation with a psychiatrist.

Phony Sex Abuse Charge

Q: I didn't believe it when I heard about it. And now the judge's verdict is in: My brother has been cleared of sexual abuse charges that were brought by Marcella, his former wife. She claimed that he had molested their 5-year-old daughter, Lori. I thought from the beginning that Marcella was just trying to eliminate my brother's visitation rights. But how could she be so cruel? And even though he has been cleared of all charges, won't this damage his relationship with Lori—who is certainly aware of the court proceedings and is now "afraid" of her father.

A: What a tragedy. Yes, Lori could be damaged, and your brother, though innocent, could obviously be damaged too.

I'm aware of other such cases. And I'm afraid we're going to see still more. Why? Child sexual abuse is in the news. Disgruntled ex-spouses (and older children too) have a new weapon: charges or threatened charges of sexual abuse as a means of "getting back." And who ultimately suffers most? The children involved. They are bewildered, caught in a vicious web of deceit. They're trapped. Whom can they trust? They're asked to take sides with one parent against the other. The stakes are high, the consequences grim.

In one case like the one you describe, the judge has threatened to take custody away from a mother who brought phony charges against her ex-husband. In your case I suggest that your brother consult with a child psychiatrist about how to reestablish trust with Lori. Perhaps a few sessions for Lori and Dad together would also help.

Italian vs. Irish

Q: I'm Italian, my wife is Irish, and we're both proud of our heritage. But we've got a problem. Our $5\frac{1}{2}$-year-old daughter, Christina, insists that she's 100 percent Italian. She's always after me to teach her words and phrases. Her favorite food is pasta and pizza. She even keeps an Italian flag in her room. My wife thought it was cute at first, but now she's getting offended; she says I'm trying to "outinfluence" her with Christina. Believe me, it's not my fault. Please help. *Mille grazie.*

A: *Prego.*

What might look like an international incident of sorts on the surface is probably just a case of individual psychology. Christina's preference for things Italiano symbolizes her relative preference for you over her mother at this point in her psychological development. Her identification with Italy over Ireland symbolizes her attraction to you and her competition with Mom. But don't worry, she'll get over it. Her psychological task, in a sense, will be to merge the flags of her parentage into a single identity; she should be able to combine the best of both worlds—traits and values from Dad and Mom; Italy *and* Ireland. But be careful. Be sensitive to your wife's concern. Examine your behavior. Are you, even unwittingly, encouraging Christina's Italian style? The pasta and pizza I can understand, but where did she get the flag?

Yes, you've got a problem, but I'm pleased, by the way, that you and your wife are proud of your nationalities and that you want to pass these values on to your daughter. Christina will be enriched. *Erin go bragh; viva Italia; hurrah U.S.A.!*

A Halloween Monster?

Q: Our 5-year-old son is preoccupied with monsters. He's always asking if they're real, and he's been having nightmares about them. Now he absolutely insists on dressing up like a "monster" for Halloween. Sounds unhealthy. Agree?

A: No. It sounds to me like your son is actually trying to make monsters less frightening by making them more familiar. In more technical terms he is utilizing a common childhood mechanism of defense: identification with the aggressor. If he himself can play at being a monster, those feared creatures must be real cream puffs.

This type of behavior, within limits, is actually in the service of his healthy growth and development. It is analogous to the adult who deliberately confronts a fear (such as flying) in order to overcome it.

I would only become concerned if your son continues to identify as a monster and truly demonstrates "monstrous" behavior in his real life such as by engaging in aggressive acts toward other children. But, for now, let's assume he's trying his best to turn the tricky monsters of his unconscious world into real-life treats!

Letters to Santa

Q: Here we go again, those horrible letters to Santa Claus. My wife and I are both fed up with the long laundry lists of gifts that our children (aged 5, 7, and 8) demand each year. You'd think that Santa runs a mail-order house. We'd like to forbid any letters to the North Pole this year. Would this be harmful to our children?

A: I agree that too many letters to Santa Claus look more like a series of bargaining demands than a child's dream list. This attitude flows from the general commercialization of Christmas.

The problem, though, isn't the concept of those letters to the North Pole, but, rather, what's happened to them in some families. Where the emphasis is on getting rather than giving, or consuming rather than celebrating a religious holiday, the result is one of those laundry lists.

Why not encourage the children to ask for some "spiritual" gifts (family health, happiness, peace, etc.) along with the video games and dolls? It would also help if you put the emphasis on giving rather than getting. You might tell the children that Santa Claus, as the spirit of Christmas, prefers youngsters who plan to give—and only hope to get.

Explain Punishment?

Q: My husband prides himself on being a reasonable man. But I think he carries it too far. For example, every time he disciplines the children (aged 6 and 7), he explains to them, in great detail, just why he's doing it.

I wouldn't be opposed to his technique if it was really beneficial, but it's not. They don't usually care why they're being punished; they just want their father to change his mind, and—this is the worst part—sometimes he does. He "listens to their point of view" and sometimes agrees that he was off base in the first place.

Any comments?

A: Explaining punishment, in principle, is a good thing, but not if it erodes a parent's ability to discipline the children. As you describe the situation, I'm afraid your husband's reasonableness is getting him into trouble. The children may be misinterpreting it for uncertainty and softness. Being children, they will try to take advantage and to avoid punishment.

In general, a parent shouldn't announce a punishment unless he or she fully intends to follow through on it. Once you've made up your mind, go for it. Yes, you may, on occasion, find that you erred...that your punishment was too strict or not strict enough... but no one's perfect. The best policy is to learn from your mistakes and vow to do better next time.

Should you admit these mistakes to the children? Only in rare circumstances where an important principle or family value is at stake. The best "apologizing" you can do for your mistakes is to improve your disciplinary skills for the next time—and there *will* be a next time.

God Will Punish You

Q: My husband and I are deeply religious. We feel a great responsibility to raise our children, aged 6 and 9, to be religious too. But sometimes I'm afraid my husband overdoes it. For example, he's always threatening the children that if they don't obey him, God will punish them. I fear that the children will get turned off to God and our beliefs by this tough approach. Am I right?

A: Putting the fear of the Lord into children can backfire. While religion can and should be a powerful force in family life, it is sometimes used against children. How? When a parent threatens a child that God will punish him if he doesn't pick up his clothes, do his homework, take out the trash, etc., this not only trivializes religious beliefs, but the parent is himself revealed as a powerless figure. It is as though he says: "Here, God, I give up. You take care of it." The result? Children may experience the parent as impotent and God as vengeful. Not a healthy combination.

How to Criticize

Q: When it comes to praising my 6-year-old son, Thomas, I do a pretty good job. When it comes to criticizing him, however, I'm a flop. I tend to overreact, to get angry, and to attack him verbally. What I intend, initially, as constructive for him ends up with his tears and my frustration. Any advice?

A: Praise and criticism are really two sides of the same coin. If you can successfully praise your son, you should be able to effectively criticize him too. And, let's face it, youngsters do need to learn how to accept reasonable criticism.

Begin by reviewing your success in the praise department. What makes it work? Apply some of those principles to your criticism of Thomas. Then try these additional tips:

1. *Don't personalize it:* When Thomas misbehaves, be sure that you limit your criticism to the specific act itself; do not attack his total personality. For example, if he doesn't keep his room clean, let him know that you do not appreciate this behavior but do not call him "sloppy" or "lazy." Name-calling is never constructive.

2. *Leave him an escape hatch:* Criticism for the sake of criticism is shortsighted. It stings but does not allow a child to learn from his mistakes. Next time you must criticize Thomas, give him a chance to come up with a plan to improve himself. Better that he comes up with solutions himself.

3. *Preserve love:* Some criticism can be sandwiched between genuine praise and cushioned in words of warmth and love; for example, "Thomas, you know that we love you, but your tantrums toward Grandpa cannot be tolerated. What can you do to improve?"

4. *Anger is okay:* If Thomas's misbehavior angers you, it's okay to admit it. In fact, denying anger when you are obviously angry will only confuse him. Anger is a natural human emotion. So admit it but keep "ownership" of it yourself. Get angry at Thomas's specific misbehavior but not at Thomas as a person.

Blow Off Steam?

Q: I'm a shy, quiet person. My husband, Rudy, is very expressive. We get along fine, but we disagree on one thing. Rudy says we should encourage our children, aged 6 and 9, to "blow off steam," to "let it all hang out" when they're angry about something. I say that it only raises the noise level around the house, that it doesn't benefit anyone. What do you say?

A: Generally speaking, child psychiatrists are in favor of youngsters being able to express their feelings in words.

Why? The active repression of feelings requires a lot of psychological energy. Children who repress tend to be like tightly sealed pressure cookers; something's got to give sometime. These youngsters tend to wear their problems on the inside; that is, they may develop physical symptoms if they cannot vent their feelings appropriately.

Appropriately. That's the key. I'm not in favor of more noise— if that's the only result. And I'm not in favor of angry outbursts that take the form of verbal abuse or that leave another person (such as you, perhaps) feeling uneasy and tense. Studies of couples, for example, suggest that husbands and wives tend to feel *more* angry, not less, after shouting at each other.

Also keep in mind that children must be taught that expressing anger may work in some situations but not in others. It's a good lesson for life.

So the basic question that should be asked is, How can I express myself to this particular person, in this situation, so that he or she will understand that I'm angry but will be able to respond in a useful way to me without feeling defensive or angry in return?

I think both you *and* Rudy have something to teach the children about the expression of anger.

Love Letters

Q: Is it a problem? Our 6-year-old, Annie, is constantly writing love letters to everyone in the family. At first it was cute, but now I'm a little worried. It's become an obsession. She spends hours at it. Even in school, she'll rush to complete her work so she can write her letters. And she throws a fit if any of us dare discard any of her notes into the trash. Is it a phase? Is it a problem?

A: It may be a little of both. Annie may feel an unconscious need to reassure herself that she loves everyone as a defense against some competitive feelings toward you or another family member. She then looks to your appreciative response that she is indeed lovable and that her underlying conflicts (which are probably normal developmental conflicts) can be contained and conquered. On the other hand, she may be a very insecure girl who seeks constant reassurance that you love her just as she loves you.

Her letter writing has also taken on the tone of a ritual. I bet, for example, that she also throws a "fit" if you attempt to interrupt or stop her from writing a letter.

Is it a problem? Hard to say without more information. I suggest you look to the bottom line. Consider Annie's overall behavior, attitude, physical health, maturity, school performance, friends, family relationships, and any other symptoms. If her love letters are the only concern, you don't have to worry; gently discourage them and reassure her of your love in other ways. If the letters are one symptom among others, I'd suggest a consultation with a child psychiatrist.

Attention Deficit Disorder

Q: We've suspected that Roger, our 6-year-old, is hyperactive so we took him to his pediatrician for a checkup. The doctor thinks that Roger may have "attention deficit disorder." We've been referred to a child psychiatrist, but we'd like to know more about it.

A: *Attention deficit disorder* (ADD) is a relatively new diagnostic category. In addition to hyperactivity, it includes two other major symptoms: inattention and impulsivity.

The symptoms of inattention include:

1. Often fails to finish things he starts

2. Often doesn't seem to listen

3. Is easily distracted

4. Has difficulty concentrating on work

5. Has difficulty sticking to a play activity

If Roger exhibits three or more of these symptoms on a regular basis, he may, indeed, be inattentive.

The symptoms of impulsivity include:

1. Often acts before he thinks

2. Shifts excessively from one activity to another

3. Has difficulty organizing work

4. Needs a lot of supervision

5. Often calls out in class

6. Has difficulty awaiting his turn in play

Three or more of these symptoms, again on a regular basis, may qualify Roger as impulsive.

I suggest you quietly observe your son for these symptoms and report the results to the psychiatrist. He or she will need good data to arrive at an accurate diagnosis and, more importantly, to design a good treatment plan for Roger.

Causes of Hyperactivity

Q: Our 6-year-old, Harvey, is hyperactive. I've read a lot about this disorder, and I realize that no one really knows the cause of hyperactivity for sure. But I wonder. I had toxemia during Harvey's pregnancy. Could that have caused it?

A: As you say, no one knows for sure what causes hyperactivity. We do know, however, that children with *attention deficit disorder* (ADD), which is the new name for hyperactivity, frequently have suggestive medical histories. A recent study, for example, substantiates this conclusion. Researchers at the University of California at Berkeley studied 5000 ADD youngsters over a period of ten years and compared their early histories to a nonhyperactive control group. Here are the factors that were found more frequently among the ADD group:

1. *Pregnancy:* Poor maternal health during pregnancy, toxemia, eclampsia, maternal age below 20

2. *Delivery:* Fetal distress, postmature fetus (born late)

3. *Medical:* Congenital anomalies, health problems during infancy

4. *Developmental:* Crawling late, delayed bowel training, and delayed speech

A word of caution: These early problems should be considered risk factors, not causes. Since you experienced toxemia, for example, we can conclude that Harvey, on a probability basis, was more *at risk* for ADD, but we can't say, with absolute certainty, that the toxemia caused his hyperactivity. This is an important distinction. First of all, there's no reason for you to feel guilty. Second, let's remember that many youngsters born with one or more of these risk factors never develop the symptoms of ADD (distractibility, hyperactivity, learning disabilities, etc.). So let's focus on Harvey's special needs: medical, emotional, social, and academic. There's plenty of help available. Make sure he gets what he needs.

Hyperactivity and Medication

Q: Our 6-year-old son has just been diagnosed as "hyperactive." We have been told that he will require medication. We are concerned about side effects and the possibility of his becoming hooked on a drug at such an early age.

A: Proper medication prescribed under the watchful eye of your physician could do wonders for your son. Nevertheless, I do appreciate your concern. The medications commonly used for hyperactivity, as with virtually all medications, do carry some risk of side effects.

Many youngsters complain of diminished appetite and difficulty with sleeping, especially in the first few weeks. Fortunately, these symptoms tend to disappear quickly. The most worrisome side effect, however, is growth suppression. Some children who must take drugs such as Ritalin or amphetamines may suffer slower growth rates than other children. Your pediatrician, however, can closely monitor your son's height and weight and discontinue the medication if problems arise. In such a case you would probably witness a growth spurt soon after the medication was stopped.

I'm pleased that I can reassure you about your son becoming "hooked" on this medication. First of all, these medications, properly prescribed and monitored, are not addictive to children. Yet you may also worry that your boy will somehow become psychologically accustomed to taking pills as a solution to his problems and that, as a result of this innocent childhood experience, he may turn to serious drug abuse in adolescence. Research studies have shown that hyperactive children who have been treated with medication actually have a lower incidence of teenage drug abuse than other children.

Because medication can be so successful in the treatment of hyperactivity, I urge you to talk things over with your pediatrician if you have further doubts. Remember, though, that medication alone is not enough. Your son will require some form of psychotherapy or counseling and a great deal of patient understanding mixed with clearly defined discipline at home.

Hyperactivity and Behavior Modification

Q: Juan, our 6-year-old, was diagnosed hyperactive about three months ago. His pediatrician prescribed medication which has helped. His teachers, however, say that he's still very jumpy and inattentive in the classroom and they would like to place him on a behavior modification plan. Is this a good idea?

A: Yes, it probably is. The plan will probably be based on a reward system. The teacher will identify target behaviors and then provide Juan some positive reinforcement (tokens, privileges, etc.) for good behavior, such as remaining in his seat and paying attention. A report in *Archives of General Psychiatry* describes a similar plan that was used in the classroom with twenty-eight hyperactive children. Interestingly, the behavioral techniques were most successful in curing aggressive behavior but were not particularly helpful with impulsivity or inattentiveness. In most cases youngsters such as Juan require a combination of medication, supportive counseling, and behavior modification—all mixed with lots of parental understanding and patience.

Kiddie Music Craze

Q: I've heard of teenagers spending their lunch money for records but my 6-year-old, Donna, takes the cake. She's got a bigger record collection than her 15-year-old sister. Thank goodness she likes children's records, not rock and roll, but I'm concerned. Is she precocious, or is this a new trend?

A: Donna may be in the forefront of a new trend—and the record industry is ecstatic. Sales of children's records are zooming. The Recording Industry Association of America reports that sales have soared from $87 million in 1976 to over $250 million in 1982.

Most of the discs being sold to Donna's age-mates are traditional fairy tales and some new twists such as *Miss Piggy Aerobique*, an exercise album for the small fry. Other favorites include education records.

Music is a powerful force in the lives of children. Parents should know, therefore, what their youngsters are tuning in. Get the beat. Listen to the lyrics. Exercise control right from the start.

Childhood Rituals

Q: Our 6-year-old son, Gary, is very ritualistic. For example, he walks around with his fingers crossed, and he'll cross the street, if he has to, in order to avoid a crack in the sidewalk. We ask him what he's afraid of, but he just shrugs; he says he doesn't know. Should we be worried?

A: Not necessarily. Gary's rituals sound a bit excessive, but I'd have to know more about him. Rituals serve a defensive purpose for children. They are a magical way of keeping unwelcome thoughts or behavior from erupting into action. When Gary says he "doesn't know" why he does these things, however, you can believe him. These phenomena are unconscious.

What happens if you interrupt one of his rituals? If he becomes flooded with anxiety, it is a bad sign. If, on the other hand, he can handle the diversion, I'd be less concerned.

More importantly, how is the rest of Gary's life going? Is he happy? What kind of reports do you get from school? In other words, it's important to assess Gary's entire life space. A certain amount of ritualistic behavior is to be expected in early childhood, but when it becomes excessive, it can be the symptom of an obsessive-compulsive disorder that may well require a psychiatric evaluation.

Death of a Parent

Q: My sister-in-law just died, leaving behind her husband, John, and her 6-year-old daughter, Becky. John is very depressed. Cries all the time. I know it's natural. He has to grieve. But I'm worried about Becky. Won't her father's grief rub off on her?

A: Yes, it probably will, but that's not such a bad thing as long as Dad has something left to give Becky. She needs his help. She needs his assurance that she can count on him. Shared grief, coupled with fatherly protection, can actually bring them closer together and make each stronger because of it.

Children, by the way, tend to handle the death of a parent better than the surviving spouse. In one study of 105 such youngsters, only six were found to have suffered clinically significant depression. Interestingly, in five of these cases, the surviving parent was also severely depressed.

So you have a point. If John becomes truly depressed as a result of his grief, he may (so to speak) pass it on to his daughter.

Both father and daughter need the active support of friends and family during this difficult time. If John's symptoms persist or if Becky should develop symptoms such as sleep disturbance, bedwetting, school refusal, temper tantrums, or other behavioral problems, a professional consultation would be in order.

When the Puppy Dies

Q: Our pet cocker spaniel, just a puppy, died one morning when our children (aged 6 and 8) were at school. I was moved to tears and called my husband immediately. His solution was for me to go out immediately and buy another puppy as a "replacement" so that the children would not become too upset. I did it, but now I'm having second thoughts. The children, for example, still keep talking about Clyde, the first cocker. Any reaction?

A: Although I'm sure that your husband was well-intentioned, I believe he made a mistake. He loves the children, and he tried to cushion them from the loss of their beloved pet. But in doing so, he eliminated their chance to feel some very real feelings, to express their thoughts, and to grieve the loss of their puppy. The fact that your children are still talking so much about Clyde is a tip-off to me that they still have some unresolved conflicts and unexpressed feelings.

Actually, the death of a pet can be a growth experience for youngsters. For many boys and girls such an event is their first experience with the phenomenon of death. Most parents find that they, as well as their children, are very saddened and that it is healthy for them and good modeling for the children to express this sadness in front of the youngsters. In this way children learn that it is natural to feel very sad at such moments, that the feelings can be expressed and shared, and that it feels better, in fact, to get it all out.

Bringing in an immediate replacement also devalues the deceased pet and may actually cause resentment on the part of some youngsters. One such 13-year-old girl explained it to me like this: "When Muffy died they bought another cat the next day. That's the thing that really got me, okay? They didn't respect my feelings. They didn't see that I could really love something. Pets are like people. You know. You have attachments to them. You don't replace them overnight like a worn stereo needle."

I suggest that you make it clear that the new puppy is not a replacement for Clyde. After all, Clyde was special. Encourage the children to express their feelings about their deceased pet. Accept their feelings. And don't leave your husband out of this family grieving process either. He may miss Clyde more than the kids.

The Child with Chronic Illness

Q: Our 6-year-old son, Clark, was born with congenital heart disease. He has spent a great deal of his life in hospitals because of

cardiac surgery and complications of his illness. He is still frail and
underdeveloped physically. Our greatest concerns at this time, however, are that he avoids children at school and does not even get
along well with his brother and sister. His psychological problems
seem to be becoming greater than his physical problems. Do you
have any suggestions?

A: Clark is not alone. About 5 to 10 percent of all American children suffer from some form of chronic illness: asthma, epilepsy,
heart disease, diabetes, etc. Research studies have shown that such
children are, indeed, more vulnerable to emotional conflicts than
other children. It is interesting, by the way, that the severity of
the psychiatric problem is related less to the actual severity of the
medical illness than it is to the length or chronicity of the medical
illness. Clark, therefore, is more in jeopardy because his heart disease has been present since birth.

Such youngsters with congenital illness may suffer from delayed
intellectual and motor development. They may have great difficulty
in establishing trusting relationships with anyone except their parents and their doctors and nurses. They may become excessively
dependent.

On the other hand, parents can exert a great deal of positive
influence. In fact, the single most important factor is generally how
realistic mom and dad are in their expectations for the child. For
example, parents who are excessively protective may create overdependency, mistrust, lack of self-confidence, and pessimism in a
child; parents who tend to deny their youngster's medical illness
may push him beyond his capabilities, leading to frustration and a
sense of abandonment. The answer, obviously, is to steer a middle
course. Consult with Clark's physician about his cardiac status and
ask for realistic projections of his future functioning. Then gently
insist that he performs up to his physical potential. Help him out
when he needs it, but don't do things for him that he can do for
himself.

I have also found that children with congenital illness tend to
blame their parents for it—whether or not the condition is actually
due to hereditary factors. Be prepared to confront this unspoken
assumption at some point down the line. A nondefensive, factual
discussion can clear the air.

Finally, Clark's hassles with his brother and sister may well be a garden variety case of sibling rivalry exacerbated by the dynamics of having a chronically ill child in the family. On one level Clark probably resents the good health enjoyed by his brother and sister. Yet he also loves them and may feel guilty about wishing his heart disease on them. So, being a 6-year-old, he puts all of this into action by externalizing this inner conflict into an external battle with the objects of his love-resentment. A similar dynamic, of course, may be at work in Clark's siblings, who may resent all the time that you and your husband have probably had to spend away from them because of Clark's hospitalizations.

No, you don't have to become an instant child psychiatrist to help the children work through this maze. Just help all of them express their feelings: resentment and love too. Respond to each of them as someone special. After all, nobody's perfect. I bet Clark has some skills that even his brother and sister lack. Build upon these individual successes for Clark—and for your other children too.

School Phobia

Q: Our 6-year-old daughter, an only child, seems to be deathly afraid of school. We thought we had prepared her well, but she refuses to go to school. Sometimes it's a stomach ache. Sometimes she just clings to me and cries. What can we do?

A: From what you've described, it seems that your daughter may well be suffering from "school phobia."

As you may know, the problem is not really a phobia (or fear) of school at all but, rather, a fear of leaving home—otherwise known as *separation anxiety*. Children who have been excessively dependent on their mothers (and sometimes fathers) are prone to this condition. Your daughter, an only child, may find it difficult to leave the joys of mother for the uncertainties of school.

Sometimes, by the way, it is just as difficult for a mother to "let go" of a child as it is for a youngster to go off to school. Be sure, then, that you are not telegraphing this to your daughter. If, for example, you are telling her that she must go to school while you are clutching her to your bosom, she will pick up your nonverbal message: Don't leave me! The key is to make sure she gets to school every day. Empathize with her, but make sure that she gets to school. The longer she stays home, the more difficult your job becomes.

Even when she complains of physical symptoms, I would urge you to take her to school. The school nurse should be alerted to the problem. For more severe symptoms you might simply stop off at the pediatrician's office on the way to school. Pediatricians are well-versed in how to deal with this condition.

Most cases of school phobia respond to a combination of empathy, understanding, and firmness. Most severe and prolonged cases require the consultation of a child psychiatrist.

Signs of Sexual Abuse

Q: I am a second-grade teacher. I know that my students should have some general interest in sex, but, from time to time, I have a boy or girl in my class who is just overwhelmed by sexual interest. Could this be a sign of sexual abuse?

A: Yes. The more common signals include:

1. Masturbatory activity

2. Preoccupation with sexual talk or touching other children

3. Fear of going to the bathroom

4. Artwork that depicts explicit sexual scenes

5. Excessive absences from school

And finally, juvenile court judges point out that a father-daughter incest may be indicated when the school receives written excuses for absences from dad rather than mom.

Grandmothering

Q: At 45, I'm a relatively young grandmother. I have a beautiful 6-year-old grandson who adores me. The trouble is his mother, my daughter. I think she's jealous that Scotty and I get along so well. She seems to keep him away from me deliberately. What can I do?

A: It has been said that sometimes children get along so well with grandparents because the two of them have a common enemy!

Seriously, though, I believe that grandparents can be a very important factor in youngsters' lives. Unfortunately, very few children today have this wonderful opportunity. In their book *Grandparents/ Grandchildren: The Vital Connection*, Kornhaber and Woodward report that only 5 percent of American children have regular and intimate contact with at least one grandparent. This is a shame. Grandparents can teach wisdom and patience and something about the flow of life and the family's history.

On the other hand, of course, the intrusive grandparent who insists on directing the parenting, rather than just the grandparenting, of a child can create unnecessary family conflicts.

A frank discussion with your daughter is in order. Let her hear your side of the story. But be sure to listen to hers as well. It may well be that the two of you have some unfinished business remaining from your daughter's own childhood. If so, Scotty is simply a pawn in the psychological game. It's not fair to any of you—especially your grandson. Try to work things out.

How to Praise Your Child

Q: It seems strange to my husband and me but our 7-year-old daughter just cannot handle praise. Whenever we compliment her or try to give her a little boost, she gets very turned off and irritated. Do you have any suggestions?

A: I have found that some parents have difficulty when it comes to praising their children. These boys and girls, in turn, become uncomfortable when they are on the receiving end of compliments from mom and dad.

Try the following guidelines:

1. *Praise, not puffery:* There is nothing like flattery or puffery to really turn off kids. Therefore, try to avoid superlatives ("best," "greatest," etc.) when praising children. Since youngsters know

they're not the greatest thing to hit the streets since steel-belted radials, flattery and puffery will get you nowhere. In fact, most youngsters get suspicious of this dishonest tactic. "What's Mom after?" they'll ask. Or, "I must really be a miserable creature if Mom has to go to such great lengths to find something good to say about me." Kids know instinctively that flattery is an empty gesture; it is easier to flatter than to praise. Flattery is aimed at artificially puffing up a child's self-esteem ("You must be one of the fastest runners in all of New England"), while effective praise is a realistic statement about a specific accomplishment ("You ran a nifty race"). Effective praise does more than just create good feelings between parent and child; it gives the youngster some realistic feedback about herself and assists her in finding her honest place in the world. Hype jobs may work on TV for laundry detergents, but they won't cut the grease with children.

2. *Praise the event, not the child:* Most children struggle against self-doubts and secrets about their imperfect inner worlds. Telling a youngster that he's a "wonderful boy" because he was so nice to the minister when he visited the house may make the boy cringe. He probably doesn't feel wonderful and may have secretly resented the minister's presence since it kept him from watching football Monday night. But expressing pride in the way he helped to serve the carrot cake will accomplish your purpose: to reward his positive behavior with a kind word.

3. *Beware the golden handcuffs:* Praise can be a weapon that ensnarls and traps. Youngsters who are continually overpraised for accomplishments learn instinctively to resent it because it implies that they are expected to do better and better, perhaps to be perfect. This can be frightening to children. It also implies that love and good feelings from mom and dad are contingent on what children *do,* not on who they *are.* Such tactics trap kids into a tight set of parental expectations. It's like locking them into golden handcuffs. Children start wondering if mom and dad can *ever* really be satisfied. They begin to worry about failing for fear that they will lose the parental praise that they come to equate with love. Such youngsters may be driven to continuous accomplishment which empties of meaning as soon as it is attained, for once they have received their parents' praise, they must go right back to work and

get more A's or win another race. These poor kids are always clutching emptiness in search of parental love. Some youngsters, on the other hand, feel so pressured to succeed that they simply stop trying; they take revenge on their parents not through success but through failure. Beware the golden handcuffs.

Fighting in Front of the Children

Q: My husband thinks that it's a good thing for us to fight or argue in front of our children, aged 7 and 10. He says we have to be "honest," that no subject should be off-limits. I'm a very private person. I believe that differences between a husband and wife should be kept away from the children. Who's right?

A: Neither one of you is completely right. To your husband I would say: Yes, it's good for children to see that their mother and father can disagree and then work things out. It's a good lesson in growing up. But there are certainly subjects, such as sex, that should be considered taboo for "public" disagreement. Kids will not thank you for this kind of honesty; it scares them.

To you I would say: It is unwise to hide all parental disagreements from children. In fact, you just can't do it. The kids will always pick up the nonverbal signals that say something's wrong. Then they've got a double burden: "Something's wrong between Mom and Dad, and it must be so horrible that none of us can even talk about it!" Children growing up in this type of atmosphere learn to repress their conflicts and feelings, to keep things in, to fear confrontation.

The answer? Try to steer a middle course. Disagreements in front of the children are fine as long as you and your husband respect each other and your children enough to follow these rules:

1. No verbal abuse

2. No physical abuse

3. An honest effort at resolution and compromise

4. Good sense about the subjects you tackle

Daydreamer

Q: Our son daydreams a lot. Brad is 6 years old. His older brother (aged 14) and sister (aged 13) never did this when they were younger. I ask him about it, of course, but he won't tell me what he's thinking about. Could it mean that he's unhappy? How can we break him of the habit?

A: All children daydream. Kids, in fact, need daydreams to fuel their fantasy life and imagination. But how much is too much? Tough to answer.

You should be alarmed if Brad tends to blur fantasy and reality. You should be alarmed if Brad *prefers* daydreaming to relating to other people. You should be alarmed if there are other signs or symptoms of trouble, such as sleep difficulty, appetite problems, behavior difficulties, poor grades, few friends, unhappiness.

Comparing Brad to his brother and sister probably won't help very much. After all, his world is different than theirs. For one thing, the age difference is such that Brad is almost an only child. In a sense, you have two families within a family. That, in fact, may be a key. Is Brad lonely? Is he using fantasy as an escape from loneliness? If so, it's a problem.

The solution? Don't try to pry into Brad's secret reveries. He won't let you in anyway. Instead, make plans to keep him actively engaged with family members and friends. Limit his amount of unstructured time. More reality time. Less fantasy time.

Repeating Children's Words

Q: My girlfriend Jennifer and I both have 6-year-old daughters. Jennifer reads a lot of how-to-parent books. Lately, she's picked up a new technique of repeating her daughter's words back to her. Jennifer says this is good communication. I think it sounds silly. Comments?

A: Techniques are okay, but they're just things to use until the parent arrives. By this I mean there is no substitute for knowing and understanding your own child and no "technique" can accomplish it for you.

Repeating a youngster's last words is a legitimate communication technique. Child psychiatrists, for example, use it frequently:

CHILD: "I'm upset."

DOCTOR: "You're upset."

This technique tends to keep the conversation in the child's hands, and it helps him or her clarify feelings and ideas. Parents can use it too, of course, but don't overdo it. If you do, you risk sounding like a caricature of a psychotherapist. Parents should talk like parents.

Paradox

Q: At first I thought the psychiatrist was nuts, but we tried it and it worked. Let me explain. We took our 6-year-old, Paul, to a psychiatrist because of temper tantrums. After three sessions the doctor told Paul he wasn't trying hard enough; he should have *more* tantrums. The doctor told him to schedule them four times a day but he could only have them at the specific times they were scheduled. I was dumbfounded, but my husband and I went along with it. What do you think happened? In about one week, Paul lost all interest in temper tantrums. He hasn't had one in a long time. How do you explain this strange treatment?

A: The treatment isn't so strange, but it is not commonly used. The technique is called *paradoxical intervention.* The therapist removes the restriction to undesirable behavior, in this case Paul's tantrums. In a sense the technique allowed Paul to learn that his misbehavior was certainly under his control. In planning for it, he subjected himself to ridicule. In essence, the fun was taken out of it.

I also presume that you and your husband were told not to get upset—maybe even to remind Paul when it was tantrum time and to compliment him if he pulled off an especially good one.

Paradoxical intervention works in some cases, but it can backfire in others. I don't recommend it for routine use in parental discipline or in professional treatment.

Religion by Coin Flip?

Q: My husband and I have been married six years. I'm Catholic and he's Protestant. No problem. No problem up until *now*, I mean. Jack and I love and respect each other, and we've each worshipped in our own church. The problem is what to do about our daughter, Melanie, who's 6 years old. It's time for her to get some religious instruction—but which religion? I say Catholic because she's a girl and she's closer to me, but I realize that my reasoning doesn't make a lot of sense. Jack doesn't buy it anyway. Should we let Melanie decide? We've even considered tossing a coin. Obviously we could use some guidance.

A: First, the obvious. The time to decide such things is before you get married or, certainly, before the birth of a first child. So much for the obvious.

Letting Melanie decide is not a good idea. She can't possibly understand what she's being asked to decide. She'll see it as a choice between Mom and Dad. Don't do that to her. Don't place her in a loyalty bind.

Some parents caught in this dilemma opt to both change their religious affiliations as a compromise. It's worked for some families, failed for others.

Some parents choose to split the difference and raise the child in both religions until she's old enough to make up her own mind. This works sometimes, but it can lead to the same loyalty bind as inviting a young child such as Melanie to decide on her own.

Religion is an important and vital factor in the development of a child. You recognize this fact. Both you and Jack actively practice your faith. Excellent. My suggestion is that you reach a thoughtful decision now if possible. I believe it's best for Melanie to be raised in her early formative years in one religion. As she grows, you can respectfully teach her the difference between Mom's and Dad's worship. Make it clear that she herself can convert to the other faith if she chooses when she's older—say, 16.

Which religion to choose? The answer would be obvious if one of you were less ardent about your own particular faith. But you know something? I'm glad you're both strong believers. As long as the love, tolerance, and respect for your differences remains intact, Melanie will do fine—whichever religion you choose for her.

Don't Be So Shy

Q: "Don't be so shy. Don't be so shy." That's all my husband says to Kevin, our 6-year-old. I know it's exasperating. Jack, my husband, is a hard charger, a topflight salesman, very popular. He's frustrated that Kevin is so timid. But I say his approach is all wrong. What should I do to help?

A: Shyness, of course, is a relative term. What's shy to Jack probably wouldn't be shy to someone less outgoing. All children have different temperaments. Although Jack might like Kevin to be a chip off the old block, Kevin might be predestined for a more introspective personality and lifestyle.

One possibility, therefore, may be some father-son conflict based on Kevin's failure to measure up to Dad's expectations. If so, Dad will have to take the lead by readjusting to Kevin's speed. What are Kevin's strengths? Better to build upon them than to criticize his weaknesses.

On the other hand, true shyness can be a problem. Is Kevin visibly upset in the presence of other people? Does he avoid situations that make him anxious? How does he get along in school? If there are some bona fide problems, better to face them. Excessive shyness in early childhood can be a predictor of later problems such as poor school performance, loneliness, and depression. So I'm not ready to blame it all on Jack by a long shot. Take a fresh look. Keep an open mind. Your pediatrician should be able to determine if a psychological consultation is indicated.

Chores

Q: Please settle an argument for my husband and me. Our son is 6 years old. Is he too young to be doing some chores around the house?

A: Most children are ready to handle some chores by the age of 6. Children, by the way, are more eager to accept these responsibilities if they are seen as something of a "rite of passage." Children wish to be seen as helpful contributors to the family's welfare. Welcome your son into the joys of family responsibility.

Pay for Chores?

Q: We have two daughters, aged 6 and 8. Should they be paid to do their chores?

A: No. Everyone in the family has certain responsibilities. Your daughter's chores (assuming they are reasonable tasks) fall into this category. Chores are their own personal contribution to the smooth working of the family.

Paying youngsters to do things that should be done anyway smacks of bribery—not payment. And, worse, it can lead to emotional blackmail; it's just a matter of time before you ask one of the girls to do something and she turns to you and says: "How much will you pay me for it?"

On the other hand, a youngster who volunteers to take on a special project (especially one that you might otherwise pay to have done) should be considered for some sort of financial reward. Such special projects, however, should be carefully distinguished from routine, assigned chores.

How to Choose Christmas Toys

Q: My husband and I could use some help with that annual ritual: How do we choose the right Christmas toys for our children, aged 6 and 9. Any guidelines?

A: Try these seven steps to successful toy selection, which I've adapted from various sources and my own discussions with children:

1. *Safety first:* Check for sharp edges, flammability, and parts that can be detached and swallowed. Some toys intended for older children (over the age of 6) may be physically safe but hazardous to household maintenance, such as the celebrated "egg from outer space" that spills forth green slime when the youngster inevitably manages to pry apart the plastic shell.

2. *Toys should be fun:* While it's a good idea to select some educational toys for children, remember that if a child is not in-

terested in a toy, it will collect a lot of dust—no matter how "educational" it might seem to you.

3. *Buy toys for your child, not for yourself:* Too many parents try to recapture the Christmases of their youth by selecting toys through their own eyes. Let your child's own interests be your guide.

4. *Select toys that are appropriate for your child's stage of development:* This is a most important guideline. Experts point out, for example, that infants delight in changing colors, patterns, and sounds; 2-year-olds love toys that can be hit or hammered; 3-year-olds should be given toys and games that allow for a high level of physical activity; and 5-year-olds thrive on games of mastery and themes of "pretend" or "let's tell a story." Elementary school youngsters should be given opportunities to develop hobbies; since these children are also so peer-related, they like simple board games, especially if they require teams or cooperative play. Preteens generally like to project themselves ahead into adolescence through their gift preferences and usually appreciate things like wall posters, record albums, sports equipment, and high-tech computer games. Teenagers have some of the residual interests of preteens plus clothes and, of course, high-ticket items such as stereo components and portable radios. One word of caution: Do not let yourself be stampeded into buying gifts beyond your established budget.

5. *Plan to give, hope to receive:* Many parents complain that Christmas gift giving has gotten out of hand. Their children's letters to Santa sound less like a cautious wish list and more like a strident set of nonnegotiable demands. These parents are understandably worried that the holiday of Christmas is becoming too commercialized and materialistic in their homes. The best antidote is to focus not on receiving—but on giving. Help youngsters make and select little gifts for family and friends. Remind them of the spiritual meaning of Christmas.

6. *Avoid super-duper, gimmicky toys:* The worst toy is the one with a single purpose. After the child passively watches it "perform" a few times (or after the batteries wear out, whichever comes first), he'll probably lose interest and start playing with the card-

board box in which the toy had been packaged! Ask not what a toy can do for your child but what your child can do with the toy.

7. *Give a gift of yourself:* Many parents tend to overwhelm kids with Christmas gifts. Why? Some parents, feeling guilty, try to make up for the neglect of the entire previous year. Some try to compensate for their own blue Christmases of the past. Others feel a sense of competition with other parents and try to outshop the Joneses at Yuletide. Better to concentrate on a few carefully selected gifts and to spread the spirit of giving and receiving throughout the year. In this way you'll be able to personalize your gifts and give them meaning. Remember, whatever gifts and toys you select, the best gift any child can ever receive is the attention, warmth, and love of a parent. Give a gift of yourself.

Working Mothers

Q: I have recently decided to go back to work. I'd like the diversion, and we could sure use the money. The problem is that my 7-year-old son and 10-year-old daughter continuously call me at the office, sometimes just to complain that there's no coke in the refrigerator. I realize that they're sending me a "message," but what should I do about it?

A: If your job is financially necessary or if it is personally important to you, don't let yourself come down with a quick case of the "guilties." Let's think it over. First of all, you should be aware that you're not the only working mother out there. In fact, 62 percent of American mothers who have school-age children are currently employed.

Try this step-by-step approach:

1. Begin by listening to your children. Let them put any anger or resentment about your working into words. Accept their feelings.

2. After they've gotten their feelings out, explain to them why you're working. Patiently.

3. Next, you need the kids' cooperation. Everybody in the family is like a spoke on a wheel. Every spoke has to do its job for the wheel to turn. Make it a real team effort. You need to work, and you need them to be a part of the solution—not a part of the problem.

4. Your husband is also one of these spokes on the wheel. You should also have his help and support. He may have to pick up some of the slack at home. Make sure he's a part of your team too.

5. Finally, it would help if you would look for ways to improve the "quality" of the time you do spend with the youngsters now that they do not have as much quantity of time with you. Ask for their ideas. They'll probably come up with some good ones.

But whatever you do, I would urge you to resist throwing in the towel too soon. Most 7- and 10-year-olds can tolerate Mom's working. Sure they miss you. That's to be expected. Reassure them of your love and the fact that your working is not a matter of abandoning them or of changing your priorities.

Remember, there are positive aspects of your going back to work: the financial rewards and probably the fact that it makes you feel better and more productive. It will help the children to ultimately see their mother as happy and resourceful. It will also help them experience themselves as being somewhat more independent and self-reliant. In fact, many working mothers and their children end up feeling closer together *because* of Mom's job.

Effects of Divorce

Q: My husband and I have been separated for six months. The divorce will be final in another six months. We have two children, Jimmy (aged 7) and Janet (aged 9). I keep reading about all the problems that divorce creates for children, but some of the reports seem to be contradictory. What are the true effects of divorce on children?

A: Divorce itself is not a reliable predictor of mental health or mental illness in a child. There are so many other factors to consider:

the child's own strengths and weaknesses and the preseparation relationship with both parents, to name a couple.

On the other hand, a recent review of the divorce literature by two researchers does point to some interesting basic data:

1. *Sex:* Boys generally have a tougher time than girls. This is probably because the mother is typically the custodial parent and boys feel the loss of their father more painfully than girls.

2. *Custody:* As a corollary, youngsters appear to fare better when they're in the custody of the same-sex parent—all other things being equal.

3. *Age:* As a general rule, the younger the child, the greater the trauma.

4. *Visitation:* Children do best when the noncustodial parent (usually the father) visits regularly and remains a positive part of their lives.

I hope these points are helpful. They're based on statistical analysis. Jimmy and Janet, however, are not statistics. Their reaction will be based largely on the amount of ongoing love and support that you and their father will give them—now and in the years ahead.

Divorce Fantasy

Q: I knew it would be tough on the children but I had to do it. Divorce was the only solution for me. Surprisingly, the kids (aged 7, 9, and 10) all seem to be taking it pretty well. I expected that they'd be filled with wishes for their Daddy and me to get back together again—but they're not. In fact, I think they're relieved. Could I be missing something?

A: Maybe—maybe not. There are several factors that determine how children react to divorce and whether they clutch to the fantasy that somehow, someday Mommy and Daddy will be reunited and we'll all live happily ever after.

The most important variables are the ages of the children during the predivorce turmoil, their awareness of the difficulties, the effects of the bad marriage on them, their relationships with each of the parents, their confidence in the custodial parent, and the nature of their continuing relationship with the noncustodial parent.

Children who are old enough to see for themselves and make up their own minds often do feel relieved by the divorce. Of course, if the postdivorce relationship continues to be marred by conflict between their parents, it never really ends for them.

You're correct in assuming that, for the most part, children do indeed harbor the fantasy that Mom and Dad will get back together again. But a recent study suggests that we might have to look again. In a survey of 368 children of divorce, Glynnis Walker found that 76 percent said it was just as well that their parents were not still together. (But whether their reaction is so much defense bravado or whether they're reflecting mature responses based on their own special situations is very difficult to determine.)

My advice: Give the children plenty of opportunity to talk about it but, at the same time, try to put the divorce behind you. Get on with life. It's the best medicine for you—and for your children.

Divorce Ceremony

Q: My husband and I are getting divorced. I'd like to have the children (aged 7 and 10) join us for a divorce ceremony where a minister would remove our rings and formally end the marriage. Do you think this would help or hurt the children?

A: First of all, you might have a problem finding a minister to perform the task. Divorce ceremonies are uncommon and controversial too.

From the standpoint of the children it is important that they understand that (1) the divorce is not their fault, (2) regardless of their wishes for Mom and Dad to reunite, the divorce is final, and (3) they can still count on both of you to take care of them. These things can be accomplished without a formal ceremony.

Hypnosis for Children of Divorce?

Q: I've recently been divorced. It's been tough on my 7-year-old, Patty. I've heard that hypnosis is being used for kids who go through a divorce. It's supposed to make them feel better about themselves. Does it work?

A: I have no doubt that some psychotherapists have used hypnosis in some of these cases, but generally speaking it is not widely used in child therapy except for very specific symptoms such as phobias, bed-wetting, and pain.

The best treatment for children of divorce is to help them express their feelings and to reassure them that they are not the cause of the divorce and that they will be taken care of. While hypnosis wouldn't harm these youngsters, any therapy that ignores the *expressive* needs of these children is incomplete.

One-Year Custody?

Q: My husband and I are in the midst of a divorce. He has agreed to give me custody of our 7-year-old daughter but insists that he must have her for one year sometime during her childhood. What do you think?

A: As a child psychiatrist I prefer to approach these matters from the perspective of what is in the best interests of the child. From this perspective, your husband's plan is not a good idea. Such an arrangement could be confusing and disruptive to your daughter's development. On the other hand, her father will always be her father. She needs him, and he needs her too. A liberal visitation policy would be best. I suggest you go back to the drawing board.

Ex-husband Snatches Child

Q: I never thought it would happen even though my ex-husband warned he was going to do it. Last week when Laura (my 7-year-old) was on her way to school, her father pulled her into his car and drove away with her. Later he called to say she's "safe," but I've had no direct contact with her at all. My lawyer is on the case, of course, but I'm desperate. What can I do?

A: Child snatching is a growing phenomenon. The typical abductor is a 30-year-old white male. Most abductions (65 percent) occur before the divorce and custody settlement. As in your situation, there is usually (60 percent) a threat before the actual abduction occurs. Most children who are abducted are between the ages of 3 and 9, as is Laura. Further research also suggests that the primary motivation for child snatching is not love of the child—but revenge against the other parent.

What can you do? I would urge you to be aggressive in your efforts to find Laura and to make contact with her. While she's probably safe physically, she must be confused and frightened. Your ex-husband, of course, may be feeding her untruths about you— even to the point of suggesting that the abduction is okay with you or that you don't love her anymore. Do everything in your power to locate her—I know you will.

An Absentee Father's Day

Q: My former husband generally neglects our children (aged 7 and 9) most of the year except to send gifts for birthdays and Christmas—usually a week or two late, at that. The problem is that when the kids don't call to wish him "Happy Father's Day," he goes into a tirade and makes my life miserable for weeks, threatening to cut off the support payments. The children are confused and I'm angry.

A: Your former husband seems to be confusing the biological fact of his fatherhood with the psychological, emotional, and legal responsibilities that go along with it.

Such situations are, indeed, confusing for children, especially if their relationship with their father was very positive before the divorce. They don't understand. They feel as though they themselves have been divorced. And, being children, they often assume that *they* must somehow be at fault. These "children of divorce" are vulnerable to low self-esteem and depression.

I would suggest that you start not with your former husband but with the children. Encourage them to express their feelings. Encourage them to ask their father questions. Do not make excuses for their father. Assure them that they are not at fault. Assure them that while their father may be having some problems with his life and with the divorce, they can count on you.

Your former husband probably needs some special understanding too. At least he still wants to be seen as a respected person in the eyes of his children. He'll have to be reminded, however, that good fathers don't command respect from children—they have to earn it.

Grandparents of Divorce

Q: My husband and I are the proud grandparents of a 7-year-old girl named Brenda. Our son, however, has recently divorced Brenda's mother and has moved from our hometown to another state. Our problem is that our former daughter-in-law refuses to let us see our granddaughter! We love Brenda, and we know that she loves us too. She is the joy of our lives. We've pleaded and pleaded, but Brenda's mother says that she wants to erase all memories of our son from her life and that she is too "uncomfortable" for us to see her daughter. Are we being unreasonable? What should we do?

A: My heart goes out to you. Both you and your granddaughter are being cheated from a very important relationship because of the leftover business that still exists between your son and his former wife.

Unfortunately, this is not an uncommon problem in today's divorce-prone society, particularly between paternal grandparents and a custodial mother. The phenomenon is so frequent, as a matter of fact, that over thirty states have enacted visitation rights for grandparents of divorce. You might check to see if your own state is among them.

Regardless of your legal standing, I would suggest a calm, reasonable approach—for Brenda's sake. If the situation is very volatile, for example, you might suggest some family therapy in which all parties (you, your husband, Brenda, and Brenda's mother) might participate. The goal would be to iron out differences and to work toward regular visitation with your granddaughter. Children lose a lot when they lose their grandparents to divorce. They lose a loving ally at a time when their world is turbulent and confused. They also lose that important link to their family roots and to their own personal identity. These aspects are worth preserving. I admire your determination.

Diet and Hyperactivity

Q: I think that our 7-year-old son, Marshall, is hyperactive. I've heard about a special diet for this problem. What is it? Does it cure hyperactivity?

A: The diet you're probably referring to is based on the elimination of two food groups that some researchers believe to be responsible for some cases of hyperactivity. The first food group consists of foods that are high in salicylate, such as tomatoes, cucumbers, and apples. The second group consists of foods that contain artificial food colors, flavors, and the preservative butylated hydroxytoluene (BHT).

When the diet was first introduced, it was trumpeted as a major breakthrough in the treatment of hyperactivity. Like so many other hopeful discoveries, however, it has fallen far short of being a panacea. A special research group at the National Institutes of Health (NIH), in fact, has cautioned that dietary treatment of hyperactivity has a very limited usefulness.

The NIH group warns that dietary approaches should be used only if traditional treatment methods such as psychotherapy and medication do not work.

The first stop for Marshall should be at his pediatrician for a thorough evaluation. Hyperactivity comes in many sizes and shapes. The treatment plan must be tailored to Marshall's specific needs.

Magnesium Treatment for Hyperactivity?

Q: Larry, my 7-year-old, is hyperactive. He's currently taking medication prescribed by his pediatrician. One of my neighbors has told me that she read somewhere that supplemental magnesium tablets are now being used to treat hyperactivity. What do you think?

A: Hyperactivity is a frustrating and complex symptom. Because a precise cause is not always diagnosable and because no single treatment is effective in all cases, you will hear, from time to time, about numerous new "cures." None of them, as yet, has proved to be effective. Yes, your neighbor probably read correctly. Supplemental magnesium has received some press. So has supplemental copper, zinc, and manganese. So has megavitamin therapy. So has the hypoglycemic diet.

On the basis of current research none of these approaches appears to be the answer. My advice: Talk it over with your pediatrician. If you're not satisfied, seek a second opinion, probably with a child psychiatrist. But hang in there. Work closely with Larry's doctor(s) as a true partner in his treatment.

Cure for Dyslexia?

Q: Our 7-year-old son, Michael, has been diagnosed as dyslexic. He has problems with reversing letters, spelling errors, and remembering things that he's read. The school has put him in a special resource classroom, and it seems to be helping—but is there any cure? I've heard about medication, diets, even "patterning exercises." Does any of it work?

A: There is no cure for dyslexia, but there are a number of special educational techniques that can help youngsters such as Michael. Researchers from Johns Hopkins University recently reported that more than half the dyslexics who graduate from special schools enjoy a high degree of success. At one special high school, for example, 58 percent of the graduates went on to earn college degrees and 10 percent went on to graduate degrees.

Pills and diets? No, there are no quick cures. Dyslexia, or specific learning disability (SLD), is complex and requires skill and patience on everybody's part.

For more information I recommend a book by Sally Smith: *No Easy Answers: The Learning Disabled Child at Home and at School.*

Stuffed Animals for Boys?

Q: My son, Mark, wanted a stuffed lion for his seventh birthday. I bought one for him, but his father doesn't approve. He says boys shouldn't play with dolls. What do you say?

A: First of all, there's nothing harmful about boys (or girls) playing with dolls. Second, a stuffed lion, king of the fantasy jungle, isn't exactly a doll.

How does Mark play with the doll, that's what I'd like to know. Does he identify with it and use it aggressively? If so, the lion may symbolize his own assertiveness. Does he attempt to "tame" it? If so, he may be attempting through play and fantasy to curb his own aggressiveness. Does he use it as a pacifier, perhaps to get to sleep at night? If so, it may be a substitute security blanket. All these behaviors are within the normal range.

Play is the work of childhood. It's the way that Mark and other children resolve their normal developmental conflicts.

Watch and learn.

Asthma and the Mind

Q: Our 7-year-old, Bryan, has a terrible case of asthma. He's allergic to many things that trigger severe attacks. He takes medication and uses an inhaler frequently. He also has to go to the emergency room a lot. As you might guess, all this has him extremely frightened. In fact, I think his worrying about it constantly is making it worse. We try to reassure him, but let's face it: If you're 7 and you can't breathe, reassurances can't count for much, right?

A: The mind-body connection is very powerful in asthma. Yes, the fear of an impending attack can itself precipitate an attack or exacerbate an attack that strikes spontaneously.

This is why it's so important to treat youngsters like Bryan not as "asthmatics" but as whole children. His therapy, therefore, should include some form of psychological support. And let's not forget things like self-hypnosis and biofeedback; they can be powerful additions to Bryan's treatment program. Check with your doctor for details.

Telephone Manners

Q: I hate it, but I can't stop it. Stewart, my 7-year-old, has absolutely no manners on the telephone. "Hey Ma, it's for you," he screams at the top of his voice. Whatever happened to "Just a moment please" or "May I take a message?"

A: Manners are not a trivial concern. Stewart's telephone behavior probably reflects other aspects of his personality and perhaps his relationship with you. If you can, therefore, help him clean up his act a bit on the phone, you'll be teaching him skills and behavior that will serve him well in other areas of his life.

Here's my four-step formula:

1. *Example:* The best teacher of good manners is parental example. Hearing Mom say those magic words *please* and *thank you* is powerful teaching. It works.

2. *Ground rules:* It helps to have a few basic rules of manners and to patiently instruct your child in them. But don't go too fast. Stewart, after all, is only 7. This type of instruction (such as how to use a soup spoon) is the old-fashioned way of teaching manners—but it still works over the long term.

3. *Timing:* Kids will be kids. If Stewart messes up and gets upset, wait for him to recover his composure. The worst time to teach manners is in the teeth of a temper tantrum.

4. *Praise:* Catch him being good. That's right. Modern child psychology teaches that praise and encouragement for desired behavior far outdistances punishment in its effectiveness. So the next time Stewart demonstrates good manners, be sure to praise him for it. Who knows? He may even say "thank you" in return. Now *that's* good manners.

Winner at School, Loser at Home

Q: Our daughter, Stanton, is 7 years old. At school she's a winner: straight A's, the teacher's pet. At home she's a loser: fights with her brother, calls us all names. We've tried everything from kissing her feet to spanking her. Nothing works. We're getting tired of this. Suggestions?

A: First of all, you and your husband seem to be reacting in extremes. Kiss her feet? No way. Don't pamper Stanton's misbehavior. Spanking? Another mistake. It won't solve the problem, but it may well make it worse since Stanton will have even more reason for revenge.

Try this four-step formula.

1. Fighting and verbal abuse cannot be allowed. Tell Stanton that. Then tell her what the consequences will be every time she breaks the rules. Make her punishment consistent, nonabusive, time-limited, and relevant to the offense. Time-outs in her room and loss of privileges are two good techniques.

2. Try to keep things as positive as you can. Reward Stanton for her good behavior. Praise her.

3. Examine yourselves. Are there conflicts in the home that could be contributing to your daughter's unhappiness? If so, try to resolve them.

4. If the problems continue or get significantly worse, don't hesitate to consult with a child psychiatrist.

Back Talk

Q: The problem is our 7-year-old, Darryl. He's always talking back to us. We can't ask him to do anything without getting some kind of snappy response. What should we do?

A: The first thing to do is to distinguish between run-of-the-mill back talk and true disrespect or verbal abuse. All children indulge themselves in some amount of back talk; it's what they use to object to parental advice, requests, suggestions, and demands. But back talk is not the same as disrespect: the name-calling or other abuse (verbal or nonverbal) to a parent.

The difference is absolutely crucial. I suggest, for example, that you ignore back talk—as long as Darryl eventually does what you want him to do. You might even joke about it—"Yes. I guess you're not too happy with my little suggestion, right?" but disrespect cannot be tolerated. It must be met with some form of punishment and education.

Tokens

Q: My sister is having trouble with her 7-year-old son, Michael. He's very fidgety, can't sit still, and misbehaves all the time. She's come up with a new gimmick, though, that seems to help. When Michael behaves well, she gives him a plastic token. At the end of the week he can trade in his tokens for a prize. What do you think of this technique?

A: The so-called token economy system is a form of behavior modification. It can work wonders with children. By the way, Madison Avenue knows that it can work with adults too—witness all the save-the-box-top and clip-the-coupon campaigns.

But I do have some concerns. First of all, tokens and other behavior modification techniques are no substitutes for *understanding* a child's behavior. Second, behavior modification, even when it *is* used, should be just one of several devices that a parent should be able to use, flexibly, in the task of teaching self-discipline to a child.

On the basis of your letter, for example, Michael might be suffering from an attention deficit disorder and hyperactivity. If so, he may require a number of additional approaches including specific academic techniques, diet, and perhaps even medication. Tokens do work, but don't mistake them for magic bullets.

Oldest Daughters Less Successful?

Q: I've read that oldest sons tend to be high achievers. What about oldest daughters? Paula, aged 7, is our oldest child. Any comments?

A: Much of the early research in birth order was directed toward males—especially when it comes to measuring the "success" of firstborns. This was probably understandable given the fact that not until recent years have females pursued traditional "male" avenues of success. But things have changed. Medical schools, law schools, business schools, you name it, are packed with female students. Women are succeeding from outer space to the ocean's floor and at all levels in between. And you know something? A disproportionately high percentage of these women are, you guessed it, firstborns. One study conducted by Bernstein and Brambs of students enrolled in graduate school addressed this issue directly. They found that oldest sons *and* daughters are statistically overrepresented in a number of fields: science, humanities, and social sciences. So move over big brother. Being firstborn apparently carries the same advantages, and disadvantages, for girls as it does for boys.

My Son Loves Chores

Q: You keep hearing that today's kids don't want to work. But don't tell it to our son, Eddie (aged 7) He loves to do chores around the house. Comments?

A: Bravo! Eddie is on his way to success. Children who cherish chores and the value of work grow up into happier adults.

A forty-year Harvard study of over 400 boys concluded that those who did household chores as youngsters and who had part-time jobs as teenagers grew up happier and more productive. For example, they were twice as likely to have warm relationships with people and five times more likely to be better paid.

Comments? Sure. Keep it up, Eddie!

Creativity or Originality?

Q: Everyone says our 7-year-old, Albert, is very "creative." He's very novel about the way he uses words. He's always drawing fascinating pictures. How can we encourage these skills? How can we increase the odds of his being a creative adult?

A: First of all, some distinctions are necessary. Strictly speaking, a 7-year-old cannot be truly creative. Why? Experts in this field insist that the definition of creativity is the capacity to do something *original* that is accepted as *significant* by society. Children, therefore, may be original and use their imagination well, but they usually do so by accident. They are not capable of judging the true worth of their efforts.

This distinction is important for Albert's future. If you want him to be truly creative you should (1) encourage the development of specific skills, (2) praise him for his efforts, and (3) stimulate him to ask questions and to view things from many perspectives and angles.

It all comes down to motivation and skill. With these two tools he'll be prepared to become a truly creative adult—and make a contribution to the world.

TV at the Dinner Table?

Q: My husband is a worse TV addict than our children, aged 7 and 9. He allows them to watch television while we're having dinner. What do you think of this practice?

A: I don't like it at all. Dinner time, for most families, is often the only time that everyone is together. It should be used to develop family values and cohesion. It should be a time of listening, talking, touching each other's lives. When you invite a television set to join you for dinner, you rob yourselves of something very important in family life.

Surrogate Mother?

Q: I'm 34. I've been married for thirteen years, and we have two children, aged 7 and 11. I've been kicking around an idea for over a year, and I've made up my mind: I want to be a surrogate mother. I think it would be marvelous to give the gift of a baby to a childless couple. Frankly, I thought my husband would put his foot down, but he's been wonderful. He says it's okay with him, but he's worried about our children. "How will they react," he asks? We haven't said anything to them yet. Do you have any advice?

A: This is a tough one. We have so little data at this time. I suggest that you and your husband ask the agency that you'll work with for permission to contact other couples who have gone through the experience. They should be able to shed some light on the issues. As a matter of principle, my own advice would be to definitely talk it over with your children *before* you decide.

You'll have to be very aware of their levels of understanding. Don't expect them to absorb it in one sitting. Give them a few weeks. Be sure to answer their questions and really sound them out. Then make your decision. While you needn't give your youngsters a veto over your plans, you should certainly weigh their reactions heavily in making your final decision.

I salute your selflessness in considering the surrogate option and your sensitivity to your own children. But, as I said, it's a tough one. Ultimately only you and your husband can decide.

Too Shy?

Q: My mother-in-law thinks that Richard, our 7-year-old, is too shy. She keeps pushing him to assert himself. She even embarrasses him in public by saying things like: "What will that nice lady think of you? Go up and say hello."

Now I admit that Richard is very shy, but isn't Grandma making things worse?

A: Yes. And I wonder why Richard's shyness bothers her so much? There are many possibilities. Here are some:

1. *Projection:* She might be projecting her own basic shyness onto Richard.

2. *Identification:* Does she identify Richard with someone else such as her own husband or Richard's father?

3. *Displacement:* Is she covertly angry at you or your husband and simply displacing that anger onto a handy scapegoat, Richard?

One type of shyness results from low self-esteem. The child who doesn't feel good about himself obviously lacks the courage to approach other people; he figures they won't like him since he doesn't like himself in the first place.

Another type is a variant of performance anxiety. Some children are fairly comfortable with themselves, until they are put "on show." They fear being made to perform.

I can't diagnose Richard's type of shyness based on what you've told me, but it's clear that Grandma's cajoling and public embarrassments are not helping.

Shared Room

Q: We have three children. Our boy (aged 7) has his own room. The two girls (aged 5 and 9) have to share a room. And that's the problem. They each want their own room. It's more than just jealousy over their brother's having his own room. The two girls just don't get along very well. Any suggestions?

A: All children need some space to call their very own. Some privacy. Why not try to make the best of the situation by dividing the girls' room with bookcases, or a curtain, or a room divider? You could also paint each half of the room a distinct color and coordinate the colors to their own possessions.

One word of warning: Things are apt to get worse rather than better. The four-year age difference will be more of a factor when your oldest daughter becomes a teenager. Better start working on some creative solutions now.

Me First

Q: We have three children: James (aged 7), Jessica (aged 4), and Jerome (aged 2). The problem is James. He always has to be first. The first fed, the first into the car, the first to do everything. How can we cure him of "me first"?

A: James, as your oldest child, is doing what comes naturally: trying to be first. But like some firstborns, he may be taking things too far. How can you help?

First, try to understand that what might look like competition between him and his younger siblings is really competition for your own love and attention. One way you can help, therefore, is to find some special time alone with him so he doesn't feel that the other children are stealing you from him. (Jessica and Jerome, by the way, should also get some private time.) You might also appeal to James's position as the oldest. Ask him to help his brother and sister do this and that because he knows how to do it better, because he's the oldest.

On the other hand, you'll have to teach James that he can't expect to be first all the time. Give him opportunities to defer to the younger children. He may not like it, but it will be good for him.

Why Do Children Lie?

Q: My grandchildren, aged 7 and 10, tell a lot of lies. I know that my son and daughter-in-law are doing their best to prevent it, but why should it be necessary? Why do children lie?

A: There are many reasons. First of all, it's important to remember that all children tell a few fibs from time to time. It's part of growing up.

Here's a list of six common types of childhood lies:

1. *The magical lie:* The best example is the 2-year-old's attempt to blame some misbehavior on an imaginary friend or to deny he did something even when you catch him with his hand in the cookie jar.

2. *Test the limits:* Most of us told these lies at the age of 5 or 6. They're designed to test Mom's and Dad's omniscience. "Do they really know everything I say and do? Can I fool them? How far can I go?" Not too far, I hope.

3. *Blaming lie:* This lie is calculated to get someone else in trouble. It's manipulative and it's more dangerous. This youngster is out for revenge. He feels picked on and misunderstood.

4. *Perfection lie:* Typically this is a favorite of the 9- or 10-year-old who thinks he has to be perfect. He won't admit to any flaw or

imperfection in himself. He's very sensitive and doesn't take criticism very well.

5. *Attention-getting lie:* Some kids tell tall tales about themselves or their parents in order to get attention. "My Dad's a pro football player" or "We have four cars and a van too." This type of lie is a favorite of preadolescents whose world is about to change radically; lying may be their way of staying in control and boosting themselves psychologically.

6. *The cover-up:* This is the most serious type of lie. It's told to protect against discovery of a misbehavior. Teenagers are often pros at it, but younger children can master it too. If a youngster leaves a trail of coldly calculated cover-ups, she might be in trouble; either because she doesn't trust her parents to deal with the truth or because she's under tremendous peer pressure to go against parental values.

Democracy at Home?

Q: My husband and I would like to prepare our children, aged 7 and 10, for the real world. We'd like to give them a taste of democracy at home so they'll be ready to assume responsibilities as citizens when they leave us. We both realize, though, that a family cannot run like a true democracy: There are things that only we as parents can decide. Our question is this: Where do you draw the line?

A: Winston Churchill once remarked that democracy is the worst form of government—except for all the rest. You seem to have a very good sense of balance about the place of "democracy" in your own family, and I applaud you for it.

Clearly, you can't open up every family decision to a vote. Yet you want to give the children a sense of participating in the decisions of the family. Where do you draw the line?

Start with issues of health and safety, clearly matters of parental responsibility. Add any issues which involve core family values; you must retain control over such matters. Then you can sketch out some areas which can be brought to a vote and other issues on which you will seek the youngster's advice and ideas but which will not be subject to vote (such as "where do we go for our next summer vacation").

Don't try to commit all of this to writing—your own familial "constitution"—you may regret it because of the complexity. Instead, be reasonable about giving the children a bona fide mechanism for participation in matters that directly concern them. Turn over progressively more responsibility to them as they grow older. That's a good plan to help them grow as individuals and as citizens in a democracy.

Overcoming Fears

Q: Our 7-year-old son is afraid of dogs. Would it be better to force him to confront his fears directly, or should we go along and protect him from encountering dogs?

A: I do not recommend either approach. Direct confrontation can be cruel and dangerous. Not only might your son end up even more afraid of dogs than ever, he'll add a new fear to his collection: you.

On the other hand, it is equally unreasonable to shield a child from his fears. First of all, you'll never succeed at protecting him from all the dogs in his little world. Second, he's going to have to face his fears sometime—with or without you.

The solution? A middle course. You can try a program of desensitization, similar to what a behavioral specialist might prescribe. Plan to introduce your son to dogs in a positive, gentle, step-by-step manner. For example, you can start by showing him pictures of dogs and even having him touch the pictures. Next, give him the opportunity of watching you pet some dogs. Then take his hand in yours and pet a dog. You get the idea. Step by step. Slowly. If your son balks at any step or becomes panicked, do not despair. Calmly back off and return to the previous step. Don't rush it. But if things don't work out, I'd definitely recommend consultation with a child psychiatrist.

Fear of the Dentist

Q: Warner, our 7-year-old, has never seen a dentist. It's about time that he had a checkup. The problem is that he absolutely refuses to go. I don't understand. He doesn't mind visiting the pediatrician. Should I force the issue or just wait for him to get used to the idea?

A: Fear of the dentist, of course, is not unusual. I bet Warner has been influenced by some of his peers who may have had a bad experience in the dental chair.

Here's what I suggest. First, ask around among your own friends who have children: Is there a local dentist who is especially known for his skill in working with children? I'm talking about sensitivity and warmth toward children as well. You might also consider a dentist who specializes in children's dentistry, pedodontics. You can be sure that such a dentist has had a lot of training in the science and art of helping children, and parents too.

After you've found the dentist, why not make arrangements to stop in for a visit with Warner. Not a professional appointment, mind you, but just to meet the dentist and look around the office. Then when Warner goes back for his appointment, he'll be returning to a familiar person; he'll know the lay of the land.

Are Phobias Contagious?

Q: My younger sister is a real phobic, and I'm afraid that her little boy, aged $7\frac{1}{2}$, will grow right into her fears; he's already afraid of being left alone. Am I right—are parental fears contagious? What can my sister do about it?

A: Yes, in a sense, parental fears are "contagious." Children look to their parents for reassurance; if, instead of reassurance, they encounter fear, they, too, will be afraid. I can't specifically diagnose your sister's problem with such little information. Phobias are *irrational* fears. Phobics are panicked by relatively safe things like elevators, heights, driving an automobile, etc. Phobias are based upon displaced fears of other objects and are deeply rooted psychological matters.

Although children are not apt to develop a parent's specific phobia because their psychological world is different from Mom's or

Dad's, they do pick up the general trait of being afraid, of lacking confidence, of mistrusting the unknown.

What can your sister do? True phobics become motivated for therapy when their fears have mushroomed so large that their ability to enjoy life is threatened. How much is her life circumscribed by her phobias? That's the key.

You might try to convince her to go for treatment for the sake of her son. It might work. But rational approaches to irrational problems often fall short of the mark.

Monster Movies

Q: Our two sons, aged 7 and 9, are absolutely hooked on TV monster movies. They never miss a one. At first my husband and I were afraid that the boys would have nightmares, but they seem to thrive on this stuff. Is it harmful?

A: Although I wouldn't prescribe a steady diet of them for any children, monster movies are not necessarily harmful. Your boys, for example, may be using them to overcome their fears of the unknown. They may be utilizing what is sometimes referred to as a *counterphobic mechanism:* By confronting a fear and making it familiar, they make it a friend. It is something like the adult who driven by a fear of heights takes flying lessons. These confrontations take place, of course, on an unconscious basis.

Some kids actually use horror films to test their ability to tolerate anxiety, fear, or aggression. The celluloid monsters stir up monstrous feelings in the unconscious which threaten to erupt, only to be beaten back by the mounting forces of the young ego. Thus tested, children feel a sense of relief and mastery. Other children identify with the violent drives of the monsters but use this mechanism of identification to harmlessly channel (or sublimate) these natural drives. Again, this is not necessarily a bad thing.

But what about children whose defensive abilities are not so strong or who are too young to understand that werewolves and Godzillas don't really stalk the back alleys of the real world? There's the problem. These youngsters are genuinely fearful of monster movies and often do experience chilling nightmares.

Your own boys seem to be using the monster movies in the service of their own psychological growth and development. Still, a preoccupation with these grade C thrillers is not the best way for them to be spending their time. Although they'll outgrow this phase eventually, I would suggest some reasonable limits on these films—and some limits on how much TV they watch in general. Two possible approaches:

1. Make a list of "acceptable" programs for them to watch.

2. Limit their TV watching to approximately one hour per day, with exceptions for wholesome special events.

Advertising and Children

Q: Our children, aged 7 and 9, are advertising junkies. I mean they can sing more commercial jingles and recite more Madison Avenue punch lines than nursery rhymes or camp songs. I guess this isn't the end of the world or anything, but it's just not wholesome. Is it?

A: It's been estimated that the average child sees about 20,000 TV commercials every year. Staggering, isn't it?

It should come as no surprise, therefore, that children pick up the slogans, the lyrics, and the catchy tunes of TV commercials—both those that are specially "targeted" for children and those intended for the adult audience.

No, it's not the end of the world, and there are some potentially positive benefits of your youngsters' fascination with commercials. Why not seize the opportunity to teach them how to be intelligent consumers? I'd suggest that you discuss their favorite commercials with them. What makes them effective? What is the function of advertising in our society? What distinguishes a "good" commercial from a "bad" commercial? How can advertising inform? And how can it mislead?

You might even have a little fun by "inventing" a make-believe product and having the children design an advertising campaign for it.

Sure, advertising can be a nuisance and too much of it can be unwholesome, but you can turn the tables on Madison Avenue by using it as an educational tool.

More Books, Less TV

Q: How can we get our children, aged 7 and 9, to watch less television and to read more books?

A: Research into the reading habits of school-age children reveals that youngsters who do the most reading have at least four things in common:

1. Their parents began reading aloud to them when they were very young.
2. Their parents actively discuss books with them.
3. Their parents are avid readers themselves.
4. Their access to television is limited by Mom and Dad.

Don't String Your Child Along

Q: Missy is my 7-year-old. She minds me pretty well but gets very negative with my husband. I've been studying the situation, and I think I have the answer: He overloads her with directions. For example, rather than telling her one thing like "clean the dishes," he heaps a string of commands together like "clean the dishes, feed the dog, and do your homework." No wonder Missy tunes him out. What do you think?

A: I take my hat off to you. I admire your powers of observation. Your husband is utilizing what we sometimes call *string commands*. Yes, they are overwhelming to a child. (By the way, they're overwhelming to adults also.)

Your husband will get better results if he limits his directions to one simple command; for example, "Missy, please clean the dishes." He should also look for ways to recognize and reward Missy when she does things without being told. After all, the goal of discipline is to create a child who has self-discipline.

Coed Sports

Q: Our daughter (aged 7) and our son (aged 8) will be transferring soon to a new school that has an optional coed sports program. We've heard a lot of pros and cons. Our children aren't sure themselves about participating. What do you think?

A: The jury is still out on coed sports. In my opinion, the grade school is probably the best place to experience it. Why? Boys and girls can compete more equally at this stage of development. Furthermore, the undoing of old sex stereotypes is better accomplished in such an early setting.

At puberty, however, the picture becomes clouded. Girls, for example, tend to enter puberty earlier; their growth spurt may allow them, temporarily, to outperform the boys. While this may be great for the girls, the boys are easily humiliated. Some experts, of course, say that this "reversal" is a good thing. The bad news for the girls, however, is that most boys catch up quickly and outstrip them in athletic prowess. Hence the girls' superiority is fleeting and temporary. Role confusion for the boys and the girls can easily result.

I'm not knocking coed sports. I'm only urging caution until more research is completed.

Burned Out

Q: I'm still shaking. Our house burned down last week. I got the children (aged 7, 9, and 10) out of bed when I smelled the smoke. Then they stood out on the lawn and watched the firefighters battle the flames. It was futile. The house went up like a matchbox. My youngest (Rourke, 7) has started wetting the bed. I try to get him to talk about the fire, but he won't do it. Any suggestions? Does he need counseling?

A: The psychiatric literature on children who have been displaced from their homes by fire is sparse. Some researchers in New York, however, have reported that such children, predictably, do tend to regress. Symptoms such as sleep disorders, tics, and even bedwetting are not uncommon in the early postfire stages.

Other children become preoccupied with fire. They talk about it, fantasize about it, and even play fire-related games such as "Firefighters."

Common dynamics in these children include fear of annihilation and loss of control over their lives.

One might speculate that the symbolic meaning of Rourke's bedwetting is an unconscious urge to "put out the fire" and to protect himself at night.

Keep trying to get through to Rourke. It's okay to share your own fears with him—but be sure to project a picture of confidence: He can count on you to go on protecting him.

Counseling? Only if the symptom persists for more than a month or if other symptoms (nightmares, physical aches and pains, school problems, behavior problems, etc.) appear. The best medicine: Mom's reassurance to quench the flames of Rourke's fears.

Fire Setting

Q: Ross, our 7-year-old son, has set two fires in the last three weeks. The first was started in a corner of the basement. He panicked and fortunately ran upstairs to call my husband. The second fire was set against the side of the house. Again, he could have burned the house down if he didn't yell for help. At this point we're worried and scared. The other children are afraid to go to sleep at night. What should we do?

A: If I was consulting with you face to face, I'd ask several other questions including:

1. Does Ross set fires at school or anywhere else outside the home?

2. Has Ross been having other behavioral problems, especially difficulties in handling aggression?

3. Are there other family conflicts?

It is especially interesting that Ross (apparently) has limited his fire setting to home. This, of course, indicates hostility and vengeance directed at some member(s) of the family. This is the usual pattern for young fire setters.

Some parents lull themselves into believing that "he really doesn't mean it" when they focus on the fact that such youngsters most frequently become frightened of their fire, try to extinguish it, and run for help. Beware. Ross, as I'm sure you realize, could easily miscalculate next time.

Will there be a next time? The odds favor it. Ross does not seem to have a suitable outlet for his anger.

What should you do? As an immediate first step Ross should be evaluated by a child psychiatrist. The evaluation would include a detailed developmental history, family history, and interviews with Ross, you, and your husband. Psychological testing and interviews with siblings may also be a part of the evaluation.

It is most likely that psychiatric treatment will be recommended. If Ross's symptom continues at such a dangerous level, it is possible that the treatment would have to take place within the safe confines of a psychiatric hospital. The prognosis for a fire setter of Ross's age, with intensive treatment, is fairly good.

Bed-Wetting

Q: Our 7-year-old son is a bed-wetter. His pediatrician has checked him for everything and has assured us that he'll grow out of it. But in the meantime he's having a lot of problems: mostly embarrassment. Should he see a child psychiatrist?

A: Bed-wetting, or *enuresis*, is a fairly common problem. Some 41 percent of the parents or grandparents of affected children have a history of bed-wetting themselves. It affects 20 to 50 percent of all children over the age of 5. Your pediatrician is certainly correct advising that most youngsters grow out of it: By the age of 15, for example, the incidence is down to only 1 percent.

But what about your son right now?

I'm relieved to hear that you have taken him to see his pediatrician. That is obviously the sensible first step. From what you've said, I presume the pediatrician has thoroughly examined your boy and ruled out physical illness. Again, I'm relieved because the bedwetting might have been caused by some underlying anatomical or neurological disorder. Thankfully, it was not.

But what *is* causing your son's bed-wetting? Again, don't worry. A specific diagnosis is made in only about 25 percent of all cases. Most of the time, when treatable physical factors have been ruled out, the most common cause is a small bladder capacity. It is cured by tincture of time, bladder retention exercises—and parental understanding.

On the other hand, some cases of bed-wetting are caused by underlying psychological conflicts. Ask your pediatrician if he feels that an evaluation by a child psychiatrist might be indicated. Most of the psychological damage, by the way, is not caused directly by the bed-wetting but by secondary parental overreaction and shaming of the child. This can cause problems with self-esteem and restrict his life away from peers who might discover his "secret."

Try to be natural about your son's symptoms. Do not punish him for it. He is not doing it on purpose. Invite him to work with you toward solving the problem: fluid restriction and so forth. Invite your son to be part of the solution. It sure beats being labeled as "the problem"! He may have some good ideas. If this intervention isn't enough, your pediatrician or a child psychiatrist can suggest other forms of treatment such as medication, behavior modification, the buzzer alarm, psychotherapy, or hypnosis.

All the Other Kids Can Do It!

Q: Our 7-year-old son, Marty, has always been well-behaved. He has always accepted our somewhat firm rules. Now, however, he is more influenced by his peers and he's getting stubborn. He answers back: "Why do I have to go to bed now? All the other kids can stay up late," etc. My question is, How far should a parent be influenced by how *other* parents are raising their children?

A: A very good question. As a child like Marty moves out into the world of peers, your relationship with him is going to become complicated. He will bring home many new ideas and influences: some good and some bad. These new influences can be enriching—if you act as a kind of information sifter: taking the good and eliminating the bad.

Start by defining your core family values. These cornerstones of your family life should not be compromised no matter what the other parents are doing. Second, keep in touch with the parents of Marty's friends. Just what are their rules for such things as bed-time, TV watching, chores, and homework? Don't take Marty's word for it; he does have a vested interest in these matters. Try to be reasonable. Apart from your basic (nonnegotiable) family values, are you being too strict with Marty as compared to the other parents? If so, you might wish to loosen up a bit. Or you might find yourself giving some slack in some areas but actually tightening up in others. After all, as Marty's parents *you* should be in charge, not the neighbors.

The Oldest Child

Q: Kimberly, aged 7, is our oldest child. The younger children (aged 4 and 5) resent her because she's so *bossy*. Will she outgrow this tendency, or is it part and parcel of being an oldest child?

A: Kimberly's personality makeup, of course, is much more than the luck of the birth-order draw. Yet her bossiness is certainly a trait that is associated with many oldest children.

Firstborns have a strong tendency toward being in charge. A significant number of firstborns eventually rise to positions of leadership and prominence. For example, twenty-two of the first twenty-nine American astronauts were firstborns. It is also a fact that firstborns are strongly represented among airline pilots, corporate executives, and even U.S. presidents. Statistically, firstborns even tend to have higher IQs than younger siblings.

But being the oldest child can have mixed blessings. Firstborns can be victims of their own drive to achieve and to lead. They tend to be more tense, worried, neurotic. They tend to be less people-oriented than younger brothers and sisters. The most bossy among them, if they rise to positions of leadership, do not tend to be very popular leaders.

Maybe you can help Kimberly on this last matter. Teach her to be a graceful and sensitive leader of her siblings. Make sure that she learns to follow as well as to lead. The best leaders know when to lead—and when to follow. In this way Kimberly may grow up to be a confident, successful, and popular leader. And she may have her younger siblings to thank for it.

Should We Allow Our Gifted Child to Go with the Flow?

Q: Our son, Rob, is 7 years old. We've been told that he's gifted, that his IQ is over 140. You'd think that Rob would be a star in the classroom. He's not. His work is erratic, and he's something of a cutup in class.

My husband and I are disappointed. Rob is so intelligent, but he just wants to go with the flow, to be normal, as he sees it. What should we do?

A: I believe that all children should be expected to work up to their maximum academic potential. For some children, this means average work. For Rob and other gifted children, this means superior achievement.

Why is Rob so intent on cutting up and going with the flow? Some gifted children actually get bored with regular classroom learning that is geared to the slower learners in class. This boredom can become translated into tension, which can easily become expressed in misbehavior. Be sure that Rob is being sufficiently challenged and stimulated in the classroom. Discuss the matter with his teachers. Remember that as many as 30 percent of all high school dropouts are gifted children who never really get turned on to learning. Don't let this tragedy strike Rob. If necessary, tackle this problem yourself: You should check on the availability of resource rooms, accelerated programs, and specialized classes for the gifted within your school system. If such programs are not available and if a suitable private school is not an alternative, you might try some type of after-school or Saturday enrichment program. Also consider enrolling Rob in evening classes or other programs that would stimulate his interests and allow him to develop his skills more fully. Above all, make it your business to see that Rob receives sufficient learning opportunities. Too many parents make the mistake of adopting a laissez faire attitude: "Let him find himself." Too many such children only "find themselves" when it's too late.

Rob also needs your sensitivity and understanding. To be 7 years old means to be increasingly dependent on peer acceptance. Rob wants to be one of the boys. Unfortunately he seems to think that he has to be average in order to be normal. Have a talk with him about this dilemma. Normality comes in all sizes and shapes. I bet there are guys in Rob's class that play baseball better than he does. Do they intentionally strike out just so they'll be well liked? No way. They try their darndest to smash home runs every time they come up to the plate. Rob should be hitting "home runs" in the classroom.

Finally, gifted children require gifted parents. You'll have to be creative in providing Rob creative opportunities. Find ways to support and encourage his growth and his self-esteem. Your toughest job may be in walking the fine line between promoting his intellectual and psychological growth on the one hand and not pressuring him beyond his limits on the other.

Adjusting to a New School

Q: We just moved to a new house late this summer. This means that our 7-year-old son, Jeremy, will be attending a new school. He does well academically, but he's always been slow to make friends, and we're concerned about his adjustment. How can we help?

A: Why not get a jump on the school bell, if there's still time, by having a back-to-school party for the youngsters in the neighborhood—especially the children that may be in Jeremy's class? If there are very few potential classmates in the immediate neighborhood, encourage each of the neighborhood youngsters to invite one or two of his or her own friends from Jeremy's new classroom.

I would also suggest a private chat with Jeremy. What are his worst fears about going off to a new school? Do not let him become overwhelmed. Cut each of his fears down to manageable size; then help him construct a game plan for tackling these fears head on.

Bathroom Humor

Q: Nicholas, our 7-year-old, has become a terrific comedian, but his jokes are usually of the tasteless, "bathroom" variety. Why this fascination?

A: Nicholas is probably just whistling in the dark. By this I mean he is compensating, through humor, against something which may actually threaten or disgust him. Such a reaction is not uncommon among boys and girls Nick's age. They are not far removed from toilet training themselves. Such regressive memories are a bit threatening; these threats are then tamed through laughter. Actually, Nick's unconscious way of defending against the underlying anxiety is a rather sophisticated and "high-level" solution. Comedy, after all, requires intelligence and creativity.

"But," I can almost hear you saying at this point, "enough is enough—especially at the dinner table!" You're quite right. Praise Nick's creativity, but let him know that his brand of humor is not universally appreciated. Of course, as he gets older, he'll probably have less fascination with this subject material. But why wait? He might as well start now to clean up his act.

Why, Mommy, Why?

Q: Nicole, our 7-year-old, is a bright, inquisitive child. But sometimes she's just *too* inquisitive. What do you do with a child who insists on asking "Why?" to almost everything you tell her?

A: "Why?" is a child's favorite question. But why?

The *whys* of children fall into three basic sizes and shapes. The first might be called the *informational why:* Why does it rain? Why does every state have two senators? Why do airplanes fly? These *whys* are wonderful. They express a budding awareness of the world and a zest for learning. And, fortunately for mom and dad, the answers to most of these questions can be found in a good encyclopedia. These *whys* should be taken seriously. The parent who takes the time to answer these questions will learn with her child—and grow with her child.

A second type of *why* is not, however, a question at all—it is a thinly camouflaged *no!* Consider these plaintive "questions": "But *why* do I have to eat all my salad?" "*Why* do I have to go to bed now. Why?" In these situations the child is not looking for an answer at all. The questions cannot be researched in the *Encyclopaedia Britannica.* In fact, no reasonable answer will satisfy. My advice: Give a straightforward answer, but do not get drawn into the looming power struggle. And, if you possibly can, try to avoid the ultimate retort: "Because I say so and I'm your mother—that's why!" Simply state your reason and back off confidently.

A third type of *why* is used primarily for *getting attention.* If Nicole falls into this category, ask yourself why she needs to seek your attention in this way. Is she unable to engage you in a more positive or productive manner? You might try to turn the tables on her by initiating the attention yourself in the form of encouragement and praise for her accomplishments.

Is Santa Claus Real?

Q: Wendy, our 7-year-old, still believes in Santa Claus. Most of the children in her class, though, have figured the truth out by now. They're starting to tease her. When she comes to me, tears in her eyes, and begs me to reassure her that Santa is real and that her classmates are all wet, I've been telling her, "Yes, honey, Santa is real." Am I doing the right thing?

A: All parents can empathize with you and your dilemma. The belief in Santa Claus is part of the magical innocence of childhood. You hate to see Wendy lose it—yet you know that she must. Most children learn the truth about Santa by the age of 7—somewhat earlier if they have older brothers or sisters to guide the way. Many children make this discovery with a certain sense of sadness; it's like losing a good friend.

Don't jump to immediately reassure Wendy. Instead, ask her what she thinks about it. In this way, you might be able to ease her into her own discovery.

It's not easy being the only kid in the class who still believes in Kriss Kringle. But it's amazing how youngsters are able to reach their own Santa solutions. A 9-year-old once announced her discovery to me in this way: "No, Dr. Novello, everybody knows that Santa Claus is not a real person—he's the spirit of Christmas, the symbol of giving and sharing."

Coal for Christmas?

Q: My husband is planning to put coal into the Christmas stocking of our 7-year-old son, Lee. My husband has threatened Lee that if he wasn't good, Santa would leave coal for him. I thought it was a joke. You know, the usual kind of pre-Christmas warning. Well, it's no joke this time. My husband says that because he's warned Lee and he hasn't responded, we have to "hang tough" or our credibility will be destroyed. What do you think?

A: Your husband is obviously overreacting. He's defined a win-lose situation from which he's allowed himself little room to step down. It's a shame.

As a matter of principle, Christmas gifts should be given without strings attached. Gifts should not be used to intimidate, to bribe, or even to reward. Christmas gifts should be given unconditionally, out of love and in the spirit of Christmas.

Don't let your husband play Scrooge to his own son.

Should Children Make New Year's Resolutions?

Q: My husband and I are great ones for making New Year's resolutions. We find it helps us take stock of ourselves and set goals for the New Year. We've never asked the kids (aged 7, 9, and 12) to join in the process. What do you think? Should children make New Year's resolutions?

A: Your children are a bit young to reflect upon their personal strengths and weaknesses or to observe their own behavioral patterns in the way that adults commonly do at year-end. Yet they certainly should be able to make a modest list of "things I'd like to accomplish next year."

Encourage them to keep it simple, concrete, and, above all, attainable. It would also be a good idea to write down each child's list of goals and to review them some time during the year—perhaps on each youngster's birthday.

Make the occasion upbeat and fun. Be clear that they will not be punished if they break their resolution—after all, how many adults really succeed at this game?

I would also encourage you to invite the youngster's participation in establishing some purely "family" goals for the New Year. In this way you can enhance the values of your family and stress that, while each individual person may have some specific goals, the family unit itself has great importance and that it will take all five of you working together to succeed as a family. Happy New Year!

Be Your Child's Best Friend?

Q: My daughter is 8 years old. Is it wrong for me to want to be her best friend?

A: Yes. Children need parents who are parents—first, last, and always. The role of a parent is very often incompatible with the role of a best friend. A parent establishes family values, sets limits, and does a thousand and one other tasks while maintaining a distinct parent-child boundary. Best friends, on the other hand, are useful supports and sounding boards for youngsters when they feel that the adult world is unfair to them. Best friends need peer support in return. You cannot be your child's peer and her parent simultaneously. The parent who attempts such a tactic will fail at both roles.

The acid test, however, is that children themselves do not really want parents to be their best friends. One 15-year-old girl complained to me once: "My Ma should quit butting into my life like this.... It's nice to be close with her, but she shouldn't use me as a friend. I need her for a mother."

Your daughter will always need you to be her mother. The nature of her need will change as the years go by, but it will always be there. Be a friendly mother, not a best friend.

No Child Support

Q: I was divorced three years ago. My ex-husband is supposed to pay monthly support for our children, aged 8 and 9, but he's been impossible about it. In fact, I've gone to court twice, but it doesn't seem to help very much. So far, I've kept all this from the children. Even though their father is deserting them, I don't feel it will help them to know about it. What is your opinion?

A: You are not alone. In a recent year it was estimated that 3.4 million women were due child support but only 49 percent actually received the full amount; 28 percent received nothing at all. Unfortunately, many courts are lax in enforcing child support payments. Ex-husbands learn very quickly that they are essentially immune from the law.

But should your husband remain immune from his children? I respect your position. You are considering the welfare of the children in shielding them from their father's neglect. I only wish their father had such concern for them.

My answer: At their ages they should not be vulnerable to fears of abandonment. They should know that you will protect them. But if they feel that Daddy doesn't love them, they'll tend to assume that it's because they, not Daddy, are bad. Therefore, keep these developmental issues in mind. I'm assuming that the children know something is wrong. Better, then, to be straight with them. If you participate in an obvious cover-up for their father, they could end up mistrusting you too. Give them the facts but don't unleash an attack on their father: With time they'll draw their own conclusions about him.

Wicked Witch?

Q: My stepdaughter, Annie (aged 8), is fascinated with Hansel and Gretel, and it concerns me. You see I'm the stepmother and Annie sometimes slips and confuses *me* with the wicked witch. Should I encourage her to talk it out with me directly, or should I just ignore it as a phase?

A: Talk it out, by all means. It's not unusual at all for children to harbor resentments against stepparents. In this case Annie may view you as a rival for Daddy's attention or as a pretender to the role of her "real" mother. There are many other possibilities depending on information that is not available to me.

Stepfamilies are made, not born. It takes a lot of work on everyone's part. This means actively pursuing "hints" like Annie's symbolic references to the wicked witch. Encourage her to express her feelings about you. Where do they come from? You'll probably learn that they're not as personally directed at you as you think: You're simply the object of Annie's fears, anger, and other jumbled feelings.

If you can help Annie understand her feelings and master them, you'll be helping her write her own fable: the true-life story of how Annie and you become friends and live happily ever after.

TV Violence and Children

Q: Our kids, like most kids these days, are TV addicts. The main difference, I guess, is that we're trying to do something about it. We limit Tuesday (aged 8) to a half hour per day and Jason (aged 10) to one hour per day. What's more, my husband and I go through the *TV Guide* every week and select the shows they're allowed to watch. They complain—boy, do they complain. But we're convinced we're doing the right thing. What do you say?

A: You'll get no complaints from me. Television is a force for great good in our lives if we use it wisely. The parent who limits and controls the viewing habits of children is a wise parent.

In case you'd like some backup, here's the essence of a review of research conducted over the past ten years by Murray, Zuckerman, and Zuckerman on the influence of TV violence on the behavior of children:

1. Children learn and remember aggressive behavior from what they see on TV.

2. Children who are exposed to repetitive violence on TV become desensitized to it. They then tend to become more accepting of aggressive behavior in real life.

On the other hand, it should be pointed out that some children learn to *inhibit* their own aggression as a result of TV violence—but only if they're made aware of the negative and painful *consequences* of this type of behavior. The best tonic, therefore, is a concerned parent who is available to talk to kids about what they're experiencing on the tube...a parent who is ready to undo some of the damage done by excessively violent TV programming...a parent, I'm sure, like you.

Hyperactivity Outcome

Q: Our 8-year-old son, Edward, has been diagnosed as hyperactive. We're not surprised. We've been through it before with our oldest son, Donald. The pediatrician wants to put Edward on medication, but I'm not so sure. Donald was treated on medication between the ages of 9 and 13, but he eventually outgrew his need for it. It makes me wonder if treatment with medication does any good.

A: First of all, I'm not surprised that Donald "outgrew" his need for medication. This is what usually happens at or about the onset of puberty. In fact, the symptoms of hyperactivity (lack of concentration, agitation, poor impulse control) tend to burn themselves out in adolescence, with or without treatment. It's erroneous, however, to conclude that such a self-limiting illness should not be treated at all.

Children who do not receive proper treatment for hyperactivity pay a great price. They fall behind in school, suffer a loss of self-esteem, and tend to get branded as bad children. You might be interested in a study reported in the *Journal of the American Academy of Child Psychiatry*. A group of men and women in their early 20s who were treated as children with stimulant medication for hyperactivity were compared to a similar group who did not receive medication. The group that had received medication had less delinquency, fewer problems with aggression, better social skills, and higher self-esteem than the untreated group.

The researchers concluded that the medication had allowed them a brighter adult life by giving them an easier childhood, a better foundation upon which to build their lives.

Hyperactivity and Sugar

Q: I think my son, Sammy (aged $8\frac{1}{2}$), is hyperactive. He just can't sit still. It seems to get worse whenever he eats anything sweet. I've read somewhere that sugar can cause hyperactivity. But when I took Sammy to his pediatrician, she dismissed the idea. Instead, she gave me some rating scales to fill out at home along with a similar set for Sammy's teacher. Am I getting the runaround or what?

A: I don't doubt that you've read that sugar (and certain food additives) are believed to be implicated in the cause of hyperactivity by some researchers and clinicians. The link, however, has not yet been proved conclusively—at least to the satisfaction of most pediatricians.

Sammy's doctor was following the majority of her colleagues in her response to you. In one study conducted by the University of Iowa, for example, it was found that only 12 percent of the practicing pediatricians surveyed recommended sugar restriction as a treatment for hyperactivity. On the other hand, there are some physicians who do prescribe specific diets, including sugar restriction, for hyperactivity. There are also a number of parents, like yourself, who have apparently observed firsthand reactions like Sammy's.

The rating scales, by the way, are a good idea. They'll help your doctor make a specific diagnosis—always the first step toward proper treatment.

In the meantime, why not conduct a little experiment of your own? Use the rating scales for several days with Sammy on an unrestricted diet; then use them for several days while Sammy is on a diet that eliminates as much sugar as possible. But be careful: You'll have to be sure that Sammy doesn't cheat on the diet. If he secretly eats a lot of sweets while he's supposed to be restricted from them, he'll sabotage your efforts. Finally, take your findings back to the pediatrician. It's the kind of data she'll need to really help your son.

Medication for Obsessive Children

Q: Walter, our 8-year-old, has been diagnosed as obsessive-compulsive. He has a lot of rituals such as washing his hands exactly three times before he eats, cleaning doorknobs before he touches them, and reciting magical words before he crosses the street. He's been to several doctors, but nothing has helped. Recently we saw a specialist who recommends medication. We were surprised. No one has suggested drug treatment before. Is this new?

A: No. Child psychiatrists have been using certain antidepressant medications in the treatment of obsessive-compulsive disorder for some time. This treatment is usually reserved for the most serious cases; those that do not respond to talking therapy and behavior modification alone. The results have been mixed, and it is not entirely clear why antidepressant medication should have a specific effect in these cases.

Researchers at the National Institute of Mental Health have recently concluded a study of a medication called clomipramine hydrochloride, an antidepressant not yet approved for clinical use in this country but which has been used for the past fifteen years in Canada, South America, and Europe. The results were promising, but there were some undesirable side effects.

Be sure the specialist briefs you fully on the medication, including goals of treatment and possible side effects. Make Walter a partner in the plan too. I'm sure he wants relief. It's no fun being saddled by magical thinking and ritualistic behavior.

Specific Learning Disability

Q: My grandson, aged 8, has something called *specific learning disability*. What is it? Does it mean that he's below average in intelligence?

A: Specific learning disabilities are weaknesses in particular areas of functioning such as reading, or writing, or visual memory, or memory for sound, and a number of other things. For example, some children have a tough time learning to read or write because their brain confuses or reverses letters such as *b* and *d* or *p* and *q*. A child might read "dog" for "bog." Children who have trouble processing sounds also have a tough time learning; imagine, for example, mistaking "bun" for "gun."

Sometimes the term *dyslexia* is used to describe these disabilities.

Special educational techniques can be used to help these young-sters. I hope your grandson will have such an opportunity.

By the way, you might tell him that he's in some pretty good com-pany. Albert Einstein didn't speak until he was 6; Thomas Edison was a school failure; and Nelson Rockefeller overcame his lifelong reading problem by becoming a master at speaking off the cuff.

Left-Right Confusion

Q: Judith, our 8-year-old, can't tell left from right. We've known about it for several years, and we've never given much thought to it. We've even joked about it—maybe just to make her feel better. She doesn't have any other problems except she's a slow reader. I read a magazine article last week about reading problems (dyslex-ia). Do you think Judi may be dyslexic? What should we do?

A: Dyslexia is a subcategory of learning disability which affects 5 to 10 percent of the population. Most dyslexics (such as Albert Einstein, Leonardo da Vinci, and Woodrow Wilson) are male, but you'll be interested to know that left-right problems are more com-mon among females. Yes, left-right confusion is usually a subtle form of learning disability.

The cause of learning disability has been a hotly contested and hotly pursued matter among scientists and physicians. Most recent evidence suggests that abnormalities in the language center of the brain are probably at fault. Somewhere in the embryological de-velopment of the brain, certain cells do not get lined up correctly. The "wiring" of the brain, therefore, becomes tangled. The result can be left-right confusion, difficulty in distinguishing certain shapes or letters of the alphabet, and other disabilities. As I have indicat-ed, some very intelligent people in history have suffered learning problems. These individuals learned how to compensate for their problem and to maximize their other intellectual skills.

Educators know much more about helping dyslexic children to-day. Special teaching techniques are available in most school sys-tems.

The first step, though, is to have Judith tested by an expert. From what you've told me, I believe there is a strong likelihood of dyslexia. But don't worry. Help is available, and Judi is in good company!

Switch to a Male Teacher?

Q: My son, Marc, is 8 years old. He's in a special reading class for slow learners and also attends a resource class for extra help in math. The school psychologist says he has trouble in audio and visual memory. The thing that puzzles me is that if he reads or does math problems for his father at home, he does just fine. It's also interesting that all his teachers are female. Should we insist on a male teacher for Marc? Do you see a connection here?

A: You may be on to something important here, but don't jump to conclusions.

Marc has probably undergone some pretty sophisticated testing. The test results should be relatively free of bias—such as the sex of the examiner and the sex of the teachers. But there well may be some element of psychological conflict between Marc and female authority figures—or a very fine relationship with his father specifically that allows him to overcome performance anxiety when Dad is working with him at home. You don't mention, though, how Marc does with you when you work with him. If he's not able to perform well with you, it would help build the case for a psychological block.

At any rate, I like the detective work you're doing here. You want to help Marc and so do his teachers. That's the key. Let them know about your observations. They may go along with a little experiment: the retesting of Marc by a male psychologist and possible trial with a male resource teacher. Of course, if that intervention makes a difference, you're still faced with the question: "Why?" A clinical evaluation by a child psychiatrist may provide the ultimate answer.

Afraid to Make Friends

Q: Our Carole, aged 8, is so shy. She's afraid of strangers. She can't make friends easily. She panics when she has to answer a question at school. Sometimes she even feigns illness to avoid school. We're starting to worry. At first, we thought it was just a stage, but, if anything, it's getting worse. What do you advise?

A: It is definitely not a stage. Stranger anxiety, for example, is normal late in the first year of life but not at the age of 8. Carole should be happily peer-related at this time, and even though any child gets upset occasionally in school if they don't know the answer to a question, frequent panic attacks are abnormal.

Carole's problems go beyond simple shyness. There are elements of both stranger anxiety and performance anxiety in the painful picture you paint. Carole may also be on the verge of a school refusal problem and appears to be developing psychosomatic symptoms as well.

The clincher is your observation that Carole is getting worse—not better. The time to intervene is now. Carole is suffering from a combination of developmental and psychological problems. The first step is a thorough diagnostic evaluation by a child psychiatrist or psychologist to identify the problem. Then the solution won't be far behind.

The Instigator

Q: Our son is a real instigator. Frankie is only 8 years old, but he's very clever about getting his two brothers and his friends to do what he wants them to do. The strange thing is that while the other boys often get in trouble as a result of Frankie's manipulations, he never seems to get in trouble at all. Is this a problem, or will this behavior be good for him when he gets to be an adult?

A: Cynics might say that Frankie is well on his way to a successful adult life. They would point out that the skillful manipulation of other people is the hallmark of the successful businessperson, politician, manager, or bureaucrat.

I don't agree. Frankie, at 8, is mostly motivated not by what's good for the other guy but what's in it for him. His motto may be: "Let's you and him fight." Such behavior will only earn him the resentment and anger of his siblings and peers...just as such behavior from adults usually ends not with their success but with their alienation from other people.

Yes, Frankie's little victories are shallow and short-lived. Don't encourage him. Don't let him get away with it.

Delay of Gratification

Q: Elizabeth is 8 years old. She's very demanding. I mean, when she gets it into her mind that she wants something, she wants it *right now!* She'll pester me until I either give it to her or send her to her room. When will she get over this phase?

A: Watch out. This is *not* a phase. Elizabeth's behavior would be typical ("phase-specific") for a 2- or 3-year-old, but it is inappropriate for an 8-year-old. For some reason she has not matured to the point where she can delay gratification and tolerate the everyday frustrations of life. The infant and toddler operate on the basis of the *pleasure principle:* I want what I want when I want it. They have very little ability to delay gratification or to distinguish what they *want* from what they *need.* With time, however, parents teach frustration tolerance by saying "no" and by teaching the difference between wants and needs.

We have a problem here. Can you imagine what kind of teenager or adult Elizabeth will grow into unless she changes? I can. She'll make a lot of people unhappy—especially herself.

I don't have enough information to diagnose the problem fully but one key may be in your own inconsistent response to Elizabeth: capitulation or punishment. There are other effective ways of dealing with this kind of misbehavior. I strongly recommend consultation with a child psychiatrist.

Should Parents Apologize?

Q: The other day I was about thirty minutes late in picking up our son, Russell (aged 8), from soccer practice. All the other boys had left the practice field. Russ was scared—and he was angry with me. I was angry at myself and frustrated, too, because my delay was due to unexpected traffic. As soon as Russ got into the car, he began criticizing me. Instead of simply apologizing, I got very defensive. I actually blamed *him* for playing on the soccer team in the first place! We ended up in angry silence. My question is, Should I go back to Russell now and apologize?

A: Yes. You can use the incident constructively and creatively. Sit down with Russ and recall the incident. Be careful not to blame him. Tell him you wish you could do it all over again; that, if you could, you'd start by telling him you were very sorry for being late. Then ask him how he would have responded. You can make a game out of it; sometimes we call this technique *role playing*.

But don't heap all the guilt upon yourself. After all, Russ blew it too. He started by criticizing you. Help him find a better way to deal with such disappointments.

Grow Out of It?

Q: My 8-year-old nephew, Steven, is a bully. There's no other way to describe him. He pushes other children around and threatens them constantly. He doesn't have a friend in the world except for his mother who smiles and says that boys will be boys. She's convinced that it's just a phase and that Stevie will grow out of it. I'm not so sure. Will he grow out of it?

A: There's a good chance that he won't. As a child psychiatrist I can tell you story after story about youngsters like Steven who do not grow out of it at all.

A recent study in New York backs up my own observation. Over 500 children, identified as "bullies," were followed over a period of several years. The result? Most of them ended up as aggressive, friendless, unhappy 18-year-olds.

Why? The aggressive child is usually struggling with some powerful underlying psychological conflict. He's very unhappy with himself, but as a defense against his fears and low self-esteem, he externalizes his pain onto other children in his environment. He struggles to puff himself up at the expense of others' misery. These youngsters need help.

Even if Steven miraculously grows out of it without therapeutic intervention, he may pay a big price along the way. His behavior is, no doubt, interfering with his natural development already.

Steven should, at the very least, have the benefit of a psychiatric evaluation. It may save him a lot of misery later on since all that aggression ultimately comes home to roost.

What Price Obedience?

Q: My husband runs the family like a drill instructor. He's obsessed with obedience. "You have to train the kids to obey, obey, obey," he says. Well, our children (aged 8 and 9) obey, but I'm not sure it's so good for them. They're like little robots. They can't think for themselves. They bring everything to Dad to decide. What do you think about this?

A: You can force children into blind obedience, but as you suggest, you (and they) pay a price for it.

Researchers at the University of North Carolina, after studying over 100 youngsters, concluded that children who are raised by do-it-because-I-say-so parents tend to be distractible and uncreative; they have little intellectual curiosity and tend to be passive and apathetic.

Children, of course, must be taught to respect the core values of the family, to keep the basic rules. At the same time, however, it's important to instill in them a healthy skepticism. Kids should be encouraged to ask questions, to express their ideas and their feelings.

Steer a middle course between being authoritarian and permissive. That's your best bet for raising children who will have a healthy respect for authority but who can, and will, think for themselves.

Calls at the Office

Q: Our son, Jimbo, is 8 years old. He's very attached to his father—too attached. He calls my husband at the office two or three times a day—more often on Saturday and in the summer. Jim, my husband, tries to explain that he has to work, and we've even threatened to punish Jimbo by taking away certain privileges, but nothing seems to work. Jimbo complains that he misses his Daddy and that he needs to talk to him. Any ideas?

A: There are several things here that do not meet the eye.

First of all, Jimbo's almost obsessive attachment to his father is unusual, especially in an 8-year-old. At this time he should have a strong identification with his father, but this is not the same as his suffering what almost sounds like separation anxiety when he is out of touch with Dad.

Second, your efforts to "solve" this problem sound very tentative and too cautious. You've "threatened" to eliminate privileges. Why haven't you done it? Jimbo has seen through your threats. He knows he's in the driver's seat.

What to do? It's not an easy question to answer in this case since I can't be sure if we're dealing with a rather superficial conduct problem that will respond to some behavioral manipulations or with a more profound psychological problem that's going to require psychotherapy.

Let's assume, though, that the problem is a simple behavioral one. Jimbo has gotten into the *habit* of calling Dad. How to break the habit? Sit down with Jimbo, and tell him that things must change. Starting next Monday he will be allowed one call per day. The next week it will be three calls per week, and ultimately he will be limited to one call per week—for emergency use only. At the same time, Dad should listen to Jimbo's complaints about missing him. Is there some truth in it? Is there some way that Dad could spend some special time with Jimbo?

One word of caution: Don't expect Jimbo to comply immediately with this plan. He'll put Dad's new resolve to a test. The key, therefore, is your husband. When Jimbo breaks the rules by calling too often, Jim should simply refuse to answer.

This plan, of course, may fail. Either Jim will be unable to keep up his end of the bargain or Jimbo will become very anxious and maybe even develop other symptoms or habits. In either case the answer is a consultation with a child psychiatrist.

When in Doubt, Punish Them Both?

Q: We have an 8-year-old son and a 10-year-old daughter. As you might guess, the two of them get into a lot of squabbles. Most of the time one of them comes running to us insisting that we punish the other one. My husband and I continually tell them to leave us out of it, to fight their own battles, but they often seem to get us involved. Our usual solution, when that happens, is to punish both of them. For example: "If you can't agree what to watch, *neither* of you can have the TV tonight." What do you think of this approach?

A: This is a last-ditch approach. As you yourself acknowledge, it is born of defeat. You're using it because another approach failed. But the other approach was destined to fail. Why? Asking 8- and 10-year-olds to fight their own battles is asking them to do more than they're capable of. Inevitably, they will turn to Mom and Dad for the solution.

Of course, they want a quick fix; they want you to determine the guilty party and to pass out the punishment. Maybe you are also searching for a quick fix. If so, you, too, will be disappointed. Sibling rivalry takes some time and patience from parents. But if you invest some time now, if you use these incidents as an opportunity to teach the youngsters *how* to solve their problems, you'll be doing them and yourselves a big favor.

So next time the kids disagree and run to you as judge and jury, sit down with them and express concern over *their* problem. They own it. You don't. But you'll help them decide how to solve it. Then invite them to suggest their own solutions. What they finally decide is not as important as the fact that they both agree to abide by their decision. Thus you will be teaching them the art of negotiation and compromise: an important lesson in life. The beauty of this approach is that, with time, your role as a nonpartial mediator will be required less and less. You can work yourself out of a job.

Black Sheep

Q: There's one black sheep in every family, right? In our family, it's Doria (aged 8). Her brother and sisters (aged 6, 9, and 11) are all energetic and high achievers. Doria operates at only two speeds: slow and stop. She never completes her chores or her schoolwork. Should we just accept this as her way of being "different" or should we do something about it?

A: Do something about it. Forget the black sheep myth. Doria is probably being scapegoated. She wants to be special, and she's found her special niche on the negative side of life. The longer you let the scenario continue, the harder it will be to change your daughter.

You might start with a realistic assessment of her abilities. Consult with her teacher and pediatrician. Does she have the potential to do better? If not, adjust your expectations and help her develop some useful skills she can be proud of. If she's got the potential, better find out now what's blocking her. A consultation with a child psychiatrist could help.

Why Can't You Be Like Your Brother and Sister?

Q: Our youngest daughter, Katie, is 8 years old. She's just the opposite of her older brother and sister. They're neat and tidy. She's, well, sloppy. They do their chores on time. Katie always has to be reminded. The list goes on and on. My husband tries to encourage her to imitate the good behavior of the other two, but his efforts seem to backfire. Any suggestions?

A: Telling Katie to keep her room clean just like her older sister or to be ready for school on time just like her brother is certainly well-intentioned, but I'm afraid the tactic is doomed to failure. Katie already feels enough rivalry with her big brother and big sister. Why reinforce it? In fact, her dawdling, oppositional behavior is her own imperfect attempt to be "different" from them. By constantly calling her attention to those differences, you are unwittingly encouraging her to exaggerate them even further.

Treat each of the children as unique individuals. While it is good for Katie to be different, you want her difference to be on the positive side of life. Reward her for success, not failure.

Let Them Fight It Out?

Q: We've got two girls, aged 8 and 10. You know what this means: squabbles, squabbles, squabbles. They can't agree on anything. Unfortunately, I think I've been fueling the fire by letting myself get involved too often. One of them will always run up to me and tattle on her sister. Then I tend to take the bait. I go right in and punish the offender. This quiets them down—but only for a little while. Only until the one I've just punished tries to get even by tattling on the other one. Then I've got to hand out another punishment. It's a vicious cycle. Shouldn't I just let them fight it out on their own?

A: You're learning.

If you let yourself get pulled into these sibling battles, you're choosing to become part of the problem, not part of the solution. Why? The girls will learn to get your attention on the negative side of life. "If we fight, we get Mom's attention" will be their conclusion. Also, you invite retaliation when you punish one child at the instigation of the other.

Yes, it is a vicious cycle. But how do you get out of it? Some parents would opt to punish both children if they can't get along. I don't recommend this approach as a first step. Save it. Use it only if all else fails.

Instead, encourage the children to resolve their differences between themselves. Next time, for example, one of the girls complains that her sister won't let her watch *her* TV program, just nod with understanding and ask: "I wonder how you two can solve the problem?" Don't expect miracles at first. You may have to help them problem-solve in the beginning. But getting involved on the side of the solution sure beats playing the punishment game.

Should Children Take Sides?

Q: My husband has an annoying habit. Every time we have a serious disagreement, he goes to our children (aged 8 and 9) and tells them about it in detail. Then he asks them to take sides, to decide who's right and who's wrong. He thinks it's good for them. I say it's terrible. Who's right?

A: You are. When children are asked to decide a parental argument, they are placed in a loyalty bind; they are being asked to choose between Mom and Dad. This is impossible, and it's harmful too.

Do not allow your children to become pawns in a marital conflict.

Adoption Grief

Q: My child, wherever he is, is 8 years old today. I think about him often—especially on his birthday. You see, I placed him for adoption at birth. I was unwed, a teenager, in no position to have a child. I did what I had to do—at the time. But now it's different. I'm married to a wonderful man and my world is complete, except for a painful hole in my heart. I miss my son. What can I do?

A: Your grief is understandable. And you are not alone. A Harvard researcher recently interviewed 321 women, aged 19 to 76. She found that women who gave up their babies for adoption often suffer unresolved grief over many years. Interestingly, 96 percent of the women surveyed had considered searching for their child, and 65 percent actually began a search. While I don't know how many of these women were actually successful in finding their children, most of them searched only to find information, not to reclaim their offspring. As one such woman told me, "It's the not knowing that's most painful." What can you do? I suggest that you contact some local adoption agencies. Ask if they have any counseling groups for women like yourself. Talking to other women who share your experience will help you work things out and put things into perspective. If you can't find a support group, I suggest you consider psychotherapy. Why? Your pain is not only harmful to you, but it could spill over into your marriage. Over 70 percent of the women in the survey reported marital problems as a result of their unresolved grief. Best to get it resolved.

Adoption and Self-Esteem

Q: We adopted Erik (aged 8) a year ago. We're worried about him. He's not doing well in school and seems sad a lot of the time. The school psychologist says Erik has low self-esteem. We try to praise him whenever we can. What else can we do?

A: Be careful. Your praise is well-intentioned, but it may backfire. You can't bestow self-esteem on a child. It has to be earned. The key, therefore, is for you to provide Erik with plenty of opportunities to earn his own self-esteem. Help him find a hobby or activity that he likes and that he will feel good about. Ask his opinion of things. Praise him, sure, but don't reach too far for it. As long as Erik feels badly about himself, you may make him feel worse if you try to pump him up artificially.

Soccer Father

Q: My husband is a typical "soccer father," and it's really getting to our 8-year-old, Noah. My husband is at every game: baiting the referees, shouting insults to Noah if he doesn't play up to par. Last week he shouted repeatedly to "kill" a boy on the other team. Noah tries to ignore these things, but sometimes he comes home and cries. What can I do?

A: This is a sign of the times. The theater has always had its share of stage mothers. Soccer now has its sideline fathers—and mothers too. Your husband probably means well, but he's projected so much of himself into Noah's soccer playing that I'm afraid he's blurred the boundary between son and self. Yes, he's shouting at an extension of himself out on the field. As with a stage mother, Noah's success may really represent self-accomplishment to his soccer father. And, of course, this is a heavy trip to lay on any 8-year-old. Noah probably wants to play well, but he also wants to have fun, and, above all, he doesn't want to be ridiculed in front of his buddies.

Have a talk with your husband. He's going overboard.

No Girls Allowed

Q: Our sons, Brian (aged 8) and Kevin (aged 10), have started a club in the neighborhood. They call it the Comets. They've recruited about a dozen other boys to join. I don't know what it's all about, but they seem to have fun, and I think it's healthy for them. The only thing I'm uneasy about is that they refuse to let girls join. I mean this goes against the trends in our society, right? I wonder if I should force the issue. I don't want my sons to grow up with out-of-date sexist attitudes, but they are very young, and the Comets will probably be just a transient, harmless experience in their lives. What should I do?

A: My own observations are that many of the artificial barriers between boys and girls are being broken and that, in general, this is good for both sexes. Some team sports, for example, and other recreational activities in schools are increasingly open to coed participation. Both boys and girls benefit since it gives them a proving ground for developing skills in cooperation and teamwork that they'll need in later life.

Yet, as you suggest, both boys and girls, left to their own devices, crave a certain amount of exclusive same-sex activity. This is especially so for preteens and youngsters in the latency stage (from 5 to 10 years old) like Brian and Kevin. It's normal and it's healthy. Attitude and balance are the keys.

Computer Kids

Q: Diane, my 8-year-old, is rusty in math. She just doesn't solve problems very well. She likes to work on the computer at school, and I wonder if I should buy an inexpensive computer for her use at home? A salesman told me that children learn how to be better problem solvers and develop more analytical skills if they have a lot of computer exposure. Comments?

A: The jury is still out. In fact, some initial findings fail to support the salesman's claims. Researchers at the Bank Street College's Education Center for Children and Technology are studying the matter; at this point they caution that a child's ability to program a computer may not translate at all into better problem-solving or analytical skills.

I'm not saying that computer education is a bad thing. It's a wonderful opportunity for Diane and other children and increasingly necessary in our high-tech world. I am saying that many claims are being made for computers that may not stand up to scientific scrutiny. Analytical children will be analytical with or without computers. Nonanalytical children may not be helped very much in the desired way even by the best of those desktop marvels.

A conference with Diane's teacher would be a good first step. Discuss the nature of her problem and the best way to deal with it. Then "compute" the data yourself before dishing out the bucks for a home computer.

Kinetic Family Drawings

Q: Adam, my 8-year-old, just had some psychological testing because of some behavior problems at school. One of the tests was called Kinetic Family Drawing. What is it? What does it show about a child?

A: The directions for a Kinetic Family Drawing (KFD) are deceptively simple. The psychologist asks the youngster to "draw a picture of your family doing something." The child then is free to select the theme and is given about fifteen minutes to complete the drawing.

The psychologist can learn a great deal from a KFD. He or she analyzes the drawing for the basic theme communicated in the drawing, for who is pictured and who may be left out of the picture, the size of the various family members, for who is drawn closer to whom (alliances versus competition), and a host of other important factors.

There are, in addition, certain symbols that tend to recur in the drawings of children; the sun often represents warmth and nurturance; a ball being thrown between two people may represent attraction or aggression. There is some danger, though, in reading too much into these symbols; they are not universal.

Any psychological assessment must be geared to the individual child. Adam's KFD, along with the rest of the tests in the battery, will be analyzed in the context of his own problems and developmental history.

What Kids Worry About

Q: When I was a girl I used to worry about things like strangers and monsters. My children, aged 8 and 10, though, seem to worry about things like environmental pollution and nuclear war. Are children changing or what?

A: The underlying psychodynamics of why children worry and what they ultimately fear (annihilation, abandonment, bodily harm, loss of self-esteem, etc.) remain quite constant. Nevertheless, these fears tend to get dressed up in contemporary clothing in each generation.

A study conducted in 1935 showed that children worried about animals, dark rooms, strangers, loud sounds, and loneliness. A recent study in New York revealed these as the most common childhood fears: death of a parent, parental cancer, divorce, nuclear war, and poor grades.

Study the two lists. At first glance the items appear to have almost nothing in common. But on closer examination the basic similarities are rather striking, aren't they? The consistent themes include loss, loneliness, fear of physical injury, and loss of self-esteem.

Precocious Puberty

Q: Our 8-year-old son, Gordon, has been diagnosed by his pediatrician as having precocious puberty. I became concerned when I noted some hair under his armpits about a month ago. My husband then noticed that Gordon was developing pubic hair too. We have been told not to worry. Can you tell us more?

A: Precocious puberty is the onset of physical changes of puberty before the age of 9 in girls and 10 in boys. Most cases are due to benign and unknown causes, although about 10 percent are due to abnormalities in the central nervous system (such as benign tumors) and overactivity of the adrenal gland. Boys like Gordon tend to develop axillary and pubic hair. In many cases there is enlargement of the penis and testicles and even sperm production. Boys tend to develop acne as well.

From a psychological standpoint there are obviously some pit-falls since the excessive production of sex hormones can cause emotional crises similar to the familiar mood swings of the typical 12- or 13-year-old. A 9-year-old, of course, is even less ready for these psychological roller coaster rides than a teenager.

I have found that physically precocious children tend to suffer shame and guilt, often precipitated by the teasing of "friends." It is important, therefore, to reassure Gordon and to be available to him for support.

Clinicians at the National Institute of Child Health and Human Development have used an experimental drug to arrest precocious puberty. The drug is related to a common contraceptive pill. The drug acts by putting a brake on the pituitary gland's release of hormones which trigger the changes of puberty. These researcher-clinicians have reported a 90 percent success rate—but they have followed only ten children for as long as four years, and the longer-term effects of the treatment have not yet been determined.

Workaholic Father

Q: My husband, Barton, is a workaholic. He loves his job. He's at the office every night until 8 o'clock. He's there on Saturday mornings and sometimes even on Sundays. In the early years of our marriage I didn't mind it too much: He was working hard so we could save for a home. Well, we have the home now but no home life. The biggest problem is the children, 8 and 10 years old. They complain that they never see their father. I'm getting tired of covering for him. When I talk to Bart about it, he shrugs and agrees with me. He says he misses them too, but he's got an important job and the company depends on him. He promises that he'll get off the merry-go-round in a couple of years and that he'll make it up to the children.

A: Barton may decide to make it up to the children some day—but it may be too late.

In my practice of child psychiatry I've encountered this phenomenon too many times. Men like Barton do love their wives and their children and, when pressed, will say that the family is their top priority, but then they hurry out of my office and right back to theirs.

Men (and women) become workaholics for many reasons. Some of them are driven to achievement as a matter of security or self-esteem. It's as though they are still striving to please a disapproving parent who continually asks, "What have you done for me lately?" Each new achievement is empty; it must immediately be topped by something else.

Other workaholics hide behind their work. They hide from intimacy and love. For them, work becomes a psychological defense.

Whatever the cause of Barton's workaholism, the children will suffer. I agree that you should not be trapped into covering for him. Let him explain himself to the children. Their complaints should also go directly to him.

Yes, your husband's workaholism sounds like a chronic condition. Don't bet that he can turn a new leaf in two years.

The Class Clown

Q: My husband and I recently had our regular conference with the teacher of our 8-year-old son, Jeffrey. He seems to be doing okay, but he's described as the "class clown." Should we be concerned?

A: Not necessarily. Humor is a wonderful gift as long as it's appropriate and kept in perspective. Keep your eye on what I call the bottom line indicators: Is Jeffrey performing up to his potential academically? Is his behavior acceptable at school and at home? Does he get along with family, friends, teachers? Is he happy with himself?

Some children lean on comedy as a cover-up for their shortcomings. Others use humor as a defense against fear or aggression. On the other hand, many class clowns are very well adjusted children. A few even grow up to become network stars.

Videotape Replay Technique

Q: I have a lot of blowups with my 8-year-old, Anne. I wish there was some way we could both learn from our mistakes.

A: Try what I call the *videotape replay technique.* After everything has quieted down between the two of you, call Anne back into the room. Tell her that you both "blew it" and you'd like to go over the incident again—to make it come out *right* this time. Set the scene and reenact the incident, trying your best to give it a more desirable ending. It's like running a videotape except you don't really need any fancy equipment—just some goodwill and imagination. This technique, a form of psychodrama or role playing, is especially appealing to youngsters of Anne's age.

Watching the Cat Have Kittens

Q: Our cat is going to have kittens. As you can imagine, our two children (an 8-year-old boy and 9-year-old girl) are excited and curious. Would it be harmful for them to witness the birth?

A: Not if you and your husband prepare them, emotionally and factually, for the event. In fact, your youngsters (and your cat!) are presenting you with a nice opportunity to do some sexual education.

Do not, however, allow your children to force your decision unless you are ready to make it. Both you and your husband should be in agreement, and both of you should be comfortable with the idea. If you decide to go ahead with it, be sure to spend several short "sessions" with the children. Do not overwhelm them with details at any one time. Be sure to answer any questions that are asked, but do not go beyond their level of understanding. In other words, do not answer questions that are *not* being asked. The sexual education of youngsters is a process that spans several years; children should grow gently into a full factual and emotional understanding of such things.

Middle-Child Syndrome

Q: We have three children: a 10-year-old girl, an 8-year-old boy, and a 7-year-old boy. They're all doing well—except the 8-year-old. He's jealous and envious of his brother and sister. He insists that they get all the advantages. He's miserable much of the time. Is he suffering from the middle-child syndrome?

A: He's certainly caught in the middle and seems to be having a hard time with it. Many middle children grow up believing that they always get the fuzzy side of life's lollipop. When you're the second of three siblings, somebody else is obviously always the oldest, but you were once the youngest—only to be displaced by the arrival of number 3—the new "baby of the family." The middle child, then, may be trapped forever into attempting to carve out his special place in the family. His identity may be tough to establish.

The worst scenario is when the middle child becomes so discouraged at establishing a positive role for himself that he makes failure and misery his secret goals. This can lead to continuous conflict with siblings since each skirmish only serves to convince him that he's right: Life is unfair; he always gets the dirty deal. No amount of parental persuasion can get him to think otherwise: His mind is made up, so don't confuse him with the facts.

How to help a youngster break out of this trap? Help him define himself in positive terms. What can he do better than his brother and sister? What are his special skills and interests? Accentuate the positive. Help him to become *special*.

By the way, there are some advantages to being a middle child. Such youngsters tend to develop better interpersonal skills that are useful in later life. All that experience in dealing with an older, more powerful sibling and a demanding younger one can pay off in an extraordinary ability to deal with other people. Middle children also tend to be less rigid than oldest children and less dependent than youngest.

One final word: There are many exceptions to these patterns. Not all middle children are victims of this so-called syndrome. Your 8-year-old's unhappiness may have nothing at all to do with birth order. Spend time with him, and encourage him to tell you how he really feels. He'll be your best teacher about why he's unhappy.

The Velvet Hammer

Q: My 8-year-old daughter, Cindy, admitted to me that she stole five dollars from my purse last week. I was flabbergasted and confused. I wanted to punish her, but I also wanted to hug her for having the courage to be so honest. If I punish her, do I run the risk of turning her off, of undermining her honesty?

A: A situation like this calls for the "velvet hammer." First of all, it is important to understand that your daughter's developing conscience is hard at work. Cindy feels guilty. She wants you to know about the incident because it's causing her so much internal discomfort. She wants to be absolved so that her conscience will go easier on her. Her conscience, in fact, is calling for some form of punishment. Cindy, of course, also wants your love and understanding.

I would recommend that you feel free to express your shock and disappointment. Cindy does know that she has let you down. Then explain your dilemma just as you have described it to me in your question. Cindy will understand. Ask her to tell you all about it; then invite her to join you in figuring out her punishment. One word of warning: Given such an opportunity, 8 year olds often have a tendency to be tougher on themselves than adults might be toward them. You may have to soften the revenge of Cindy's punitive conscience.

Some form of punishment, however, is advisable as long as it is done in an atmosphere of understanding and warmth: *the velvet hammer.*

He's Got the Moves

Q: I think our Freddy, aged 8, has the "moves." I mean he's very upset because we've just moved to a new city. I knew it would happen. I even warned my husband, but now we have a problem on our hands. Freddy is withdrawn, he's lost his appetite, and he's not sleeping very well. The only thing he wants to do is cling to me day and night. What should we do?

A: Freddy is depressed. He's probably reacting to a loss of friends. He may also be reacting to the family stress that usually accompanies such moves. For example, you say you "warned" your husband. Pretty strong language. Was there a major disagreement between the two of you over the move? If so, Freddy might also be reacting to tension between you.

My advice is to address these matters squarely. Help Freddy work through the loss of his friends. Help him express his feelings and help him keep in touch with postcards or letters, tapes, or phone calls. If Freddy is frightened about his new school or worried about making new friends, help him out. If there *is* tension between Mom and Dad, work it out—and be careful not to burden Freddy with it. If these measures don't work, I'd suggest a consultation with a child psychiatrist. Freddy's symptoms would be considered to be fairly serious if they don't clear up reasonably soon.

Latchkey Leftovers?

Q: We have two latchkey children, Dina (aged 8) and Morton (aged 9). They seem to handle it fairly well. I wonder, though, if the latchkey experience will cause them any problems in later years? Will they be afraid to be alone or anything like that?

A: A perceptive question. Some experts believe that latchkey children do, indeed, suffer in later years. One researcher, for example, interviewed 1000 former latchkey children and found that one-half of them were still afraid of being alone.

The best you can do for Dina and Morton is to build as much safety into their situation as you possibly can. Be sure they can reach you or a trusted adult. Educate them about safety in the home: electricity, fire, flooding, accidents. These are the biggest fears of latchkey children—anticipate them. Finally, encourage the children to express their fears. Maybe they're simply not afraid, but maybe they *are* and they're reluctant to talk about it. If the fear is there, let's get it out. The formula, then, is protection, education, and expression.

Hot Line for Kids

Q: I'm a working mother with two typical latchkey kids: aged 8 and 10. I've trained them both very carefully, and I feel reasonably secure about their safety. But I've recently heard about a nifty idea: a hot line for children that's been established somewhere. Can you tell me more about it? Are you in favor of it?

A: Several communities have established such services, perhaps based on the successful model introduced in State College, Pennsylvania, in 1982.

And why not? Over 60 percent of all mothers with school-age children are employed outside the home. A substantial number of children, like yours, are latchkey kids.

In the District of Columbia, with the highest proportion of working mothers in the country, a kiddie hot line called PhoneFriend has been popular and successful. The lines are manned every school day from 3 P.M. to 7 P.M. Trained staffers respond to requests ranging from "I just need somebody to talk to" to "what to do with a baby robin I just found in a nest" to outright emergencies.

As a child psychiatrist I'm pleased that the adult staffers are trained to stay within parental guidelines. For example, if a child asks, "Can I go outside?" the staffer would ask: "What are your parents' rules about that?"

My point: Kiddie hot lines can be useful to remove the stress and fear of being alone for some latchkey children, but they are not a substitute for mom and dad.

Ex-husband Hides behind Santa

Q: My ex-husband does it every Christmas. He shows up with a carload of gifts for the children, after ignoring them all year long. The children (aged 8 and 10) love it. They see all those expensive gifts, and they immediately forget all the times they've asked, "Why doesn't Daddy ever visit us?" But I don't forget so easily. How can I? He doesn't even pay the child support.

A: Your ex is hiding behind Santa Claus. His lavish gift giving is less in the spirit of Christmas and more in the service of obscuring his neglect during the rest of the year. This is not an uncommon phenomenon, by the way, even in intact families.

You have an additional problem here. Your ex-husband's expensive gifts may dwarf your own gifts in the eyes of the children.

This may undercut you to some extent, but remember that children are not so easily fooled. They know who's there when they need them. They know who can be counted on.

You don't mention whether or not you share your feelings with the youngsters. Do you interpret your ex-husband's behavior to them? It would be understandable if you did so. Be sure, though, that your children understand that their father's neglect has nothing to do with them—it's his problem. As they grow older, they'll put these things into perspective.

Children of Alcoholics

Q: My husband is an alcoholic. After all these years, he's finally been motivated for treatment. Two weeks ago he attended his first AA meeting. I've been going to Al-Anon for about a month, and it really helps. In fact, I'd like our children (aged 9 and 11) to attend some Ala-Teen meetings, which are specifically designed for children of alcoholics. Other parents have encouraged it, but Bob, my husband, refuses. He says it will "mess up the kids' heads." He says that if I make them go to Ala-Teen, he'll quit going to his own meetings. What should I do?

A: Bob is holding his sobriety up for ransom, a common trick of alcoholics who are not fully committed to abstinence.

While you are absolutely correct about Ala-Teen for the youngsters, I suggest that you beat a strategic retreat at this time. Let's not make waves. If Bob begins to work with the AA program in earnest, he'll soon see the wisdom of the children learning more about his illness. If it works, he himself will probably recommend Ala-Teen to the kids. If, on the other hand, Bob does *not* follow through with treatment, I would urge you to continue with Al-Anon for yourself and get the youngsters involved in Ala-Teen.

Alcoholism is a family disease. Sooner or later every member of the family is affected. You and the children will benefit from the support group. I hope Bob will let it work for him too.

Hidden Scars

Q: My 9-year-old nephew, Brian, is a perfect gentleman, and that's what worries me. The way I figure it he should have some problems. Let me explain. Brian's father is an alcoholic. His behavior is violent and unpredictable. Last week, for example, he went into a rage and broke all the dishes in the kitchen. Then he went out to the backyard and passed out in the bushes. Believe me, this is nothing new. My sister, Brian's mother, has learned to cope with it, I guess, but what about Brian? What effect will his father's drinking have on him?

A: Dad's drinking will have a profound impact on Brian now and for the rest of his life. Brian's facade of being a perfect gentleman is a typical coping mechanism of children of alcoholics. Beneath his polished veneer are the scars of his psychological wounds. Youngsters such as Brian adapt to the unpredictable violence by distancing themselves emotionally from it. They learn to accept as normal behavior such craziness as Dad breaking all the dishes and passing out in the bushes.

Brian is probably a boy without feelings. As such, he'll grow into an adult who will have problems dealing with such things as anger and frustration, joy and love.

Brian is not alone. It's estimated that 28 million American children live in homes where alcohol is abused. This means that one in four children, like Brian, must adjust, as best they can, to the ravages that alcohol can bring to family life.

I salute your sensitivity. You know that something is wrong. You're right.

What to do about it? First, the obvious. Brian's father needs treatment. Brian's Mom needs help too. What's her role in this family drama? She may well be enabling her husband's alcoholism. Her answer may well be Al-Anon, the self-help group for relatives of alcoholics. Brian needs help too. The thing that would help him most, of course, would be for the adults in his life to pull themselves together. Until that happens, he's at risk. A consultation with a child psychotherapist who understands alcoholism could also be helpful for Brian. He doesn't have to feel alone.

Family Puppet Interview

Q: Our 9-year-old, Martin, is very unhappy. We took him to a child psychiatrist last week. I thought we'd just sit around and talk. I was surprised when the doctor asked Marty, my husband, and me to select some puppets from a shelf and develop a play. It was awkward at first, but we really got into it. You could even say it was fun. But can the doctor really learn very much from this technique?

A: Yes, indeed. The family puppet interview is a variation of play therapy that is often used with children up to the age of 11 or 12. The theory, of course, is that the theme and roles expressed by the players symbolize the themes, roles, conflicts, etc., in the real life of the family.

This type of interview is usually less awkward for kids than it is for parents. It's a good icebreaker, though, and may be especially beneficial to a family that finds it difficult to verbalize ideas and feelings directly.

Fear of the Shrink

Q: We know he needs it. Boy, does he need it. But Bryan, our 9-year-old, refuses to visit a child psychiatrist as recommended by both our pediatrician and the school. Why this fear of the shrink? Any advice?

A: Most 9-year-olds can think of two dozen things they'd rather do than visit a psychiatrist. But let's look a little closer.

In my experience such resistance on the part of a 9-year-old falls into these categories:

1. *Misunderstanding:* Many children, like adults, believe that you have to be deranged or "crazy" to see a psychiatrist. It's simply not so. Child psychiatrists are "talking doctors" who help kids with the problems of everyday life.

2. *Shame:* Bryan may be afraid of what his peers will think if they know he's seeing a psychiatrist. First, you can probably reassure him that his friends don't necessarily have to know about it

at all. Second, it's nothing to be ashamed about. Third, you can be sure that several of the youngsters at his school have no doubt seen a psychiatrist themselves.

3. *Fear:* Some children fear that the psychiatrist will give them shots (not true) or shock therapy (no way) or put them in an institution (rarely needed in child therapy).

4. *Parental spillover:* Children are quick to pick up any resistance from parents. If you or your husband are reluctant about the referral, you can be sure that Bryan has absorbed your vibes. You may have to work out your own resistance first.

5. *Misbehavior:* If Bryan's problems include misbehavior such as opposition to parental control, he will surely exhibit resistance to anything you plan for him—including a visit to a doctor. My advice: Get him to the doctor. After all, he probably doesn't like to visit his dentist either, but I bet you manage to get him there, right?

6. *Fear of discovery:* As miserable as Bryan may be feeling, remember that it's a known quantity to him. He may fear anyone, such as a psychiatrist, who may discover the real reasons beneath his manifest problems.

7. *Fear of change:* Change is tough—even if it's for the good. Bryan will resist any efforts to change him. Things may be bad but— at least he knows the landscape.

Of course, there may well be some unique aspects to Bryan's fear of the psychiatrist (not "shrink" please—psychiatrists, if anything, expand people's minds; they don't "shrink" them), but start with these seven common hurdles. Help Bryan over them. But stay in charge. Make sure he keeps his appointment. Then it's up to the doctor.

Adoption Bombshell

Q: I have a serious problem. Three months ago my mother-in-law told our son, James (aged 9), that my husband is not his father. It's true. My husband adopted James when he was 6 months old. But why would my own mother-in-law do such a cruel thing? James is devastated. He's gone from A's and B's to failing grades. He cries a lot, and now he's telling lies. At first we tried punishment. It only made matters worse. Then we tried going easy on him. He just took advantage of us and got away with things. Now my daughters (4 and 6) are starting to suffer. What should we do?

A: This is a serious problem. In retrospect, of course, you would have been wise in raising James with the knowledge that he was, indeed, adopted. By making a secret of it, you contributed to James's pain when he inevitably discovered the truth. Yes, adoptees almost always learn the truth sooner or later. That's why it's so important for adoptive parents to be up front about it from the beginning. There's no shame in being adopted. But attempts to cover up the facts can contribute to a sense of shame and stigma.

Your mother-in-law has certainly created a crisis for James and the entire family. I suggest three things. First, you and your husband should sit down with James and have a frank and candid discussion. Don't be defensive. Ask him what he wants to know. Tell him. Then reassure him of your love. Second, it sounds to me like professional help is called for in this case. Ask your pediatrician to refer you to someone. Third, you might contact a local adoption agency. They could steer you to a self-help group of other adoptive parents who could provide plenty of wise advice and support for you and your husband.

Change His Name?

Q: Our son, Everett, is 9 years old. He's happy about everything except his name. He says the kids make fun of it. We've tried to humor him, thinking it would pass—but it hasn't. He insists that he wants to change his name. What do you think?

A: Don't be too quick with the humor or the reassurances. And don't latch onto a name change as a solution to your son's problems. Why are the kids *really* picking on Everett? It probably has more to do with his behavior or mannerisms than his name. The persistence of the taunts may also be due to the fact that Everett continues to react poorly—rather than to ignore the baiting.

Exotic and very unusual names *can* put a youngster at a disadvantage—but "Everett" is neither exotic nor very unusual.

As an interim measure, why not suggest "Ev" or "Rett"? But put your emphasis on helping your son win back his self-esteem. That's the real name of the game.

Cut from the Team

Q: Leonard, our 9-year-old, is brokenhearted. He failed to make the final cut for the neighborhood baseball team. The toughest part of it, of course, is that he has also been "cut" from his peer group: All his other friends apparently made the team. Lennie is a very bright boy (top of his class), and he understands that sports are not really "his thing," but he's only 9—and it hurts. Any suggestions?

A: Lennie is learning an important, but painful, fact of life: nobody's perfect—you can't have it all. While he's a hall of famer in the classroom, he has struck out on the playing field.

The best you can do is to first empathize with him. Don't be too quick with the pep talk. He feels terrible. Help him get it out of his system by listening carefully. Then I suggest a practical approach. His friends won't be playing ball *all* the time. What other activities can Lennie share with them this summer? Finally, and this is crucial, help Lennie find some way to maximize his own interests and talents over the next few months. Maybe a summer camp with an academic orientation is the answer; in this way he'll establish new peer relationships with youngsters who have similar interests—and he'll be relating to them on his own turf.

The Coach Has Problems

Q: Mark, our 9-year-old, plays football. He likes the game, and it's fine with us. At least it was fine until last Saturday. That's when my husband and I went to our first game and met the coach. We couldn't believe it. He rants, raves, shouts, and shoves. He even slapped a little guy on the helmet because he missed a tackle. The boys, of course, don't know better. They worship this guy, maybe because he's their very first "coach." But my husband and I think he's got a problem. We've asked the league officials to transfer Mark to another team. Any comments?

A: You scored a touchdown in my book. It's important to protect youngsters from well-intentioned but overzealous coaches. You're right, by the way, when you describe the hero worship. Coaches tend to be idealized by their young charges—a fact that makes them even more vulnerable to inappropriate and punitive treatment. They may need parental intervention, therefore, to save them from ridicule, shame, or even injury.

I presume you reported the coach's behavior to the league officials. Good. At the very least he needs some counseling with his supervisor. If there have been similar problems noted by other parents, he should be removed from his position. Playing the game with sportsmanlike fairness and being a member of a team are the best lessons taught by Pee Wee football. The desire to win is important too—but real winning coaches concentrate on beating their opponents, not beating up their own players.

Playing Doctor

Q: There it was. I walked into the basement yesterday afternoon, and there was my son Herbie (aged 9) playing "doctor" with two little girls from the neighborhood. One girl, the "patient," had her clothes off. The other girl, the "nurse," was "helping the doctor." I screamed. I couldn't help it. I know I should have been cool. This sort of thing is normal, right? I talked to Herbie later and got more details. As far as I can tell, nothing happened except the undressing. Also, it was the first time—Herbie swears it. My husband and I realize that children do these things, but we've taken a tough line with Herbie. He's been punished. My husband thinks we should tell the parents of the girls (aged 8 and 9). What do you think?

A: Yes, playing doctor is an age-old game of sexual exploration. It's usually a harmless way station on the road between infantile autostimulation and adolescent or adult sexuality. Yet, I agree that it should not be encouraged. To do so allies you with the unconscious sexual forces—only half the story in the child's internal struggle between his basic drives and his developing conscience.

Should you call the girls' parents? Put yourself in their place. Would *you* want to know? I think you would.

Emotional Blackmail

Q: We've just returned from a trip to Disney World with our daughter and our 9-year-old granddaughter, Helena. My husband and I are still shaking. We were shocked by Helena's behavior. She made the trip miserable with her continual talking back to her mother and us. We've seen it before, of course, but we've never had to live with it for an entire week. She called her mother names, and whenever any of us tried to discipline her, she'd threaten to go live with her father who left the home about six months ago. My daughter, I'm afraid, has not been effective with her for several years. I don't think it's just the separation. She's never been able to say "no" to Helena. What can we do?

A: I get the impression that Helena rules the family. This is not good. It's not good for you, her grandparents, or for her mother. Most of all, it's not good for Helena herself. Mom has to get back in charge. But how? First of all, she must realize that firm discipline begins by a parent feeling good about herself. If Mom finds it hard to say "no" to Helena, is it because she fears the loss of her daughter's love? If so, she's setting herself up for emotional blackmail. She's not doing anyone any favors by giving in to a child. And Helena will only expect more and more as time goes on.

Children learn more from what we do than from what we say. That's why Mom must follow through on threats of punishment. She has to say "no" and mean it.

I think you're correct by putting the emphasis on your daughter in this case. After all, children live by the pleasure principle: "I want what I want when I want it." It's up to parents to put a little reality in their lives.

On the other hand, children do suffer from marital conflict. You can be sure that Helena is hurting in some way from the recent separation of her parents. For this problem she'll need sensitivity, warmth, reassurance, and the chance to talk to Mom openly about it.

Logical Consequences

Q: We're frantic. We've tried everything. But we can't get our 9-year-old, Randy, to take his lunch to school. He insists on buying it in the cafeteria instead. Every morning is a battle. My wife hands him the lunch bag; he drops it on the table and demands lunch money instead. My wife has to give him the money, but you can be sure we punish him for this. First we took away TV—no response. Then we took away his bicycle—no response. There must be some form of punishment that works. We're in trouble.

A: Easy does it. You are in trouble. Randy's got you jumping through hoops; maybe that's the goal of his misbehavior. If so, your attempts to punish him are like putting jam on his bread.

But back to square one. You're making two basic errors: First, why punish Randy at all? What do TV and a bicycle have to do with his school lunch? Second, your wife is sabotaging her own disciplinary efforts when she hands Randy the lunch bag with one hand and his lunch money with the other. Randy is sharp. He knows he's got the upper hand in this game: He knows that Mom will back down. Why?

Let me suggest a solution. It's called logical consequences, a technique popularized by Dr. Rudolf Dreikurs. Example: What's the logical consequence of Randy's not taking his lunch bag to school? Is it loss of TV? Loss of bicycle? Money for the cafeteria? No, no, no. The logical consequence is that he won't have lunch that day.

Begin this technique tomorrow. Give Randy a choice: lunch bag or he's on his own. It's up to him. If he doesn't want the lunch bag, no problem. The next meal served will be dinner.

After a few days of this approach, Randy will know you mean business. I think you'll then see a sudden appetite for your brown bag offerings.

Boys and Dyslexia

Q: Our 9-year-old son, William, is dyslexic. He understands everything just fine, but he has a heck of a time with reading. Our daughters don't have the problem. We've been told that boys with dyslexia outnumber girls by ten to one. Why?

A: The answers aren't clear, but there is plenty of speculation and some serious research being conducted.

A Harvard research team suggests that unusually high levels of testosterone in the male fetus might delay the development of nerve cells in the left side of the brain, thus causing specific learning problems later in life.

The answer lies somewhere in the complicated circuitry of the brain. Autopsies on people with dyslexia, for example, reveal that the left hemisphere of the brain is smaller than normal.

What does all this mean for William? Cheer up. Most dyslexics have normal or even above normal intelligence. They're just stymied somewhat in some specific area of learning. With a good educational program and lots of encouragement at home, William will probably do just fine. You can tell him that many famous men of history have been dyslexic. General George Patton was dyslexic. So was Woodrow Wilson, who had so much trouble with letter discrimination that he didn't learn the alphabet until he was 9 years old. I bet William is ahead of the former president's pace already.

Fat Parent, Fat Child

Q: My husband is, well, fat. I mean he's about 150 pounds overweight. I've been after him for years to go on a diet, but he refuses, saying he's happy the way he is. Now I'm worried about our daughters, aged 9 and $10\frac{1}{2}$. Both of them are just slightly overweight, but they keep putting on pounds, and I'm scared. Is it in the genes or what? How can I help?

A: Childhood obesity is a complex and controversial matter. It's true, though, that the vast majority of cases are caused by two basic culprits: (1) excessive caloric intake (overeating) and (2) reduced exercise. Only 1 percent of youngsters have some kind of endocrine problem such as hypothyroidism or Cushing's disease.

Is childhood obesity hereditary? Consider these facts: If both parents are obese, the chances are 40 percent. But if both parents are of normal weight, the risk of childhood obesity is only 7 percent.

Of course, you could argue these facts both ways: as favoring either heredity or environment (parental-eating patterns, etc.) as the major cause.

But hold on. A recent study by the National Institute of Child Health and Human Development uncovered a fascinating discovery: Obese spouses tend to have obese adoptive children. What's more, they tend to have fat dogs and cats too. Therefore, environmental influences may well be even more important than genetics.

How can you help? Show your husband this information. Apparently, he doesn't want to help himself. Appeal to him as a father, for the sake of the girls.

Growth Shots?

Q: Our 9-year-old son, Marty, is very small for his age. It bugs him and has created a lot of psychological problems. His pediatrician says Marty is at the low end of the growth scale for his age but that he's still within the limits of normal. I've heard about "growth shots." Do you advise them?

A: No. Marty's problems are obviously more emotional than physical. Hormone injections to stimulate growth are not in routine use, but they do work. In one research study a group of fourteen youngsters were given growth hormone three times a week for six months. Two years later their growth had soared 20 to 50 percent.

Yes, growth shots work, and the treatment may bring new hope to the 2 percent of children between the ages of 5 and 10 who truly suffer from abnormally slow growth. But there are some unanswered questions: long-term side effects, patient selection, availability, and cost.

In the meantime, hang in there. Help your son adapt to his natural body image. And remind him that his natural growth spurt will probably come at age 13 or 14. Finally, make him realize that "bigness" is more a habit of mind than a physical feat.

Psychological Testing

Q: The school has suggested psychological testing for our 9-year-old son, Benjamin. Just what is it anyway?

A: Psychological testing is done by a psychologist with a masters (M.A.) or doctorate (Ph.D.) degree. There are two basic categories of tests:

1. *Cognitive:* These tests, such as the Wechsler, measure basic intelligence. The results can be used to determine a child's academic potential and other factors.

2. *Projective:* These tests, such as the Rorschach (ink blot) Test, are designed to uncover the themes of a youngster's conflicts—defenses, worries, weaknesses, and strengths too.

Be sure to tell Benjamin that testing can be fun. There's no passing or failing. It should help both of you understand him better.

He Misses Grandpa

Q: A few months ago we moved to the west coast because of my husband's job. It was difficult for both of us, but now I realize that our 9-year-old son, Patrick, has had the biggest problem of all. He's been sulking around, and until yesterday, he had refused to talk about it. Finally, it came out. He misses his grandfather. How stupid of me. I should have realized. How can we make it up to him?

A: Patrick has joined the swelling ranks of children who are separated from grandparents. In their book, *Grandparents/Grandchildren: The Vital Connection*, authors Arthur Kornhaber and Kenneth Woodward report that only 5 percent of American children have regular weekly contact with their grandparents; 80 percent have occasional contact; and 15 percent have no contact at all.

Yes, grandparents can have a profound influence on children. Even though Patrick may be separated from Grandpa by many miles, you can help by reducing the emotional distance. Help Patrick express his sadness; then help him devise ways to keep in touch through letters, tape recordings, and other means. Psychological and emotional closeness can make up for geographical distance.

Too Big for a Baby-Sitter?

Q: Our 9-year-old, Stanley, has always been independent, so I wasn't too surprised the other day when he announced that he doesn't want a baby-sitter anymore. Do you have any rules about when parents can start leaving children alone?

A: There are no hard-and-fast rules, but I'll try to give you some guidelines:

1. *Emotional maturity:* There is no chronological cutoff. Some 9- and 10-year-olds are more trustworthy and independent than some impulsive 13- and 14-year-olds. Is Stanley self-disciplined? Does he show good judgment?

2. *Your neighborhood:* Is your neighborhood safe? This is obviously a key question.

3. *Helpers:* Will an adult be immediately available if Stanley has trouble?

4. *Length of time:* Many 9-year-olds today are "latchkey" children and take care of themselves for an hour or two after school. No problem for many kids. But what do you have in mind? A 9-year-old should not be left alone for extended periods.

5. *Day vs. night:* If you choose to leave Stanley on his own for a short period while you go out, I suggest limiting your excursions to daylight hours.

All children ultimately outgrow their need for baby-sitters. It's a mark of emancipation from childhood. But Stanley still has time. Let's not rush into it.

Overachiever?

Q: Our 9-year-old, Sherrie, is a good student. We're proud of her. Imagine our surprise last week when we met with her teacher, Mrs. K., who reported that Sherrie is an "overachiever." Mrs. K. felt that Sherrie tries too hard, that her good grades come at too great a sacrifice, that she drives herself too hard. We were floored. We've always praised Sherrie for her good grades. What should we do now?

A: Take it easy. You are correct in praising Sherrie's academic accomplishments. I am also pleased that your daughter is doing well in school. But what about the rest of her life? That's the key. Is Sherrie happy? Is her health good? Does she have friends? Hobbies?

If Sherrie is putting so much of her energy into making A's that she's failing to develop other parts of her personality, then her teacher's warning should be heard.

On the other hand, if Sherrie's life is in balance and she cares enough about her schoolwork to achieve beyond what her teacher expects (perhaps based on IQ testing!), then Mrs. K. may be making a serious error. Her implicit message to Sherrie is "go slow—you're not supposed to be doing this well."

Don't let Sherrie fall victim to the testing trap. Don't let her be branded as an overachiever. Talk it over with Mrs. K., and then plan your strategy.

He Wants an Advance

Q: My 9-year-old son, Kenny, receives a weekly allowance every Monday morning. The trouble is that he spends it as fast as he gets it. By Friday he's broke. Then he comes around to me and asks for an "advance" on next week's allowance. I guess I shouldn't, but I generally give it to him. Of course, he "forgets" about the advance and expects his full allowance again on Monday—which, again, I usually give him. My sister-in-law says this is wrong. What do you suggest?

A: You are instructing Kenny in the ways of deficit spending. I'm concerned that he'll never learn how to handle money as long as

he knows that Mom is standing by to bail him out. Why not practice the principle of *logical consequences?* The consequence of
spending your allowance by Friday is that you wait until Monday
to refill the coffers. The choice is Kenny's: budget or bust.

Cruelty to Animals

Q: My 9-year-old nephew, Andy, has a very disturbing habit: He
is absolutely cruel to any animal he can get his hands on. He stran-
gles stray cats, picks the wings off flies, burns worms. My brother-
in-law, Andy's father, laughs it off. He says Andy is just "being a
boy." Is this normal?

A: No. Cruelty to animals, of the severity that you describe, is not
within the normal limits of child behavior. My best guess is that if
you inquired further, you would find that Andy probably has other
problems as well. Does Andy harm his own pets? This is more serious than injuring stray animals. Is he assaultive or provocative
toward other children? How does he get along at home? Is he unhappy? In other words, take a look at the big picture. While cruelty to animals is not normal behavior, it does not usually stand
alone as a solitary symptom. And when other problems coexist, the
plot usually thickens to spell more serious trouble that requires a
solid psychiatric evaluation.

Flames of Youth

Q: Our middle child, Christopher (aged 9), was sent home from
school last week because he set a fire in the boys' restroom. The
school won't take him back until he's been "cleared" by a psychiatrist. All kids play with matches, don't they? Chris said it was an
accident. He's never done it before. He's a good boy. Isn't the
school overreacting?

A: Probably not. Children and teens are responsible for two out of
every five cases of arson in this country. Schools are often the target. Hence educators are understandably edgy about these things.

Yes, it may turn out to be a one-time "accident," but a psychological evaluation is still a good idea.

Wooden and his colleagues studied over 100 child fire setters, and they found that these youngsters fell into four categories:

1. *The normal curious:* Children usually below the age of 10 who accidentally start fires while playing with matches.

2. *Help seekers:* Problem-ridden youngsters whose fire setting is a desperate cry for attention and help. They want mostly to be caught.

3. *Delinquents:* Angry teens who express their burning rage by setting fires.

4. *Severely ill:* Psychiatrically disturbed children and teens who set fires because voices tell them to "torch" or who try to burn themselves. These youngsters are often psychotic.

Chris, as you describe him, seems to fit in the first category. If so, nothing much to worry about. But, at the very least, he'll need some education about the dangers of fire and playing with matches.

Army Brats

Q: Our two children, aged 9 and 10, are "army brats," and we're proud of it. The Army has been good to all of us, and the children seem to be developing beautifully. My only concern is with the frequent moves that we've had to make: two in the last three years with still more to come. Will this be bad for the children?

A: Not necessarily. It is important for you and your husband to build into your family life reliability and consistency that you can take with you anywhere in the world. It is also important to teach your children to make deep and rich friendships—not to defensively remain superficial in preparation for the next move. Help them keep in touch with the friends that they make. The toughest years, of course, are still ahead. Teenagers, being so peer-related, are most resentful of being uprooted.

Latchkey Children

Q: I guess you could call our 9-year-old daughter and 10-year-old son "latchkey" children: They let themselves into the house after school and are on their own for about two hours before my husband and I return home from work. My husband and I worry about them, but they seem to be very responsible. Do you have any thoughts about the situation?

A: Latchkey children are a growing phenomenon in the present-day United States. It is estimated that 14 million children between the ages of 6 and 13 now have working mothers and that about a third of them are unsupervised for at least a few hours every day.

I have interviewed many such children, and I find that the results are mixed. Some youngsters are deathly afraid of being left alone (one prowls the house with a hammer in case burglars attack) but do not voice these fears because they have been told that Mom (and Dad) must both work to support the family. These children have a tendency to experience nightmares or develop psychosomatic symptoms. Other children feel safe and actually mature more quickly because of the added responsibility.

While police in some large cities warn that latchkey children and latchkey households are particularly vulnerable to intruders, the situation has not become nearly as desperate as some doomsayers would warn.

In fact, some of these latchkey children are actually better supervised than children whose parents are around but do not exercise proper discipline. How so? By telephone, by strict rules to remain indoors, by tasks, and even by assigned "fun" activities.

Be sure that your children understand your absence. Be sure that they can reach you and other adults by telephone. Consider resurrecting the old "block mother" or supervised "play group" in your neighborhood if adequate after-school care is not available. Try to take the youngsters to work with you, at least once, so they have a firsthand knowledge of your existence and availability when you are away from them. Improve the *quality* of your time with them. After all, *quantity* counts but it isn't everything.

An Only Child

Q: Our 9-year-old daughter seems to be doing well, but she's an only child. Are there things that we should be watching for? I've heard that only children have a tendency to become alcoholics.

A: Research studies of only children show that they do rather well throughout life and do not suffer from a higher incidence of mental illness, drug abuse, or alcoholism.

The only child, whether male or female, is most vulnerable to developmental conflicts (regression to bed-wetting, temper tantrums, etc.) at about the age of 3 to 5 because of intense alliances and conflicts with Mom and Dad. Another difficult period may be the entry into school because the child suddenly gains a roomful of "siblings"; if the only child has not had much experience with other children, she may find it very difficult to share the teacher with them.

You can anticipate many of these difficulties and, with your husband, assist your daughter to avoid the pitfalls. Since, like all children, she must ultimately leave you as a mature and independent person, give her plenty of room to grow and to experience the give-and-take of the world outside the family.

Sexual Abuse

Q: Our 9-year-old daughter has been molested by her uncle. As far as we know, it has occurred two or three times and involved touching but no intercourse. Our daughter was frightened to tell us about it but otherwise does not appear to be suffering any negative effects. Our questions come down to these: Should we have her evaluated by a child psychiatrist? What are the chances that she will develop sexual problems later in her life?

A: Surveys reveal that about 25 percent of adult women who report having been sexually molested in childhood experience sexual problems in later life. Of the many factors involved, the key is whether they were forced against their will or whether they were willing participants in the act. No other factor (age, identity of the male molester, the specific acts performed, frequency, etc.) is as important. Why? Girls who are physically forced to participate in these activities can absolve themselves of guilt. Girls who, while perhaps being frightened, allow the event to occur with little or no resistance and who may even "enjoy" the act may be left with a great deal of guilt which can hover over their conscience like a black cloud for many years.

It is important for you to, gently and lovingly, learn more about this sad situation from your little girl. Into which category does she fall? If there is any doubt in your mind, the safest course would be a consultation.

A Halloween Protection Racket

Q: Last year the teenage boys in our neighborhood "sold protection" to the younger kids on Halloween night. They would stop small children on the street corners and demand a portion of their candy, money, and other treats in return for protecting them from bad men who were allegedly out to "get" the trick-or-treaters. When Sheila, my 9-year-old daughter, told me about it two weeks later, I was enraged but it seemed too late to do anything. I've recently talked to Sheila about it and told her that I intend to alert the police next year, but she says that my actions would only make things more difficult for her. I don't believe this is happening. What would you advise?

A: I appreciate your concern. It is important for Sheila to know that you can be counted upon to take active steps to protect her. A parent is the best "protection" any child will ever have. On the other hand, your daughter's world is also a world of peers. Her reluctance to accept your well-intentioned help derives from her uncertainty about how her peer group would react if Mom got into the act.

What is a mother to do, then, in this situation? It appears as though you are trapped in the classic bind: damned if you do, damned if you don't.

If you fear for Sheila's safety or feel very strongly about what the teenage boys are getting away with, I would urge you to take action. Begin by explaining your dilemma to Sheila: You don't want to embarrass her with her friends, but you simply cannot stand back and allow this kind of thing to continue. Ask her what *she* would do if she was a mother in your shoes? Sheila may surprise you with some good solutions. Nevertheless, you should have a plan of action. Short of calling the police before the fact, you might call the parents of Sheila's friends for support.

You should also consider accompanying Sheila and her friends the next time they go trick or treating on Halloween night. If the kids object to a parental chaperon, you can always remain safely at a distance. But even from a block away, your presence should be enough to protect Sheila and the others from their would-be protectors.

Mom Starts Dating

Q: My former husband and I were divorced two years ago. I'm just starting now to rise out of my blue funk and to put my life back in order. The problem is my 10-year-old daughter. She resents the man I've started dating. Any suggestions?

A: First, it would help to realize that you are not alone. This is a fairly common problem. There are tens of thousands of women in your shoes. Most all of them manage to work out of this dilemma. Your daughter obviously resents your boyfriend because he is a competitor for your time and attention. She is accustomed to having you all to herself.

It is unreasonable, however, for her to think that she can keep Mom all to herself forever. You have needs that go beyond your relationship to your daughter. You have a right to fulfill those needs. Some of your daughter's own developmental needs, especially as she will soon enter adolescence, also go beyond her relationship with you. She must be freed of overdependency on Mom so that she too can develop her full potential.

One way to explain this to a 10-year-old is to ask her to list all the things that she "is," that is, daughter, granddaughter, niece, friend, soccer player, student, etc. Then you might list all the things that identify you, that is, mother, daughter, sister, friend, worker, etc. Your daughter should get the picture. You wouldn't ask her to give up all the various parts of herself to become exclusively your daughter. By the same token, she should not stake an exclusive claim on you. Yet the two of you are very important to each other, and you should both vow to protect your relationship.

As a child psychiatrist I am sensitive, however, to another important factor in your problem. Your daughter is a child of divorce. While most boys and girls eventually work through their parents' divorce satisfactorily, recent research shows that up to 37 percent of such youngsters are still suffering psychological symptoms up to five years after the divorce.

Have you talked to your daughter about the divorce? She was about 8 years old when it occurred. Many 8-year-olds, as incredible as it may seem to the adult mind, secretly believe that *they* were the cause of the divorce. Many of them keep this secret locked in their hearts for years. Meanwhile, they become preoccupied with being "perfect" so that Mom and Dad will somehow get back together again. Your resumption of dating, then, may be a harsh reminder that your daughter's reunion wish is doomed. She may persist, however, in conscious and unconscious attempts to block your dating, such as "getting sick" just before you leave for the theater, etc.

The solution? Allow your daughter to express her feelings about the divorce. Accept them. Reassure her, if necessary, that she was not the cause. Explore other fantasies that may lurk in her mind. Give her some facts—but stop short of details about the marriage that a 10-year-old cannot handle.

Even though your daughter may conceivably appear unaffected by the divorce, do not let appearances deceive you. Many such youngsters are vulnerable to losses (real or imagined) for a few years. For example, some children actually fear that if Mom remarries, she might go away and leave them—especially since their "badness" might have caused the first marriage to fail.

Try to put yourself in your daughter's position. Try to understand all the things that might be worrying her. That's good "mothercraft." Listen to her. Give her a chance to express all her feelings and fears, as unreasonable as they may seem to you. Then patiently express your love for her and describe your own needs.

Listen. Love. Reassure. Be a mother—but don't stop being a woman.

Reunion Fantasy

Q: My former husband and I have had a "good" divorce: no anger, no game playing. Our 10-year-old daughter, Vicki, has lived with me but has visited her father frequently. I've been dating a man for two years, and Vicki has just loved him—until last week when I told her that Bill and I are going to be married. I thought she would be thrilled. Instead, she cries every night for her Daddy. Help.

A: Many children, especially in the face of a "good" divorce, harbor the secret belief that Mom and Dad will get back together again. This is sometimes called a *reunion fantasy*. I assume that your former husband has not remarried. In that case, Vicki's wish for your reunion has enjoyed sustained life for all these years even in the presence of Bill. Your announcement, however, has burst the bubble of her dreams.

Do not despair. With patience and sensitivity you can help Vicki to resolve her pain. Begin by reassuring her of your own love, that you and Bill will not abandon her. Second, reassure her that her Daddy will always be her Daddy. No one, not even Bill, will take his place. She can still love Daddy and visit him. It would also help a great deal if you could explain the problem to your former husband. Ask for his assistance. It would be wonderful if he would reassure Vicki and give his blessing to you and Bill. Vicki will need all of you. Don't let her get trapped between what she might view as conflicting loyalties.

Blended Family

Q: My husband and I have been married for a year. Things are going well for us but not for our children. Jack, my husband, has two daughters, aged $10\frac{1}{2}$ and 7. I have two boys (aged 10 and 7) and a daughter (aged 6). We really hoped that they would all merge into one big, happy family, but it isn't working that way. Jack and I don't play favorites. We try to be reasonable with all the kids. But it's fight, fight, fight. What's happening?

A: Blended families are not that unusual these days, but they do present challenges.

It's unrealistic, for example, to assume that you will magically become one big, happy family. Look at the facts.

Blended families, first of all, are born of loss—either death or divorce. There are two biological parents who loom over your family in some way or other. Then there's the tremendous disruption in the ordinal position of the children. Your oldest son (aged 10), for example, is no longer the oldest in the family. He's been displaced by Jack's $10\frac{1}{2}$-year-old daughter. But Jack's 7-year-old daughter has also been displaced; she's given up the youngest-child slot to your 6-year-old daughter.

Who's who is the name of the game here. Where does everyone fit? You've got to expect a period of jockeying for position, for realignment. Be patient. Be firm. Be clear. And don't hesitate to seek help if things get out of hand.

Devil at Home, Angel at School

Q: Harriett (aged 10) is my only child. I love her, but she's getting impossible. She sasses me back, calls me names, and generally makes my life miserable. But at school it's a different story. Her teacher tells me she's the best behaved student in the class. By the way, it was the same last year: devil at home, angel at school. This doesn't make sense, does it?

A: Yes, it makes sense. It is not so rare for children to wear a different face at home than at school. Kids react to the cues around them. I bet, for example, that Harriett's teachers would never allow her to sass them back or to call them names. Why do you let her get away with it at home?

I don't like the sound of this at all. The root of Harriett's anger at you must be explored and identified. Your own inability to handle her defiance is also a problem. Get help now. Things are apt to get worse as Harriett enters adolescence. The "devil" lurking in her will grow up to haunt you and to damage Harriett's own happiness too. My advice: See a child psychiatrist (M.D.) or psychologist (Ph.D.)—the right "exorcist" for this case.

Booze and Children

Q: Our son, Rusty, is a fifth-grader. When he came home last night, I smelled alcohol on his breath. At first he denied it, but he finally came clean: He had been drinking wine at the home of a friend. Rusty says it's "only" the second time he's ever done it. We're shocked and we're scared. What should we do?

A: Children are experimenting with alcohol at an ever earlier age. According to a survey conducted by the National Parents' Resource Institute, 33.4 percent of sixth-graders have tried beer or wine; 9.5 percent of them have chugged hard booze. Most of these youngsters, however, try it and forget it. The problem kids are the ones who go on to regular use. This phenomenon, unfortunately, is also in the upswing. In a 1983 survey, 1.9 percent of sixth-graders consumed alcohol at least once a week. In 1984, the figure was 4.1 percent.

I'm curious that Rusty admitted to at least *two* drinking bouts. Keep in mind the fact that most youngsters tend to minimize their drinking when confronted by parents.

The best you can do at this point is to keep a close eye on Rusty. He should be punished for what he's done, of course, but don't be unreasonable about it. Most importantly, talk to your son. Why did he drink? Peer pressure? To alter his mood? Why? One more thing. I urge you to notify the parents of Rusty's "host" for these binges. You'd want to know if you were them, right?

Beauty Contests for Little Girls?

Q: Our daughter, Amber, is 10 years old. Everyone is always telling us how gorgeous she is. A couple of our friends, in fact, are pushing us to enter her in a local beauty contest. Both my husband and I have very mixed feelings about the idea. What do you think?

A: Beauty pageants for preteen girls have become a multimillion dollar business. While some of them are undoubtedly rip-offs, others are legitimate. Yet your question implies concern even about the legitimate contests. Good.

From a psychological standpoint, there is substantial risk and very little gain for Amber being thrust onto the beauty pageant runway. At 10 she should be developing a sense of self-esteem based on who she is, not on how she looks. Better to encourage her academic pursuits, interests in sports and hobbies and friendships. Beauty contests, even for the winners, can be a lonely narcissistic indulgence, full of pomp but little circumstance.

If you can't resist the plunge, I'd suggest a couple of steps. First, discuss this with Amber. What does she think? Don't push. Don't become a "beauty pageant mother." Second, try to find a legitimate contest that includes talent competition in addition to curtsies and coiffure. Finally, be sure to keep it all in perspective.

Pumping Iron

Q: Our 10-year-old son, Carl, and his buddies have become zealous weight lifters. They compete with each other to see who can "press" the most pounds. Is there any danger in this activity?

A: Yes. Unsupervised weight lifting can lead to muscle pulls and broken bones. An even greater danger is injury to bone growth centers. Preadolescents, like Carl, are especially prone to *weight lifter's fracture,* a particular fracture of the wrist or arm, because their bony structure is much weaker than older youths'.

"Pumping iron" seems to be enjoying a new spurt of popularity across the United States these days. One of the reasons is probably the burgeoning health spa industry and its emphasis on body building for adults. The younger set has caught on to the craze. Of course, preadolescent boys always have an interest in competing among themselves and demonstrating their prowess to each other. It is a kind of rite of psychological passage since being strong and having big muscles is really more of a psychological issue than a physical necessity.

As a matter of fact, medical studies have shown that while weight lifting can increase a preadolescent's strength slightly, it does not increase his muscle mass at all. Muscle building is really not possible until puberty, when the level of the male sex hormone, testosterone, increases dramatically.

Please pass this information on to Carl. He may decide that pumping iron is not for him—just yet.

Campaign Manager

Q: My older children have all worked as volunteers in political campaigns: stuffing envelopes, making phone calls, that kind of thing. My husband and I will be working as volunteers in a congressional campaign this year. Our 10-year-old, Wyndham, wants to be a volunteer too. I'm sure the candidate would okay it, but what do you think? Would she really get very much out of it?

A: Ten-year-olds love contests—especially where there's a clear-cut winner and loser, such as in political campaigns. Wyndham then will probably view the experience largely in terms of winning and losing.

There is, of course, much more to be gained from the volunteer experience, so you'll have to take extra time to teach her about campaigns and our political system. I suggest that you have her keep a diary and review it with her on a weekly basis.

By the way, I think it's great that you've involved all your children in politics. Such firsthand experiences in the American way are very valuable lessons. They create knowledgeable citizens and astute students of democracy: the ultimate safeguard of our freedoms.

Younger Friends

Q: Our daughter, Barbie (aged 10), is an only child. She seems to be getting along just fine at school (A's and B's) but just can't seem to make friends of her own age. Most of her playmates are aged 5 to 7. Any comments?

A: I understand your concern. Many only children like Barbie tend to be adult-oriented rather than peer-oriented. They are much more comfortable in the company of adults than they are in the company of classmates and age-mates.

Barbie's selection of much younger children as friends may be explained on the same basis. I'd guess, for example, that she plays the role of the authority figure with her little playmates. She probably picks the games, sets the roles, and serves as final arbiter in disputes. If she can't play *with* the adults, Barbie *becomes* the adult in her play. Clearly, her own age-mates will not tolerate such behavior. (They'd dismiss it as "bossy.") So Barbie is forced to look to compliant younger children when she wants to play.

As you must guess, this is not healthy for Barbie. It's important that she learns the give-and-take necessary in the establishing and maintaining of peer relationships. Make sure she gets plenty such opportunities.

Memories

Q: Freddy, our 10-year-old, is obsessed with a memory from his early childhood. As he describes it, he's locked outside the house during a snowstorm and almost dies. He saves himself by breaking into a candy store. I've told him again and again that the dream can't possibly be true. Why not? Well, we lived in Florida until two years ago—and Freddy's never been locked out of the house because we've never locked our doors. But the memory seems so vivid to Freddy. What does it mean?

A: Early memories are important indicators of how children (and adults too) perceive themselves and their worlds. These recollections may or may not have any basis in reality. The telling point is their psychological relevance.

Freddy's memory, therefore, is of psychological rather than historical significance. It didn't really happen, but it holds psychological reality for him. What reality? Well, Freddy, in his memory, obviously perceives himself as lonely, vulnerable, abandoned. His world is cold and uncaring. There is no one to protect him. Interestingly, no one comes to save him. He must rely upon his own devices by resourcefully finding his own refuge: the candy store.

Is this the Freddy you know? He's telling you something about how he perceives himself and you too. What to do? If things on the surface are going well in Freddy's life (school, friends, behavior, health, etc.)—do nothing. File the information away. If Freddy is experiencing some significant problems in his life at this time, his memory may be a powerful message to you that he needs help.

Hidden Feelings

Q: Our 10-year-old, Chris, is the kind of girl who holds everything in. She bottles up her feelings. I know it's not good for her. How can we help?

A: Generally speaking, it's good to be able to put feelings into words and to express those feelings to other people. But remember that everyone handles these things a little differently. Allow Chris some room for individual difference.

The best way to help is to set a good parental example. Do you and your husband openly communicate your feelings, both positive and negative? Can you do it in a way that is helpful and constructive? Do you feel better afterward? Remember, Chris is watching. If the answer to any of my questions is "no," she may have already concluded that she'll keep her feelings to herself.

You're Not My Real Mother

Q: I knew it would come sooner or later, and it did. Our 10-year-old adopted son, Richard, in a fit of anger because he was restricted for failing to do his chores, shot back those horrible words: "You're not my real mother." I handled it matter-of-factly and reminded him of the restriction. I couldn't tell him how much he had hurt me. I haven't mentioned it since. Should I?

A: Yes. As you suggest, most adopted children will resort to this device at some point, usually in preadolescence. You've probably talked to other adoptive parents. You knew it was coming, but still it hurts.

Let Richard know your reaction, but don't go overboard. Tell him that he'll have other feelings about being adopted and that you will be available to talk about them. You're not his birth mother, but you are his "real" mother.

The two of you, along with your husband, will grow together through the unfolding phases of adoption. There may be some rough spots along the way, but with respect and understanding you will travel the path successfully.

Tourette's Syndrome

Q: About two years ago our youngest son, Adam (aged 10), developed a chronic blinking of the eyes. Our pediatrician said it was just "nerves." Several months later he started having coughing fits—still "nerves" we thought. Then his whole body would twist whenever he got upset. We didn't know what to think. We even got angry at him and scolded him, which actually seemed to work for a while.

But about six months ago things got worse. Adam started swearing. I mean, he couldn't stop it. He'd shout one 4-letter word after another. It was quick, like a machine gun, like the tic of the eye, I guess.

This time our pediatrician referred Adam to a neurologist and a child psychiatrist. It was the neurologist who diagnosed Tourette's syndrome. Can you tell us more about it?

A: You've already learned much more than most people know about Tourette's syndrome. Adam's case, you see, is classic.

The earliest symptom is usually an isolated tic. But diagnosis of Tourette's on the basis of this symptom alone is rarely made. Adam's tics spread, however, just as they do in this chronic disorder. The most baffling symptom, the uncontrollable utterance of obscenities, is also a unique feature of Tourette's. In medical parlance it's called *coprolalia*.

Diagnosis of Tourette's is ultimately based on the clinical findings you've described.

I'm sure you've been told that there is no cure for this illness. The good news, however, is that there is medication available to reduce the severity and frequency of the tics. The most commonly used drug is haloperidol. If Adam is taking it, I'm sure the doctor will monitor him closely for side effects.

No, there's no use in getting angry at Adam. He can't help himself. These symptoms are neurological in nature and are largely out of his control. Be thankful he's been diagnosed at an early age. Some youngsters are subjected to a number of inappropriate treatments before the correct diagnosis is made.

Counseling Can Hurt

Q: Penny, our 10-year-old, is seeing a counselor. She's had about six sessions. After her last appointment she came out crying. She says she can't take it, that it hurts too much. We thought it was supposed to make her feel better. What's going on?

A: No pain, no gain. The work of therapy goes through many cycles, but you can be sure that, if it is to succeed, Penny will have to get in touch with some feelings. Otherwise it's just an empty intellectual exercise. So, yes, there will be some hurt. The skillful therapist, however, won't let it get out of control.

Holiday from Therapy?

Q: Our 10-year-old son, Dana, started psychiatric therapy about six months ago. He sees his doctor once a week. My husband and I thought it would be a good idea to give Dana a vacation from therapy during the Christmas holidays. When we suggested it, though, the doctor made a big deal about it. She said we're "sabotaging" Dana's treatment. What is this?

A: As you describe the situation, it sounds like Dana's doctor overreacted. It is not uncommon for some youngsters to miss an appointment over the holidays.

On the other hand, disruptions in treatment can be detrimental. Perhaps Dana is closing in on some important issues at this time. Perhaps the doctor knows that the holidays are likely to be stressful for him. Perhaps there are other factors.

I'd suggest another talk with the doctor. You might focus on what she means by "sabotage." Does she really believe that you are not 100 percent behind the therapy? Better to clarify these matters now.

Mother's Day, Sweet and Sour

Q: Mother's Day is mixed for me. I have a horrible relationship with my own mother; we haven't spoken to each other in years. Yet my 10-year-old son, Jimmy, worships me and loves to make me feel like a queen on Mother's Day. It's beautiful, but it makes me feel guilty about my own mother. It tears me up inside.

A: The raising of children brings us face to face with our own childhoods. But for Jimmy's sake, do your best to repress the matter of the relationship with your own mother—unless, of course, you really want to tackle the problem head-on.

You feel guilty about your own mother. This tells me that you might want to build a bridge back to her. Why not start with a short Mother's Day note? Someone has to take the first step. This could be healthy for Jimmy, who will begin to wonder why he never sees Grandma and why you don't remember her on Mother's Day.

Quiz

The grade school child (or latency stage youngster) is a marvelous creature. If things went well during the first five years of her life, these should be her golden days—a place for everything and everything in its place. But if things didn't go so well, if the foundation is weak, he'll struggle through these years. Whichever the case, a child's behavior in these years will be a very strong signal about what's ahead in adolescence and even about what kind of adult he'll be. Take your time, therefore, with this quiz. Study it. Go back and reread the chapter if necessary. You'll never have as good a chance again to make a difference in your child's life as you will during these few years. Use them wisely.

1. A 10-year-old girl who is upset about her mother's dating one year after divorce is (select the best response):

   ☐ A. Probably afraid of being abandoned

   ☐ B. Afraid that Mom will remarry and, therefore, her mother and father will never get together again

   ☐ C. Being unreasonable

2. True or false? Most bed-wetting is caused by psychological factors.

3. What percentage of American children have regular contact with at least one grandparent?

   ☐ A. 5 percent
   ☐ B. 25 percent
   ☐ C. 50 percent

4. If a 9-year-old confesses to stealing money from you that you haven't missed at all, you should:

   ☐ A. Thank her for being honest
   ☐ B. Thank her for being honest and punish her for stealing
   ☐ C. Help her get her angry feelings out

5. True or false? Middle children often grow up to have better "people skills" than only, oldest, or youngest children.

6. What percentage of women who were sexually molested as children later report sexual problems in their adult lives?

   ☐ A. 10 percent
   ☐ B. 25 percent
   ☐ C. 50 percent
   ☐ D. 100 percent

7. Hyperactive children who are treated with medication (select all correct responses):

   ☐ A. Could suffer growth suppression
   ☐ B. Often obtain dramatically positive results
   ☐ C. Have a higher incidence of drug abuse as teenagers

8. True or false? Often the most difficult adjustment for an only child is entering school.

9. You have two children (aged 7 and 9). Their pet kitten dies. When should you replace the pet?

   ☐ A. The same day

☐ B.   One week later

☐ C.   In two or three months

10. Latchkey children:

☐ A.   Should have very strict rules

☐ B.   Should be encouraged to use their own judgment

11. True or false? Most children grow out of being shy. There's no need to intervene.

12. An 8-year-old fire setter (select all that apply):

☐ A.   May be seriously disturbed

☐ B.   Is probably angry

☐ C.   Has a fairly good prognosis with psychiatric treatment

13. Firstborns (select the one *incorrect* answer):

☐ A.   Tend to have higher intelligence

☐ B.   Tend to be more "successful"

☐ C.   Tend to be very popular with peers

14. True or false? Children who become avid readers usually have been restricted from excessive TV watching by their parents.

15. Dietary treatment for hyperactivity:

☐ A.   Is a generally accepted treatment modality

☐ B.   Has limited usefulness, based on current research

16. A 9-year-old girl spends all her weekly allowance in one day. She wants an advance. You should:

☐ A.   Give it to her "just this once."

☐ B.   Hold the line. Wait until next week.

☐ C.   Give it to her. Kids will be kids.

17. True or false? Obese children do not usually grow into obese teenagers.

18. Hypnosis is useful in child therapy for all except:

☐ A.   Bed-wetting

☐ B. Depression due to parental divorce

☐ C. Fear of riding in cars

19. Most children are capable of doing chores by age:

☐ A. 6

☐ B. 8

☐ C. 10

20. True or false? Alternating custody (one year with one parent, then one year with the other, etc.) is generally a good solution if the parents agree on general parenting approaches.

21. School phobia in a 5-year-old is:

☐ A. Due to fear of school

☐ B. Based on anxiety over leaving mother

☐ C. Means the child should be kept at home until first grade

22. Research has shown that children suffer most:

☐ A. When they grow up in very unhappy but intact families

☐ B. From divorce

23. When parents have decided on divorce, they should:

☐ A. Tell the children together

☐ B. Approach the children separately

☐ C. Have a neutral third party break the news

24. Generally speaking, who suffers most from divorce?

☐ A. Boys

☐ B. Girls

25. How much time each week does the average American child spend watching TV?

☐ A. Five hours

☐ B. Fifteen hours

☐ C. Twenty-five hours

26. Children and television (select all correct answers):

- ☐ A. Parents should approve programs for viewing.
- ☐ B. Parents should limit the amount of TV viewing.
- ☐ C. Parents should discuss programs with children.
- ☐ D. Children who watch excessive amounts of TV may be bored or depressed.

27. True or false? Since 5-year-olds cannot comprehend the concept of death, a threat of suicide should not be taken seriously.

28. True or false? Parents should never disagree in front of their children.

29. True or false? Children should be paid to do routine chores.

30. A former husband habitually fails to remember his children's birthdays and generally neglects them. The mother should (select all that apply):

- ☐ A. Make excuses for him
- ☐ B. Tell the children they are not at fault
- ☐ C. Openly criticize him
- ☐ D. Encourage the children to ask him why he neglects them
- ☐ E. Confront him with the problem

31. True or false? The child who fears dogs should be made to pet them. Direct confrontation is the best way for children to overcome fears.

32. True or false? Children tend to "inherit" their parents' fears.

33. True or false? A parent should strive to become a child's best friend.

34. Television violence and children (select all that apply):

- ☐ A. Children learn and remember aggression on television.
- ☐ B. Children become desensitized to violence and more accepting of it.
- ☐ C. There is no link between TV violence and aggressive behavior in children.

35. True or false? Hyperactive children treated with medication tend to outgrow their need for it when they become adolescents.

36. True or false? It is not unusual for a child with a specific learning disability to have above-average intelligence.

37. Childhood bullies:

   ☐ A.   Tend to outgrow it
   ☐ B.   Tend to become unhappy, aggressive teenagers

38. If a child is adopted in infancy:

   ☐ A.   There is no need to ever tell her she's adopted.
   ☐ B.   Wait until she can understand "adoption," that is, at the age of 10 to 13.
   ☐ C.   Parents should, from the start, make references to adoption.

39. True or false? As a rule of thumb, parents should never threaten a punishment that they cannot or will not enforce.

40. True or false? In selecting gifts for children, it is generally better to pick toys that will be fun—rather than educational.

Answers

1. B	11. False	21. B	31. False
2. False	12. A, B, C	22. A	32. True
3. A	13. C	23. A	33. False
4. B	14. True	24. A	34. A, B
5. True	15. B	25. C	35. True
6. B	16. B	26. A,B,C,D	36. True
7. A, B	17. False	27. False	37. B
8. True	18. B	28. False	38. C
9. B	19. A	29. False	39. True
10. A	20. False	30. B, D, E	40. True

CHAPTER 5

Final Exam

Here's a chance to apply the facts and principles you've learned in this book. All you have to do is picture yourself in each of these vignettes and then select the one response you feel is most correct.

One word of caution: There's usually more than just one way of doing things. When two or more responses might work, I've indicated it, and I've also explained why I've selected one of them as more "correct." You might not agree with every solution I've suggested. That's okay; I only ask that you think carefully about your response, that it's consistent with your own reasonable philosophy of raising children—and that you have fun taking the quiz.

For those of you who like a contest and who insist on a grade when you take an exam, try these guidelines:

Number of Correct Answers	*Your Rating*
9, 10	*Superior:* You won't be needing this book anymore. Why not pass it along to a friend?
7, 8	*Good:* You've got a good feel for raising children. Keep working at it.
6	*Average:* You can do better. Study the questions you missed. Then go back to the text and reread the appropriate sections.

Number of Correct Answers	*Your Rating*
5 or less	*Fail:* No, you're not a failure as a parent. You only failed this particular quiz. But take it as a warning sign. Read the book again. Study it—then try the quiz again. After all, being a parent isn't supposed to be easy, you know.

Potty Training

You've begun potty training Alex, your 20-month-old. It's not going well at all. Alex won't stay on the seat. He squirms and fusses. Then almost as soon as he's off the potty, he has a bowel movement in his diaper. What do you do?

1. Put him back on the potty seat, soiled diapers and all. In this way he'll associate moving his bowels with the potty.

2. Back off. Obviously Alex is not yet ready for toilet training.

3. Keep at it, but don't be punitive. When Alex soils, call it an accident. Encourage him to do better next time.

4. This is a test of wills. You can't afford to let Alex get the upper hand. Show him who's boss. Spank him when he soils.

Potty training is an important developmental issue. In addition to body control and cleanliness, this marks the first real responsibility to a child. Which response have you chosen?

1. Not a good idea. There are other, less punitive ways to teach Alex about bowel control and the function of the potty. Doll play is one. Alex may, in fact, be close to getting the idea. His soiling immediately after being taken off the potty seat may be his way of saying that he needs more control, that he would like to be in charge. Try allowing *him* to signal *you* when he's ready for a BM. Toilet training on demand can lead to power struggles between parent and child.

2. Most children are ready for toilet training at about 18 months. There is, however, a range of normal. Alex may not be quite ready, but I wouldn't back off altogether. No child would ever become bowel-trained if he was left entirely to his own devices. Parents have to become actively involved.

3. Yes. This is more like it. Keep it positive. Don't be punitive—but don't back off altogether. Maintain the upbeat expectation that Alex can do it. Avoid power struggles. Give him some slack but keep at it.

4. This is a blueprint for disaster. The parent who sets out to "break" a youngster is looking for trouble. The result can be constipation, more "accidents," and willful disobedience. On the other hand, a child, too overwhelmed to fight back, may comply—only to get even later in some other way. Spanking has no place in toilet training—or in most aspects of raising children. It teaches hurt, fear, aggression, and revenge.

Temper Tantrums

Your $2\frac{1}{2}$-year-old is tagging along behind you in the supermarket. Suddenly she spots some candy bars and grabs them off the shelf. When you tell her to put them back, she screams, stamps her feet, and launches a full-scale tantrum. How would you react?

1. Reason with her. Explain that she has lots of candy at home.

2. Buy her the candy if she first promises to be quiet. But be clear with her that you will not do it next time she shops with you.

3. Ignore her. Continue your shopping.

4. Shout right back at her. Show her that temper tantrums are very ugly things.

Which response have you chosen? Let's review each of them.

1. This is no time for reason. It is a time for action. Trying to reason with a child who is having a full-blown temper tantrum is almost impossible. The child is consumed by blind desire and rage.

It's a classic case of "my mind is made up, don't confuse me with the facts!" This little girl could care less if you promised to buy her an entire candy factory tomorrow; as a $2\frac{1}{2}$-year-old she operates on the basis of the pleasure principle: "I want what I want when I want it." Reasoning is doomed to failure in the face of such powerful emotion.

2. The parent who resorts to such behavioral bribery is buying a short-term solution at the expense of long-term problems. Will this little girl remember your words next time you go shopping? Of course not. In fact, we should not expect it. The only thing that she has learned from this experience is that temper tantrums *equal* candy bars. If it worked once, she will quite naturally expect it to work next time too.

3. Yes. This is more like it. Temper tantrums usually require an audience. This one, as a matter of fact, is being staged for your benefit. Responding to it can be like throwing gasoline on a fire. On the other hand, by simply and confidently walking away, you allow the flames to burn themselves very quickly. Yes, it may take some courage to walk away from a crying child, especially if other shoppers are viewing the spectacle, but it is a tactic that works and that's what counts.

4. While many of us might get the urge to regress to the mentality of the "terrible 2s" ourselves in this situation, very few of us would ever give in to the impulse: We'd be guilty of creating a scenario where we have two infants in search of a parent. Yet I once heard an "expert" suggest such bizarre tactics on a television talk show. Choose your experts carefully.

Sibling Rivalry

Your 4-year-old son, Andrew, has just run into the kitchen to find you. He complains that his two older sisters, aged 6 and 7, have just changed the channel on the TV from *his* program to *their* program. He's upset. "They always get their own way," he cries.

Sound familiar? As Andrew's parent what would you do? Pick the *one* response that you think is most correct.

1. Storm right into the family room and check out Andrew's story with the girls. If he's telling the truth, turn off the TV for the rest of the evening. If the three children cannot learn to share, they should all be punished.

2. Listen patiently to Andrew, but do not get directly involved. Encourage him to go back and solve the problem on his own.

3. Call the girls into the kitchen. Acknowledge that all three youngsters seem to have a problem. Help them discuss it and come up with a reasonable solution.

4. Andrew is obviously being bullied by his older sisters. Give them a dose of their own medicine. Go in there, and put Andrew's program back on for him.

Sibling rivalry: a common but tricky problem. Let's go over each of the responses.

1. While any of us might have an initial impulse to do this very thing, it is a bit shortsighted. It is an immediate *parental* solution as it eliminates the conflict—but only for the moment. It is not a *child* solution; that is, now you will have not one but three unhappy children, all feeling that they've been treated unfairly. They're sure to try to get your attention again very soon—probably with another type of hassle. They'll want you to intervene on their side to prove that they "won."

If you chose this response, do not feel badly. It can be used effectively with older children who should be expected to demonstrate more cooperation. Such an intervention puts them on notice that they'll have to solve this kind of problem themselves; if they force you to intervene, you will not take sides, but, instead, you may set some limits on all of them.

2. Listening patiently to Andrew and accepting his feelings is certainly a good idea, but this response does not go quite far enough. Andrew, remember, is only 4 years old. He lacks experience and skill in problem solving. He feels overpowered and outmaneuvered by his two older sisters. If you try to send him back into the fray to "fight his own battle," he will feel misunderstood and unsupported by you.

3. Yes. This is very good parentcraft. You are supportive of Andrew *and* of your daughters in this response. While you might have to help Andrew a bit, you'll also listen to what his sisters have to say. Allowing all three youngsters to participate in the solution teaches them the value of cooperation and negotiation. Since the children are young and still inexperienced in these matters, you may have to disallow some of their alternatives, such as "Only girls are allowed to watch TV" or "Everybody gets their own TV." But given the chance, they will probably come up with some reasonable solution that is mutually agreeable.

Although this response obviously takes more time than the other three, it really is a time-saver in the long run. Young children will need help, at first, in these situations, but you are building a solid foundation for their future development. In later years they'll have much less need to involve you in their sibling squabbles.

4. If the girls have, indeed, been in the habit of picking on their little brother and if you've warned them repeatedly against doing it, your knee-jerk response might understandably be to rise immediately to Andrew's defense. Don't do it! In the eyes of your daughters, this business of giving them "a dose of their own medicine" is comprehended as your demonstrating to them that you can be as arbitrary and childish as they. Andrew may be the smug "winner" in such an event, but his sisters will soon be plotting their revenge.

Did you select response number 3? I hope so. But remember that there are usually several acceptable ways of dealing with these everyday parent-child problems, and there is even some merit in the "wrong" responses. Sound parentcraft requires love and understanding and flexibility. Children themselves are very forgiving. They know that nobody's perfect—not even parents.

Masturbation

Your 5-year-old son has developed a new habit: masturbation. Whenever he gets excited or anxious or whenever he just doesn't seem to have anything else to do, his hand seems to reach down instinctively into his pocket.

You've been increasingly concerned about this matter.

Tonight, while you're sitting in the living room, you see him begin to "play with himself." What would you do? Pick the *one* response that you think is most correct.

1. Grab the offending hand. Slap it.

2. Do nothing. This is part of normal development for boys and girls. He'll get over it.

3. Try to divert his attention by engaging him in conversation or handing him something.

4. Tell him that it's not nice to do these things in public. If he *must* do such things, he should limit it to the privacy of his room.

5. Scare him out of it. Warn him that boys who play with themselves go blind and become feebleminded. God will punish him.

Which response have you chosen? Let's review each of them.

1. Slapping is a real "pain game" and is not a good teaching device except that it is good for teaching children to avoid parents. Your son will need sensitivity and understanding from you in this situation. Slapping implies that what he's doing is very, very bad— so bad that not even you can deal effectively with it.

2. This is not an unreasonable solution. It certainly accepts the fact that some amount of masturbatory activity is normal for 5-year-old boys (and girls too) and avoids the pitfalls of shame or humiliation. Yet such a laissez faire attitude can have undesirable results. It allows youngsters unrestricted access to their instinctual drives and robs them of the experience of delaying gratification and channeling their childish sexual and physiological strivings into more constructive pursuits. Read on.

3. Yes, this is more like it. By unobtrusively diverting your son's attention to you in conversation or to a toy that is handed to him, you are helping him develop a crucial skill that he will need in growing up: the ability to channel, or *sublimate,* his innate drives into constructive pursuits such as interpersonal communication or cooperative play in this case.

4. I include this response because such advice has been fashionable lately. I do not agree with it. Why? This advice takes into account only *half* the situation. While it acknowledges the natural presence of the drive to self-stimulation or masturbation, it fails to recognize that every drive has, or will have, a corresponding prohibition directed from the developing conscience. The unconscious drives say, "If it feels good, do it." The conscience says, "It is not right. You will feel guilty." The would-be enlightened parent who says, "Do it, but do it in private," is taking sides with the darker faces of the unconscious drive toward masturbation. This can be especially problematic with adolescents since such a parental attitude would also be interpreted to condone the masturbation fantasies of the teenager as well. The parents' role is to help youngsters chart a course between their natural drives and a soundly developing voice of conscience.

5. Just as it is wise to avoid an unholy alliance with a youngster's unconscious desires, the thoughtful parent will avoid a holier-than-thou alliance with the punitive forces of the child's developing conscience. Gloom and doom predictions of future blindness or feeblemindedness not only are grossly inaccurate from a medical standpoint but can also cause symptoms from a psychological standpoint. One boy who had been warned about blindness, for example, was brought to me for consultation because he had developed a severe eye-blinking tic. And, finally, the ultimate power play is to invoke God's name into the situation. Such guilt trips do not generally make a child more religious or God loving at all; they create fear and repression of the normal drive developments of childhood.

Logical Consequences

Your 6-year-old daughter, Anne Marie, has gotten into a bad habit: She refuses to eat at the dinner table. You urge her to eat. She says, "I'm not hungry." Your husband says, "Eat." Anne Marie snaps, "I'm not hungry." Then her brothers and sisters get into the act. "Eat, eat," they repeat. The climax is predictable. Anne Marie cries, runs to her room, and slams the door. The rest of you are left to finish your meal in stunned silence. Now everyone's upset. How might you handle this problem more effectively?

1. Punish her. No TV if she doesn't eat.

2. Wait until dinner is completed. Then take her favorite snack to her room. Talk to her. Help her get her feelings out.

3. Admonish her. Remind her about all the starving children in the world.

4. If she's not hungry, she doesn't have to eat, but you do expect her to stay at the table. The next meal is called breakfast.

Now let's see what your responses are.

1. There is a place for punishment, but this isn't it. Discipline should teach. It should be related to the event whenever possible. What's the connection between eating and television? None. Save punishment for later—if all other techniques fail.

2. Choose this response if you want the problem to continue and if you want to raise a pampered child. What 6-year-old wouldn't trade the family dinner for favorite snacks and a private tête-à-tête with Mommy? Yes, it's always important to help a child get her feelings out—but at what a price in this scenario. Anne Marie learns only one thing here: Misbehavior pays.

3. No way. It may make you feel better, but the world's starving children are only an empty abstraction to a defiant 6-year-old. You need action here, not aphorisms.

4. Yes, this is more like it. This is the principle of logical consequences as pioneered by Rudolf Dreikurs. If you're not hungry, you don't eat. But don't expect late-night snacks either. Mom has rights too. She's worked hard to prepare dinner. After the meal she deserves a rest. Breakfast will be on the table tomorrow at the usual time. The beauty of this response is that it allows Anne Marie to learn directly from the consequences of her own behavior. She can eat or not eat—it's up to her. No punishment, no special snacks, no moralizing. Believe me, she'll get the message. Logical consequences work.

Discipline

Your 8-year-old son has just dropped an entire pepperoni pizza on your kitchen floor. You had warned him not to handle it. How do you react?

1. "I warned you. Now look what you have done."

2. "Oh honey, I'm so sorry. Let me clean it up for you."

3. "What a klutz! You can't do anything right."

4. "Quick. The mop is in the closet. You can clean it up before the cheese sticks to the floor."

5. "You must be so embarrassed."

Which response have you chosen? Let's review each of them.

1. There is little doubt in my mind that almost all of us would be tempted to use this response. "I-told-you-so" reactions are almost a reflex in such situations. Yet, clearly, this kind of parental response does not leave either party feeling any better about what has happened. And the pepperoni is still on the floor.

2. This response gets a good chuckle whenever I conduct this particular quiz with a live audience. Parents are not slaves, and children must learn to clean up their mess. Such a response, by the way, creates dependency on the part of a child. He is led to believe that he is to be pitied. Very sympathetic but not very realistic.

3. Parents would not knowingly select this response. I've included it because any of us might, in exasperation, fly off the handle once in a while. Name-calling, however, is a no-no. Criticism should be directed at the event, not at the child. You have every right to be upset over the spilled pizza and to express it, but to attack a youngster with name-calling only serves to poison the atmosphere.

4. This is more like it. Put yourself in your son's shoes. The last time you accidentally spilled something at a party, how did you want the hostess to react? To make a big fuss? No. You prob-

ably preferred to take care of it as unobtrusively as possible and to go on with the party. Allowing your son to clean up the mess similarly allows him to save face and to work his way back into your graces.

5. This response is very empathic and probably hits the target, but by itself, it does not go quite far enough. Spilled pizza calls for action as well as empathy. But if we'd allow ourselves to "cheat" on this quiz a bit and select two responses, a combination of this response and number 4 would be the best of both worlds: empathy *and* action.

Responsibility

Your 9-year-old son, Nicholas, is a good boy. He minds you well. He never gets into trouble. Imagine your surprise, then, when he comes up to you and reveals that he stole two dollars yesterday from your neighbor's house. He feels guilty. He's crying. He promises never to do it again.

This is an important issue. Family values, discipline, and responsibility are at stake. Nicholas's conscience is bothering him, and that's good. But do you let it go at that? What would you do?

1. Nicholas has done enough by confessing to you. He feels guilty. He's learned his lesson. No punishment is necessary.

2. Insist that he apologize to the neighbors and return the money. If he's already spent it, he should offer to do some chores.

3. Guilt is fine but Nicholas must also be punished. No TV for a week. No need to spill the beans to the neighbors, though; they probably won't miss the money anyway.

Which of these responses would you choose?

1. It's fine that Nicholas has confessed to you. It demonstrates that he indeed is developing a solid conscience, that inner voice of right and wrong. The child who can feel guilt is on his way to becoming a "good," self-disciplined person. But has Nicholas really learned his lesson? No. In fact, he's really asking for some additional punishment here. His impulses got the better of him. His conscience was overwhelmed and allowed him to take the money. He's frightened. He needs some reinforcement in the form of atonement—then his guilt will be relieved.

2. A fine solution. Why? You allow Nicholas to learn from the consequences of his behavior. You use the episode to teach him something about your family values and, most of all, about taking responsibility for his actions. By the way, although you should certainly voice your disappointment, this does not have to be done in a harshly punitive way. No further punishment should be needed.

3. This is not a good idea, for two basic reasons. First of all, there is no relationship between stealing from the neighbors and being restricted from TV. Nicholas learns very little from the punishment. Second, and more important, now *you* are participating in a cover-up. You've joined forces with Nicholas's impulses. Now you share the irresponsibility. Not a good parental example.

Divorce

You and your spouse have recently agreed to a divorce. Your 9-year-old daughter, Jenny, has been very tense lately. What should you do?

Pick the *one* response that you think is most correct.

1. Do nothing now. Wait until Jenny asks about the situation. Then, agree to answer any questions that she would like to ask of you.

2. Each parent should go to her separately to express his or her love and tell Jenny his or her own side of the story.

3. You and your spouse should go to Jenny together. Express your love and give her only the basics—no personal details.

The 9-year-old child of divorce: a sad, and not uncommon, phenomenon in our society. Let's go over each of the responses in an effort to help Jenny and all the other children who may become snarled in this predicament.

   1. No. While it might appear "enlightened" to wait for a child's lead and to respond, such strategy is just a handy way for parents to rationalize their own avoidance and denial. You cannot expect many 9-year-olds to initiate such a painful discussion. Like yourself, they may well prefer to avoid it. They hope against hope that their worst fear will not come true: divorce. On the other hand, they tend to interpret parental denial as proof that something is so dreadfully wrong that it cannot be acknowledged. This feeds their fantasies: "Mom and Dad are getting divorced and it's all my fault. If only I had been a good girl, none of this would have happened," etc.

   2. The danger in this response is that each parent will try to "win" Jenny over to his or her side. The child is then placed in a cruel "loyalty bind": If you love me, you have to hate your mother, or vice versa. There is also danger in flooding children with gruesome details (infidelity, etc.) in order to score points against your spouse. Jenny will need both of her parents in her corner as she grows up. Try to preserve as much for her as you can.

   3. Yes. This is more like it. It is the mature and wise husband and wife who can momentarily set aside their personal differences for the sake of their child. It would be important to reassure Jenny that (1) it's not her fault, (2) she can count on the love of both parents, (3) plans will be made with her interests in mind, and (4) while she should feel free to ask questions, you will give her only the kind of information that you feel is important for her to know; you will withhold details that concern only Mom and Dad.

   Did you select response number 3? I hope so. If not, remember that there is seldom only *one* way of responding in these difficult situations. These quizzes are designed to teach some general principles of raising children. Sound parentcraft requires love and creativity—and understanding your own "Jenny."

Lying

Your 10-year-old son, Troy, was supposed to be home at 5 o'clock for dinner. He arrives one hour late, explaining that he ate at the home of his friend Eddie. The next day you run into Eddie's mother at the shopping mall. She hasn't seen Troy in days! What would you do?

1. Forget it. All children tell fibs from time to time.

2. Casually ask Troy what he had for dinner at Eddie's house. Did he have chicken. Did Eddie's mother serve dessert? In other words, give Troy a little more rope with which to hang himself. See just how far he'll go with these lies!

3. Punish him for being late but not for lying.

4. Punish him for lying but not for being late; that is, teach him that lies are more serious than lateness.

5. Punish him for both lying and being late.

6. Tell Troy that you have learned that he lied to you. Offer him "immunity" from punishment if he will tell you what he was really doing.

Which response have you chosen? Let's review each of them.

1. All children certainly do tell lies from time to time. But this is not a harmless garden variety "fib." Troy is involved in a cover-up: the most dangerous type of lying. Bad enough that he was one hour late for dinner, now he's spinning a web of deceit. This kind of lie cannot go unpunished. If you choose to "look the other way," you'll only be encouraging more of this misbehavior.

2. No. This approach is right out of the "Perry Mason School of Parenting." If you assume the posture of a clever courtroom attorney who lures his unsuspecting quarry deeper and deeper into a trap, you'll succeed only in poisoning the atmosphere between yourself and Troy. This approach will also, over a period of time, teach Troy how to become an "expert witness": He'll hedge all his responses to your questions since he suspects that you're only out to catch him at something sinister.

3. This response is a mistake unless your purpose is to teach your son that timeliness is more important than truthfulness.

4. If honesty is an important value in your family, you would certainly stress your concern about Troy's lying over his lateness, but it would be a mistake to overlook the incident that caused the lying. It might also imply to a 10-year-old that it is tolerable for him to break rules—as long as he tells the truth about it.

5. Yes. This is good parentcraft! Two punishments, one for each act, is the order of the day. For being an hour late, Troy might be required to "pay back" the time by not going out at all the next afternoon. For lying he may lose some important privilege for a period of time. The principle is important: You take both offenses seriously. Also, Troy will learn that the next time he is late for dinner he can expect the lateness punishment but that he will not suffer any further consequence—as long as he tells the truth.

6. Some parents may be tempted to use this stratagem. Why? As adults we're interested in getting to the facts! Just where was he anyway and what was he doing? While you might certainly want to explore the facts with Troy after deciding on his punishment (as in response number 5), giving him amnesty is unnecessary and could even be harmful. Troy, like all children, needs to develop a sense of right and wrong, a sense of good and bad. He'll learn this from you. If coming home late is "wrong" and if lying is "bad," he must learn that there are consequences. Only in this way can he eventually develop his own private conscience: his internal voice of decent behavior and sound morality.

Empathy

It's Valentine's Day and your 10-year-old daughter, Marcie, has just come home from a class party. As she enters the kitchen, she throws a stack of Valentine's cards on the table, slams down her books, and recklessly pulls up a chair. When you look up and ask her "What's wrong?" she snaps: "Nothing!" How do you react?

1. Do nothing. It's her problem. Obviously she prefers not to talk about it.

2. Ask her if Freddy, her "boyfriend," forgot to send her a Valentine's card. That's probably it.

3. Tell her that it's okay to be angry but that she shouldn't take it out on her school books—they cost money.

4. Say nothing, but walk over and place your hand gently on her shoulder.

5. Say: "Marcie, it's obvious that you're upset. Maybe you'll feel like talking about it later."

Which response have you chosen? Let's review each of them.

1. No. Marcie wants to share this problem with you. Her non-verbal behavior absolutely cries for your attention. So why does she snap back at you when you ask "What's wrong?" If only 10-year-olds were rational all the time! Her behavior says one thing; her words say another. Place your bets on her behavior. Try to ignore her words. She wants you to hang in there with her.

One additional word about your initial response: "What's wrong?" It might have actually made Marcie more upset. Why? Your question asks for a factual answer at a time when your daughter is flooded by feelings. Besides, she may not know "what's wrong." Therefore, it's better to respond to her feelings rather than launching off on a search for the facts. The facts, after all, will come out soon enough.

2. While you might be right on the money about Freddy, you might be way off the target. Either way, it really doesn't matter. Even if you're right, she'll probably deny it in a fit of shame and embarrassment. Why play "twenty questions" with Marcie's feelings?

3. You might, depending on your own feelings at the moment, be tempted to respond in this way, particularly if Marcie has been very difficult lately and all your patient efforts at reaching out to her have been met by huffy rebuff. The issue, then, is your annoyance, not the cost of the school books. Try to keep these feelings to yourself for now. And, as far as the school books go, there'll be plenty of time for teaching your daughter to respect them—later, when she's worked through the present "crisis" and is in a receptive learning mood.

4. A gentle touch that says "Honey, I'm here and I want to understand" can be a marvelous gesture. You're demonstrating empathy: the ability to see with a child's eyes, to hear with a child's ears, to feel with a child's heart. This is parentcraft at its best. This type of tactile, or touching, empathy would be the preferred response for a youngster who reacts well to being touched in this way. If Marcie, on the other hand, is the kind of girl who recoils at such touching, you would opt for the next response.

5. Yes, this could also be a very satisfactory way of handling the situation. This empathic response allows Marcie some physical distance but lets her know of your interest, your availability, and your support.

In both numbers 4 and 5 you show your heart on Valentine's Day. The key to choosing between the two is in knowing something about Marcie. No technique works equally with all youngsters all the time. Techniques are handy, but they are just devices to use "until the parent arrives": There is no substitute for a parent's understanding of a daughter's unique needs.

Index